From Stonehenge to

Debates in Archaeology

Series editor: Richard Hodges

Against Cultural Property, John Carman
The Anthropology of Hunter-Gatherers, Vicki Cummings
Archaeologies of Conflict, John Carman
Archaeology: The Conceptual Challenge, Timothy Insoll
Archaeology and International Development in Africa, Colin Breen and Daniel Rhodes
Archaeology and State Theory, Bruce Routledge
Archaeology and Text, John Moreland
Archaeology and the Pan-European Romanesque, Tadhg O'Keeffe
Beyond Celts, Germans and Scythians, Peter S. Wells
Bronze Age Textiles, Klavs Randsborg
Building Colonialism, Daniel T. Rhodes
The Byzantine Dark Ages, Michael J. Decker
Changing Natures, Bill Finlayson and Graeme M. Warren
Combat Archaeology, John Schofield
Debating the Archaeological Heritage, Robin Skeates
Early European Castles, Oliver H. Creighton
Early Islamic Syria, Alan Walmsley
Empowering Communities through Archaeology and Heritage, Peter G. Gould
Ethics and Burial Archaeology, Duncan Sayer
Evidential Reasoning in Archaeology, Robert Chapman and Alison Wylie
Fishing and Shipwreck Heritage, Sean A. Kingsley
Fluid Pasts, Matthew Edgeworth
Gerasa and the Decapolis, David Kennedy
Heritage, Communities and Archaeology, Laurajane Smith and Emma Waterton
Houses and Society in the Later Roman Empire, Kim Bowes

Image and Response in Early Europe, Peter S. Wells
Indo-Roman Trade, Roberta Tomber
Loot, Legitimacy and Ownership, Colin Renfrew
Lost Civilization, James L. Boone
Museums and the Construction of Disciplines, Christopher Whitehead
The Origins of the Civilization of Angkor, Charles F. W. Higham
The Origins of the English, Catherine Hills
Pagan and Christian, David Petts
The Remembered Land, Jim Leary
Rethinking Wetland Archaeology, Robert Van de Noort and Aidan O'Sullivan
The Roman Countryside, Stephen L. Dyson
Roman Reflections, Klavs Randsborg
Shaky Ground, Elizabeth Marlowe
Shipwreck Archaeology of the Holy Land, Sean A. Kingsley
Social Evolution, Mark Pluciennik
State Formation in Early China, Li Liu and Xingcan Chen
Towns and Trade in the Age of Charlemagne, Richard Hodges
Tradition and Transformation in Anglo-Saxon England, Susan Oosthuizen
Vessels of Influence, Nicole Coolidge Rousmaniere
Villa to Village, Riccardo Francovich and Richard Hodges

From Stonehenge to Mycenae

The Challenges of Archaeological Interpretation

John C. Barrett and Michael J. Boyd

BLOOMSBURY ACADEMIC
LONDON • NEW YORK • OXFORD • NEW DELHI • SYDNEY

BLOOMSBURY ACADEMIC
Bloomsbury Publishing Plc
50 Bedford Square, London, WC1B 3DP, UK
1385 Broadway, New York, NY 10018, USA

BLOOMSBURY, BLOOMSBURY ACADEMIC and the Diana logo
are trademarks of Bloomsbury Publishing Plc

First published in Great Britain 2019
Paperback edition first published 2021

A catalogue record for this book is available from the British Library.

Library of Congress Cataloging-in-Publication Data
Names: Barrett, John C., author. | Boyd, Michael J., 1970-author.
Title: From Stonehenge to Mycenae: the challenges of archaeological
interpretation / by John C. Barrett and Michael J. Boyd.
Description: London, UK; New York, NY: Bloomsbury Academic, 2019. |
Series: Debates in archaeology | Includes bibliographical references and index.
Identifiers: LCCN 2018056532 (print) | LCCN 2019017332 (ebook) |
ISBN 9781474291903 (epub) | ISBN 9781474291910 (epdf) | ISBN 9781474291897 (hbk.)
Subjects: LCSH: Prehistoric peoples–Europe. | Social archaeology–Europe. |
Europe–Antiquities. | Stonehenge (England) | Mycenae (Extinct city) |
Europe, Western–Relations–Aegean Sea Region. | Aegean Sea
Region–Relations–Europe, Western. | Archaeology–Philosophy. | Archaeology–Methodology.
Classification: LCC GN803 (ebook) | LCC GN803.B24 2019 (print) |
DDC 936/.01–dc23
LC record available at https://lccn.loc.gov/2018056532

ISBN: HB: 978-1-4742-9189-7
PB: 978-1-3501-9082-5
ePDF: 978-1-4742-9191-0
eBook: 978-1-4742-9190-3

Series: Debates in Archaeology

Typeset by RefineCatch Limited, Bungay, Suffolk

To find out more about our authors and books
visit www.bloomsbury.com and sign up for our newsletters.

Contents

Figures

Foreword

'Obscurity and Oblivion'? The Challenge of Interpreting the Prehistoric Past

Colin Renfrew

Stonehenge, conspicuous on the Salisbury Plain in the region of southern England traditionally known as 'Wessex', has presented an enigma since time immemorial. 'Who built it?', 'Why?' and 'When?' are questions to which, over the years, many answers have been given. The early nineteenth-century antiquarian Sir Richard Colt Hoare (1807, 257), writing mainly with reference to the remarkable passage grave in Ireland at Newgrange, was pessimistic:

> I shall not unnecessarily trespass upon the time and patience of my readers in endeavouring to ascertain what tribes first peopled this country, nor to what nation the construction of this singular monument may reasonably be attributed for, I fear, both its authors and its original destination will ever remain unknown. Conjecture may wander over its wild and spacious domains but will never bring home with it either truth or conviction. Alike will the histories of those stupendous temples at Avebury and Stonehenge which grace my native country, remain involved in obscurity and oblivion.

This was an understandable assessment, but it has proved, with the passage of subsequent years, to be unduly pessimistic.

Others were less cautious, some even seeking to establish links between Stonehenge and the great fortified citadel at Mycenae in Greece, following the excavations there of Heinrich Schliemann in 1876. It was not, however, until about a century later that the application of radiocarbon dating established a secure chronological context for Stonehenge (and confirmed the rather later dating of Mycenae). This allowed the interpretation to move on, beyond the 'When?' question. The present volume is a triumphant documentation of how much more can now be said about the 'Who?' and the 'Why?' – and perhaps also hints at how much more there is still to be said about both.

This refreshing and thoughtful study by John Barrett and Michael Boyd takes these two great monuments as a starting point for a challenging consideration of what can be established today, in the early twenty-first century, about the later prehistory of Europe of several thousand years ago. First they review earlier (and sometimes contradictory) archaeological approaches to the two designated sites. Then, choosing to focus primarily on two regions of Europe, south Britain and the Aegean – where these two iconic sites lie – they consider and develop their analysis with a treatment of three major fields of interest in contemporary archaeology.

In doing so they touch on a series of problems and contemporary concerns of archaeological theory and interpretation which are of much wider relevance. These relate to issues applicable to many ancient agrarian societies across the world which flourished before the advent of writing, and therefore before written history. Their thoughtful approach will offer useful insights for archaeologists across the world who study societies which were likewise active and flourishing before the advent of literacy.

A pervasive theme in their analysis is the creation of *identity*. Identity, collective as well as personal, is often clearly expressed through the medium of material culture – that is to say in the artefacts used by earlier societies, of which tangible remains can be found today. This is discussed in Chapter 3 which forms an introduction to the succeeding trilogy of chapters where their thinking is most clearly developed: (4) Things that Mattered; (5) Places that Mattered; and (6) Bodies that Mattered. These three chapters offer a programmatic treatment of what becomes a richly documented exercise in comparative archaeology.

The consideration of the politics of the early eastern Mediterranean and of northern European metallurgy undertaken in Chapter 4 gets to grips with the evidence of the things that these people were making, things which clearly meant a lot to them. The beakers became the characteristic drinking vessels in northern Europe and the so-called 'sauceboats', ceramic drinking vessels, were a *leitmotiv* in the heyday of the Aegean early bronze age. They were clearly of symbolic significance to their makers. In both areas their users were associated with the development of copper and then bronze metallurgy. The trading networks which metallurgy brought into being are documented by the distribution of finds of these well-made pots, and by other conspicuous artefacts, including daggers, which were certainly 'things that mattered'.

In their treatment of 'Places that Mattered' (in Chapter 5) the authors consider a number of locations of ritual significance in the third and second millennia BC. Their focus moves from Orkney to Stonehenge, then south to Keros in the Aegean, and then to Knossos in Crete and finally to Mycenae. Such ritual centres were used in different ways. Each became a centre of influence and probably also of pilgrimage. The significance of each endured for several centuries.

The body is central to the concept of identity, a theme which dominates the discussion of 'Bodies that Mattered' in Chapter 6. In the context of their treatment of ancient DNA, where recent studies suggest a possible discontinuity in the population of prehistoric Britain with the arrival of the beakers, Barrett and Boyd assert that: 'archaeology needs to understand the strategies by which shared identities were constructed by people in the past, rather than by imposing identities upon past populations by means of such classes of archaeological materials as "cultures".' Cautioning against the equation of cultural inheritance with that of genetic inheritance, they review mortuary strategies of identity and the placing of the dead in a ritual landscape, focusing first on the British evidence of the third and second millennia BC (particularly in Wessex) before turning to the Shaft Graves of Mycenae to reconsider the funeral practices there.

The two authors are careful to avoid sweeping statements about the nature of culture change. Their return to two well-known sites and areas offers the occasion for fresh and illuminating discussion of the ways that material culture (i.e. 'things') has been used, systematically and often deliberately, to create identities of different kinds. Their consideration is focussed on their two chosen areas of Europe, Britain and the Aegean. Yet clearly their approach could be applied to a wide range of other contexts in prehistoric Europe and indeed in other parts of the world. It is a brilliant demonstration of how interpretations can change, and how these can require new forms and contexts of reasoning. This is a work which moves on beyond the debates of the 'processual' and 'post-processual' archaeologies prevalent at the end of the twentieth century, and takes the analysis into other fields. The treatment employed here can clearly be applied to other regions beyond those of Stonehenge or Mycenae. I predict that the approaches and issues developed and debated here will soon also find fruitful application in other regions of the world.

Colin Renfrew

Introduction

During the 1970s and the 1980s the North American archaeologist and founding figure of what was, in those days, called the 'New Archaeology', Lewis Binford, claimed to have identified both the problem, and the solution, to the conundrum that he believed bedevilled archaeological reasoning (cf. Binford 1983). Archaeologists had long accepted that the materials that they studied had resulted from different formation processes and could therefore be treated as if they were the representations of those processes and thus of the events that had happened in the past. The methodological problem was to establish what the material actually represented in ways that found general agreement amongst archaeologists. Up until the mid-1960s in North America and in much of Europe it had been assumed that archaeological materials represented the ways that people had once behaved, such as the ways that they had made pottery, built their houses and buried their dead. It was further assumed that these behaviours were the cultural products of various social conventions. This reasoning appeared to adopt a principle from the sociology of Émile Durkheim, that social solidarities were constructed through the beliefs that people had shared with each other, and archaeology deployed this reasoning to assume that such beliefs were likely to be represented by the patterns of their material residues. Binford had two problems with this seemingly uncontentious reasoning. The first was that some of the patterns that were treated as if they represented earlier human behaviour were in fact demonstrably the products of non-human processes of decay and the transformation of materials caused by animal activity. The second problem concerned the ways attempts to explain changes in the sequences of material residues, and thus to explain changes in human behaviour, seemed to depend upon the assumption that different communities would have been open to influences from others who were more socially advanced and culturally dominant. Not only was this latter assumption unexamined in any detail, but the means of tracing the path along which such supposed influences had diffused seemed to be highly speculative, with some archaeologists claiming to be able to identify cultural influences in the design of the material residues that other archaeologists were not able to recognize.

The solution to these problems, Binford suggested, was for archaeology to establish the link between past dynamics and the surviving material record

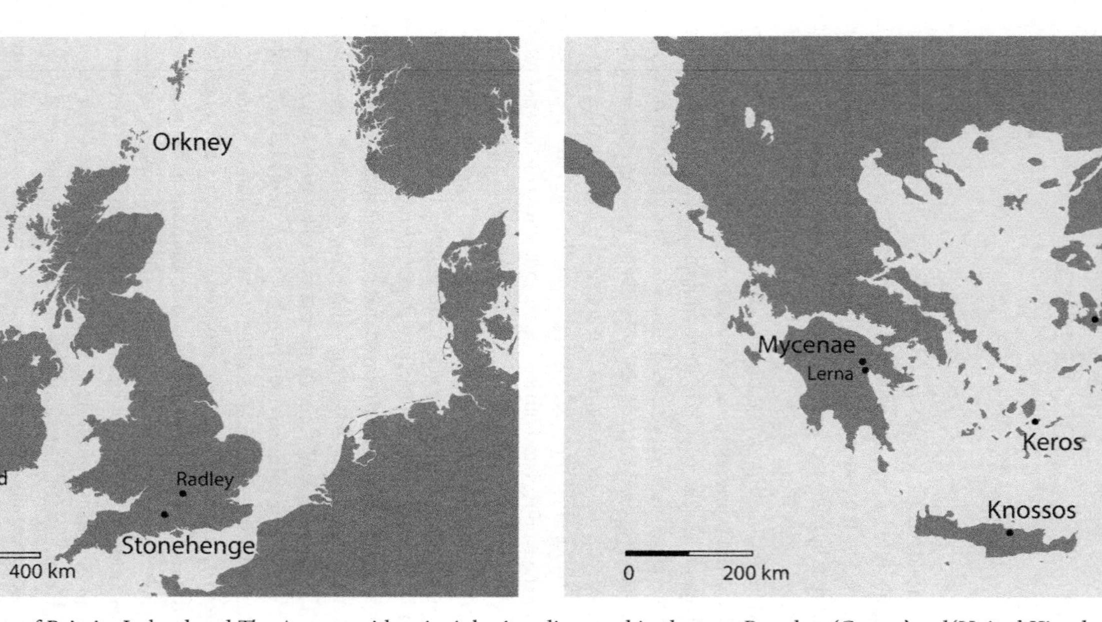

Fig. 0.1 Maps of Britain, Ireland and The Aegean with principle sites discussed in the text. Based on 'Greece' and 'United Kingdom' by FreeVectorMaps.com.

purely in terms of mechanical processes that could be replicated by means of modern experimentation or could be observed ethnographically. At the same time Binford, and the New Archaeology more generally, rejected attempts to explain cultural change as the product of influences diffusing from one social and cultural context into another, suggesting that such accounts often amounted to little more than guesswork. From one perspective these proposals represented the basis for a more secure archaeological reasoning that accepted the properties inherent in the surviving evidence, but from another perspective the resulting archaeology appeared limited in what it could say about the past and was, for example, unable to engage with the ways that human communities had actively worked to construct their own histories.

The writing of a European prehistory, extending from the closing stages of the last Ice Age until the development of the western Empire of Rome, had long depended upon the archaeological claim that it was able to recognize cultural influences that linked one region with another. Before the advent of the independent dating mechanism provided by radiocarbon these supposed links were used not only to explain cultural change within the European sequences of material but also to establish chronological ties between these sequences and the historically dated cultures of Egypt and Mesopotamia. The European prehistorian Gordon Childe followed upon the earlier work of Oscar Montelius (1903) in attempting to systematize the sequences of prehistoric material found across Europe and to establish presumed links between the different cultural sequences so established and those of Mesopotamia and Egypt (e.g. Childe 1925; 1929).

Childe's aim was to do more than simply catalogue the prehistoric sequences of cultural material in Europe. In what was his last book, he restated that the aim of all his work had been to understand the distinctive development attested by the archaeology of European prehistory. He claimed that:

> even in prehistoric times barbarian societies in Europe behaved in a distinctively European way, foreshadowing, however dimly, the contrast with African or Asiatic societies that has become manifest in the last thousand years.
>
> Childe 1958, 9

Following upon the Neolithic colonization of Europe by agriculturalists, who had originated from south-western Asia, Childe regarded the initial impetus for this uniquely European development as having lain with Europe's proximity to, and dependency upon, the civilizations of Egypt and Mesopotamia. He

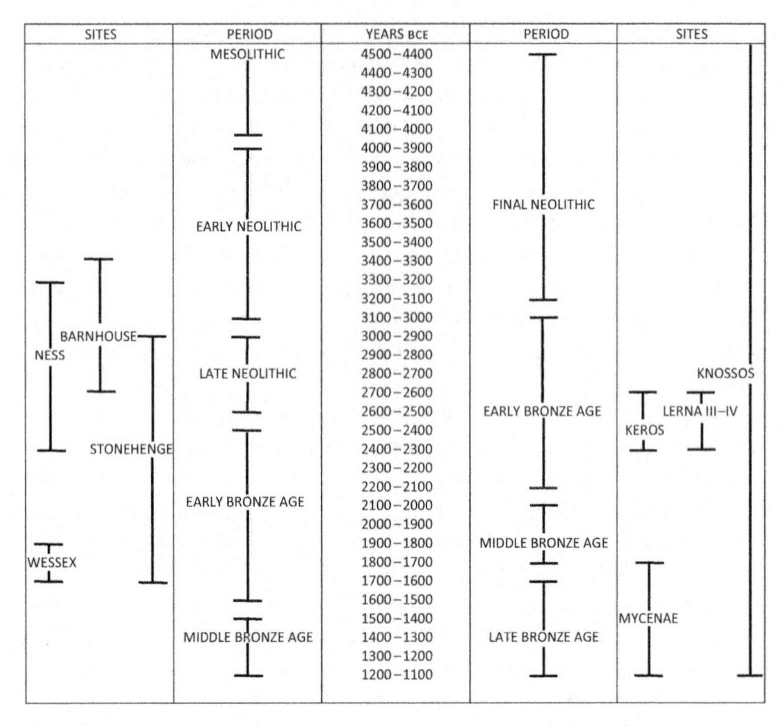

Fig. 0.2 Chronological chart giving approximate calendar dates for sites mentioned in the text and regional periods: British Isles to the left, and Aegean to the right ('Wessex' refers to the Wessex graves: see Chapter 6).

characterized the archaeological challenge as being that of understanding the historical mechanisms by which 'European barbarians outstrip their Oriental masters' (Childe 1958, 7). The 'distinctively European way' of behaviour had emerged, at least according to Childe, with the 'manifest superiority of European technology', a technology that arose 'through the application of science', the 'spiritual ancestors' of which were to be found amongst the 'operations of prehistoric potters and smelters' (Childe 1958, 9). The challenge that Childe faced was to establish how and when this 'manifest superiority of European technology' had supposedly originated. Childe proposed that:

> It was with the Bronze Age that the course of Europe's history – social and economic as well as technical and scientific – began to diverge both from that of the New World and from that of the Ancient East.
>
> Childe 1957a, 2

The significance of the European Bronze Age, as opposed to the Bronze Age of 'the Ancient East', lay, as far as Childe was concerned, with the different social contexts within which he believed that the working of metals had developed. The casting of metals required a geological knowledge of source materials, a chemical and technical knowledge that was demonstrated in the smelting, alloying and working of the metals, and the trading networks that could supply regular access to raw materials. This complex pattern of activity, Childe believed, necessitated the existence of specialist producers, and any account of the social context of production had to describe how this specialist class had been maintained. It was the difference between the Oriental and the European social contexts of production that defined, for Childe, the distinctive nature of Europe's historical relationship with that of the Orient.

In Childe's model, the specialist production of smithing would have been sustained by an economic organization capable of both generating, and managing, the distribution of food that was surplus to a community's subsistence needs, and he proposed that such a surplus could be envisaged as having been generated originally, not by the Neolithic agriculture of temperate Europe, but by the agricultural exploitation of the alluvial environments of the Tigris, the Euphrates and the Nile rivers, and to have been managed through the 'totalitarian regimes' of the early civilizations of Mesopotamia and Egypt by which this 'surplus was systematically extracted from the peasant masses and gathered into royal or temple granaries' (Childe 1957a, 6). It was therefore in the context of the emergent Oriental civilizations that Childe believed that the specialist technologies of metallurgy arose, but it was also these totalitarian regimes that, in his view, 'fettered the further development' of the very technologies that they had sustained by subsuming them under the 'complete dependence on a court or a temple' (Childe 1957a, 8).

Childe proposed that the technologies of metalworking had been carried from the Orient, first into the Aegean, and then into the western Mediterranean and on into temperate and Baltic Europe by a process of transmission driven by the movement of smiths in search of new sources of ore, and by the expansion of the exchange networks that carried both the raw materials and their products. The assumption throughout was that the technological knowledge of metalworking was part of a cultural pattern of behaviour, the transmission of which was represented in the form and distribution of archaeological finds. These metal producers were therefore thought to have brought with them the technological and scientific knowledge gained in the Orient but transferred into a European context and into relations of production that were not constrained by the restrictive class divisions that had existed in the east. This move supposedly ensured that metal producers were 'freed' by relations that facilitated innovation and the development of technology and science. The need to sustain specialist producers by means of a surplus food product none the less remained, and until such a surplus was released by the application of the new technologies upon European agricultural production, Childe claimed that this necessary support was achieved by trade relations with, and therefore dependence upon, the earlier centres of a developing metallurgy (Childe 1958).

There is much to criticize in Childe's model for the origins of metallurgy, not least his 'orientalism' which suggested that the initial technological development of the Orient had atrophied, only to be taken forward by the entrepreneurial endeavours characteristic of European culture (Rowlands 1984, 149; cf. Larsen 1989). Among the many things that were not recognized at the time was the level of geological knowledge associated with stone quarrying, mining and working, now understood as a feature of the early European Neolithic and which represents one likely foundation for the early organization of ore quarrying. Indeed, Childe simply did not accept the inherent potential for change in the agricultural systems of the European Neolithic.

It is Colin Renfrew who, from the late 1960s onwards, has been mainly instrumental in pulling apart the Childean model of prehistoric Europe in which cultural, technological and therefore social change had somehow 'diffused' out from regions that were claimed to be innovators in economic or cultural development. Renfrew instigated the need to rethink the dynamics of European prehistory by demonstrating the impact that radiocarbon dating was having on models of cultural diffusion. The independent method of dating was resulting in moving the chronologies of key European cultural sequences earlier than their supposed Oriental antecedents (Renfrew 1973a). Renfrew's argument for an indigenous, European development of metallurgy was initiated by his building of the chronological case for the indigenous development of an 'autonomous' copper metalworking tradition in the Balkans (Renfrew 1969a). This argument was spectacularly endorsed by the find, in 1972, of the fifth millennium BCE cemetery at Varna near the Black Sea coast which yielded grave assemblages containing numerous copper and gold artefacts (Ivanov 1975; 1991; Renfrew 1986; Higham et al. 2007). Renfrew then published a case for the relatively independent development of metallurgy in the Aegean (Renfrew 1972). Colin Renfrew thus laid the foundations for the development of the New Archaeology in Europe, the primary concern of which was to explain how the patterns that were observed in the material had arisen without recourse to the suggestion that change had resulted from external influences. Among other things, this required Renfrew to establish the case for cultural change to have been an inherent property of the European Neolithic, a possibility seemingly denied by Childe (cf. Renfrew 1973b; Sherratt 1981). Renfrew's approach therefore had the effect of producing a geographical distinction drawn between the regions that had contained the forces driving historical, and therefore material, change and those external relations that, whilst they may have operated between different regions, were none the less denied the diffusionist role that Childe and others had granted them in instigating cultural change (cf. Renfrew 1977; Renfrew and Cherry 1986).

The narratives of European prehistory that have developed over the past century might now be described as a series of changing geographical models and processes. It remains widely accepted that the origins of Neolithic agriculture lay with a process of colonization, lasting over some two millennia, by agriculturalists who introduced domesticated plants and animals from south-western Asia. This process extended across the European land mass that was itself already occupied by hunter-gatherers and that sustained a variety of soil, plant and animal habitats. The complex relationships between the indigenous and incoming populations are only now beginning to be understood from the result of the analysis of strontium isotopes and the ancient DNA that can be retrieved from individuals buried in the cemeteries of these earliest agriculturalists (Bickle and Whittle 2013). It was against the background of this palimpsest of human identities, material exchanges and ecological variability, that the early development of metal technologies occurred, marked by the initial working of gold and copper to be followed using lead and the alloying of copper with tin to cast bronze. Whilst indicative of a technological change, the Copper and Bronze Ages of Europe have also been taken to indicate an organizational change amongst the established agricultural communities. Thus, whilst Childe treated the foundations of a European metallurgy as the result of a further migration into Europe from the east, this time by smiths seeking out new sources of raw materials and who had originated ultimately from the early state systems of western Asia and north Africa, Renfrew countered this by placing an emphasis upon indigenous social and economic forces that resulted in the technological developments that had emerged within different regional systems across Europe.

Renfrew certainly concurred with Childe that the Bronze Age was a 'crucial period' in the prehistory of Europe, 'the only continent in which there was a true Bronze Age – that is to say a "barbarian" or pre-urban Bonze Age' (Renfrew 1994, 159), but he rejected Childe's diffusionist claims in which the 'barbarian' development of Europe depended initially upon the urban societies of the Orient. Renfrew's argument that the development of social ranking, a process that Timothy Earle (2002) was to equate with the development of a 'political economy', could be understood in terms of a series of autonomous regional developments (cf. Renfrew 1977) was also developed to counter the growing interest in the application of World Systems modelling (Wallerstein 1974) to an understanding of the ancient world (e.g. Frankenstein and Rowlands 1978). Renfrew originally argued that World Systems approaches, with their emphasis upon economically dominant core regions, simply marked the re-introduction of diffusionist narratives to explain European cultural sequences (Renfrew 1994, 158). The contrast was therefore between Renfrew's emphasis upon explaining social change by reference to mechanisms that were internal to the regional system, and a World Systems approach in which an asymmetrical relationship between a socially and economically dominant 'core' and its economically dominated 'periphery' was used to explain the structural transformations that were witnessed in both. The trajectories mapped by such asymmetrical connections between the regions comprising these larger networks of exchange, and of economic and political domination and dependency, might also have been expected to have traced a long-term path of cyclical development as the inherent demands made upon the periphery for increasing its levels of resource exploitation resulted in periods of ecological exhaustion and realignment (Friedman and Rowlands 1977; Kristiansen 1998).

The archaeological claim to recognize the 'internal' use of exotics for display and for conspicuous consumption, such as the use of copper and gold in the burial assemblages at the Varna cemetery (Renfrew 1986), assumed that these practices were key to the development not only of social rank but also to the maintenance of ideologies of authority (Miller and Tilley 1984). As such these ideas lent themselves to explanations in which the localized development of rank necessitated participation in various 'external' networks of material exchange (cf. Kristiansen 1978). Indeed, the restricted distribution across Europe of native ores when set against the evidence for widespread metal production, the distribution of numerous different types of artefact, and the evidence for water- and land-based transportation certainly imply that, whatever local processes of social differentiation and economic development might have been at work, these processes must be understood as having operated within a more extensive network of social alliances and material exchange (Harding 2013a & b; Sherratt 1993).

The archaeology of history

Archaeological narratives continue to depict the histories of the third and second millennia in Europe as if they were processes that were represented by the material evidence. From this perspective it appears as if the historical processes that matter are the very ones that resulted in the formation of archaeological deposits. But surely historical processes have always involved much more than this? Whatever we might envisage the historical processes to have been, they clearly operated across both local and regional scales in such a way that the European Bronze Age emerged in both the regional polities towards which Renfrew directed our attention, and in the larger systems of material exchange and human movement which World Systems approaches addressed (Kristiansen 1998).

Kristian Kristiansen has been one scholar who has developed an understanding of the Bronze Age world of Eurasia as a geographically integrated system of communities that was held together by the exchange of materials, the movements of traders and warriors, and by shared concepts of a world order (Kristiansen 1998; Kristiansen and Larsson 2005). This model treats the patterns of archaeological materials as if they had been generated by the large-scale organizational relationships through which materials moved and styles were copied. By way of contrast we start from the principle that archaeology is an investigation of how emergent historical conditions enabled the construction of particular kinds of human life. In other words, our archaeology is primarily concerned with the material contexts in which particular kinds of life were possible, rather than treating archaeology as primarily the study of the material consequences of large-scale structural organizations. It is in this way that we aim to address the call made by Kristian Kristiansen and Thomas Larsson for the development of a theoretical strategy that enables us to understand the human experiences that were once gained by means of the local material practices that had operated in the context of the larger regional movements of peoples and materials (Kristiansen and Larsson 2005, 4–10). These experiences enabled the construction of people's identity, such that those of the Mycenaean aristocracy, which were not the product of some spiritual, cultural or biological primordial essence, but rather were created by the strategic deployment of, or resistance to, the flows of materials and people that cut across Europe and Asia (Renfrew 1994; Rowlands 2010). In this way we can recognize that there is no conflict 'between the increasing evidence for the scale of mobility in the Bronze Age, including both movements of people and things' and the evidence for long-term patterns of regional continuity (Rowlands and Ling 2013, 517).

In the pages that follow our emphasis will be upon the archaeological understanding of the ways that human identities have been created. We follow Ingold and his colleagues in treating identity not as something given and fixed but as something that is achieved by development, it is a process of 'becoming' that uses available material conditions and traditions of practice to bring forms of life into being (Ingold 2001; Ingold and Palsson 2013). The shift we envisage is thus away from an archaeology that treats history as if it were merely the description of how archaeological deposits were formed, and towards an archaeology that is concerned with how local systems of humanity had constructed themselves, or were constructed by others, out of the flows of materials and people that were then available. The credibility of such narratives as these rest upon the competence of our characterization of the processes that we assert to be of archaeological concern, and our design of the archaeological procedures that enable their investigation. The structure of this analysis is clearly very different from that which was developed by Lewis Binford to achieve what he took to be a viable archaeological knowledge of the past. For Binford the past could only be known securely as the system of those mechanisms that had created an archaeological record. For us the past was a condition in which people found it possible to become who they were. Archaeology, from this latter perspective, seeks to understand how lives were lived given the conditions that are attested for archaeologically.

In the chapters that follow we address the conditions that developed during the third to second millennium BCE in two regions of Europe, that around Stonehenge in southern Britain, and that in the insular landscape of the southern Aegean. The reason for this selection is that it enables us to address the archaeology of two regions that were once linked by the diffusionist narratives that Colin Renfrew recognized as no longer being viable (Renfrew 1968). As we show, these were two regions of long-term cultural continuity through which people passed and whose occupants drew into their own use, by processes of creolization and hybridity, the wider movements of materials that were available to them. We set out the challenge that archaeology faces in the first three chapters before examining in later chapters the various strategies by which people's very being was constructed. We focus upon three aspects of the available archaeological material. Chapter 4 considers how lives might have been lived to build worlds of identity among the use of material things. Chapter 5 then explores the ways that the occupancy of place made certain kinds of identity possible before turning in Chapter 6 to the different ways that the lived identities of different communities might have been constructed relative to their dead.

1

Archaeological Approaches to Stonehenge

On a June day in 1668 Samuel Pepys visited Stonehenge. His diary entry records his reaction to the stones: it was a reaction that is likely to have been shared by many visitors before and since:

> Come thither, and find them as prodigious as any tales I ever heard of them, and worth going this journey to see. God knows what their use was!
>
> Pepys 1668

Whatever Stonehenge's use was, and speculations have ranged from a temple to a computer, the monument continues to challenge our understanding of the world in which it was built, used and then abandoned. Our concern in this book is to consider the issues that archaeologists face in their attempts to make sense of worlds such as this.

There was of course a time when the purpose of the monument was widely understood; when it was built with such considerable effort, when it was modified and used, and it is this world that has been the focus of

Fig. 1.1 View of Stonehenge from the south-west. Photograph by Elaine Wakefield. Copyright Wessex Archaeology.

archaeological concern and speculation. But then that use stopped, and its original purpose was forgotten, and whilst the Stonehenge of today is used as a visitor attraction, we might wonder at the circumstances that allowed the original purpose of the monument to slip from view.

Pepys was certainly not the first to record an impression of the site: the site was sketched and recorded at various times during the middle ages, and two years before Pepys' visit the antiquary John Aubrey had drawn a plan of the stones and observed some of the additional archaeological features that are part of the monument's history. Our story will begin however with the archaeological excavations and the re-setting of some of the stones that took place between 1950 and 1964. The history of the archaeological investigations of Stonehenge has not been a particularly happy one. Various 'diggings' have taken place within the circle, not all of which have produced the detailed records that might have been expected. The work that was instigated in 1950 was itself designed to evaluate an earlier programme of excavations that had taken place between 1919 and 1926. Neither of these twentieth-century programmes of investigation produced anything but the most minimal written record until all that work was finally brought together in 1995 (Cleal et al. 1995). Nonetheless the 1950–1964 excavations did result in a scheme for the architectural development of Stonehenge that remained in use until recently (Atkinson 1960). This proposed architectural sequence was reassuringly simple: three stages of building were suggested, starting with an earthwork enclosure within which lay a cremation cemetery, some evidence for a central timber structure and with stones at the enclosure's north-eastern entrance. In this scheme, the second stage of development focused upon the trans-shipment of stones, whose distinctive geology indicated an origin in the south Welsh mountains of Prescelly, and their preliminary erection at Stonehenge, along with the construction of an avenue between the north-east entrance to the earlier earthwork and the River Avon. This Avenue ran for some 2,100 metres, initially along the line of the north-eastern axis of the monument and then east and south-east. It was in the third phase of the proposed scheme that the great stone structure was erected and modified. The stones came from relatively local sources on the chalk lands, but they had been extensively shaped before being erected in what has long been regarded as an outer circle of standing stones that were linked by a continuous line of lintels, and within which five sets of trilithons had already been erected. The latter comprised closely set paired standing stones, where each pair supported a lintel. The original south Welsh stones were re-erected within this more massive and complex structure.

In the three hundred years since Pepys' visit archaeology had thus provided something of a building sequence for the history of Stonehenge, although archaeology was less forthcoming in providing an understanding of its use. Richard Atkinson, who was one of those directing the 1950–1964 programme and author of the proposed building sequence, when confronting such questions as: 'why it was built, why this particular sequence of building and, indeed, what did it all mean?' simply countered that:

> To all these questions 'Why?' there is one short, simple and perfectly correct answer: 'We do not know and we shall probably never know'.
>
> Atkinson 1960, 168

That said, Atkinson then permitted himself to conjecture that the monument developed as a temple that originated with the digging of an earthwork enclosure which may have been intended to separate the sacred activities within the enclosure from those beyond. Atkinson suggested that the initial priority of the celebrants was to communicate with a nether world and that the development of the stone architecture implied that ritual concerns were lifted towards the sky and the movement of celestial bodies. We have no need to follow Atkinson's suggestions in any detail for, as we shall see, much has changed as to how we might understand the monument and the periods of its use, but for all his doubts Atkinson was forced to allow that these questions concerning the meaning of Stonehenge, difficult as they might be to answer, were the kinds of ideas that archaeology should explore and that mark 'the growth of ideas about what archaeology is for' (Atkinson 1960, 178 original emphasis omitted).

If archaeology can provide for a securer knowledge of the sequence of Stonehenge's building than it can for the use of the monument then, as an alternative, archaeology might provide an account of the historical context in which the monument was built, used and then abandoned. After all, the building sequence itself means little historically without an understanding of the kind of world in which that sequence occurred. One of the challenges that Stonehenge poses is therefore not so much the question of 'what was its use?', but 'what kind of world could, and indeed would want to, build such a thing?'. Therefore, all the puzzling questions concerning the use of Stonehenge, or what the monument might once have meant, might simply come down to whether the world in which the building and use of Stonehenge occurred is understandable by us. By understanding that earlier world we might also come to understand 'what archaeology is for'.

Archaeology has become adept at describing what can be known of the material conditions of the past, based upon the analysis of archaeological finds and by providing an account of the mechanical processes that created and transformed those finds; but understanding the past as the historical context in which such things had occurred and, as the 'New Archaeology' sought, to explain *why* such things had come about, has proven to be much more difficult. The problem is that by treating archaeological finds as a record of human activity, archaeologists have faced the unenviable task of establishing the principles that might have determined, and therefore explained, the activities that are recorded. It is hardly surprising that the resulting claims have been contentious. The New Archaeology rejected the assertion that the ways that people had behaved simply derived from their social and cultural context by arguing that such an approach failed to offer a useable basis for explaining social and economic change. The New Archaeology developed, by way of an alternative, the idea that *what* people had done in terms of their various social and economic consequences, rather than *how* they had done those things culturally, revealed the historical context of behaviour in ways that might explain the processes of change.

Establishing a context for Stonehenge

In 1956, when Richard Atkinson first published his short book on Stonehenge, the problem of dating each stage of its construction, and thus of establishing those other things in Britain and Europe that were contemporary with the monument's development, was considerable. The first results from the radiocarbon method of dating were only just becoming available, and a single date had been obtained for organic material that was recovered in the excavation of 1950. This material came from the fill of a pit that belonged to the first stage of Atkinson's sequence (Atkinson 1960, 89), and whilst Atkinson treated this date with due reservation, the chronology for the entire sequence was estimated from it. Atkinson offered dates for the proposed sequence which he suggested ran from the earthwork enclosure first dug around 1900–1700 BCE to the erection of the stone monument that we see today, sometime around 1500 BCE. The significance of these dates is not only that we now know them to be far too late, such that the first stone monument was erected around a thousand years earlier than Atkinson had calculated, but that they therefore placed Stonehenge in the wrong historical context.

The emphasis that archaeology places upon human history, where the evidence is treated as if it recorded earlier human activities, means that if we claim to be able to explain the historical context of Stonehenge we might not only be expected to describe the ways that human activities were organized at that time, but also offer an account as to how that kind of organization had come into being. The assumption would be therefore, that by tracing the development and organization of human activity archaeology must account for not only the different technical understandings that were available and the levels of social organization within which those understandings were applied but also what had motivated those resources and that understanding to have been directed in a particular way. This would mean that the building of Stonehenge becomes understandable as not only lying within the technical and organizational capabilities of the prehistoric peoples of southern Britain but as also satisfying a certain kind of motivation. Even allowing for the late dating proposed by Atkinson for the erection of the stones, the unique nature of Stonehenge, the scale of the work undertaken, and the architectural refinements represented by the ways that the stones had been worked, all marked something of a challenge to Atkinson's expectation of what was possible for the prehistoric communities of the period.

Atkinson therefore set about seeking to understand the stone architecture of Stonehenge as if it had been built in the Early Bronze Age around 1500 BCE by assessing the technology used and the necessary level of social organization in which that technology was employed. In terms of technology, Atkinson employed experimental work, model building and an understanding of the mechanical properties of stone, to argue that the ability to transport, work and erect the standing stones and lintels of Stonehenge lay within the capability of the prehistoric communities of that period. He also noted that the mortice and tenon jointing employed to secure the lintel stones onto the uprights was a carpentry technique that had been employed here in stone-working, and that such woodworking skills were likely to have existed given that timber structures had been excavated within earlier monuments in Britain (e.g. Cunnington 1929; Piggott 1939).

If the technical achievements implied by the monument were understandable, then the social context was treated by Atkinson as if it concerned the two questions of the ethnicity of the builders and of their social organization. Ethnicity had long been a central concern for archaeological analysis and one that was addressed by the cultural style of the artefacts and monuments that were created at the time. Although the assumption was simple, that people who had shared an ethnic identity would also have shared in ways of doing things, Atkinson had in fact little evidence that might enable him to assign a cultural context to the building of the unique stone phases of Stonehenge. Nonetheless, he believed that circumstantial evidence existed to suggest that his proposed second phase of construction, that brought the so-called 'bluestones' from Pembrokeshire to their initial erection in the earthwork enclosure, could be linked ethnically to the 'beaker people'. Known from the western European distribution of a distinctive form of ceramic vessel (see Chapter 6), these so-called 'beaker people' were believed to have arrived in Britain, bringing with them not only the ceramic tradition but also a new form of single grave burial and the first traditions of metalworking. This cultural context therefore fixed the construction of the first stone architecture at Stonehenge at the key moment when copper, gold and then bronze working was introduced into Britain.

In 1938 Stuart Piggott, who excavated at Stonehenge with Richard Atkinson and J.F.S. Stone, had published a survey of the Bronze Age immediately following upon the currency of the 'beaker culture' in southern Britain. The implication for Atkinson was that the period surveyed by Piggott must have covered the final development of Stonehenge. The evidence that was then available to Piggott included individual finds of metalwork but otherwise it was mainly formed of the material from late eighteenth- and early nineteenth-century excavations into round burial mounds or 'barrows' of the Bronze Age. A major concentration of these burial monuments lies in the immediate vicinity of Stonehenge itself and they clearly imply a Bronze Age funerary association with the monument (see Chapter 6). Piggott argued that the burial rites associated with these mounds witnessed a trend from earlier beaker period inhumations to the adoption of cremation in the Bronze Age, and that the burial assemblages from these chalk uplands of Wiltshire and Dorset (comprising part of an area traditionally assigned to the region of Wessex), produced a range of artefacts that were indicative both of an 'opening up' of a wide range of Bronze Age trade routes, and of the production of items of display that included bronze daggers, necklace beads of amber and a blue vitrified material (faience) and the decorative use of gold. These developments, along with the changes in funerary rites, were indicative, Piggott suggested, of a 'Wessex Culture', the origins of which he believed lay among the communities that were represented by the 'dagger graves' of Brittany in north-west France.

The exchange relations and cultural contacts represented by this period appeared to be extensive. The daggers from some of the Wessex graves were not only comparable to finds from the Breton graves but Piggott traced further comparisons to central Europe and northern Italy. The amber in some of the graves was traced to sources in the Baltic, and the blue faience was believed to have had an Egyptian origin. Further decorative amulets and pins indicated central European contacts whilst gold sources were traced to Ireland. The 1938 study therefore established the idea of an international European Bronze Age in which the political or ethnic grouping of the Wessex Culture played a significant role. Piggott calculated this network to have occurred sometime after about 1800 BCE with the arrival of Breton migrants into southern Britain. In his final commentary on this material Piggott suggested that 'chronological and cultural equations may be made with regions even more remote and unexpected' (Piggott 1938, 95). Those regions,

Piggott suggested, lay with the Bronze Age of southern Greece and Crete, where comparative material, including the distinctive use of amber, was used to link the Wessex grave finds with some Minoan material and the finds from the shaft graves at Mycenae (cf. Harding 1984, 70–87).

The Mycenaean shaft graves comprise two grave circles, one of which is enclosed within the later walled citadel of Mycenae itself (see Chapter 6). These graves were made famous in the late nineteenth century by Heinrich Schliemann who associated the burials with the aristocracy portrayed in the epic poetry of Homer. The archaeological link Piggott made between the Mycenaean shaft graves, the Wessex burials and other European grave series depended both upon general similarities in the finds, such as the inclusion of daggers among some of the grave assemblages, but also more specific comparisons, such as the complex design of the drilled plates of Baltic amber that were used in necklaces or other settings (Harding 1984, Fig. 18).

It was therefore to this international Bronze Age that Atkinson turned in his desire to establish a historical context for the building of the massive stone structures marking the third phase in his Stonehenge sequence. He glossed the Wessex grave finds as indicating a world dominated by warrior-chieftains, the 'middlemen' who he claimed had operated on the trade routes that he assumed had run between Ireland, with its metal ores, and continental Europe. He saw these chiefdoms as having been capable of commanding 'the immense resources of labour and craftsmanship necessary for the building of Stonehenge III' (Atkinson 1960, 164). And yet he went on to wonder 'were these Wessex chieftains alone responsible for the design and construction of this last and greatest monument at Stonehenge?' (Atkinson 1960, 165 emphasis omitted). He concluded that it was surely more likely that a monument that transcended all other comparable buildings in Britain had been influenced by the only contemporary European culture in which '*architecture*, as distinct from mere construction, was already a living tradition' (Atkinson 1960, 165 emphasis original). That culture was to be found, in Atkinson's view, in the Mycenaean world with the seemingly obvious comparison between the lintelled stones of Stonehenge and the lion gate of the citadel at Mycenae, with latter's stone uprights and lintel. Rather than being the product of 'mere barbarians', the final building of Stonehenge was thus assigned by Atkinson to the design of a Mycenaean architect (Atkinson 1960, 165–166).

By the early 1960s Stonehenge and the burials beneath the round mounds that cluster around it had thus become the manifestations of a land of warrior-chieftains. It was they who supposedly organized the resources to build the final stone structures of Stonehenge, albeit under the direction of a

Fig. 1.2 The Lion Gate at Mycenae in the nineteenth century.

Mycenaean architect. By the late 1960s all this had begun to change. It now appeared possible that the sequence of Wessex burial mounds began at a time predating the construction of the Mycenaean citadel, perhaps by some centuries, although the shaft graves themselves also predated that construction. Indeed, the lintelled stone structures of Stonehenge were now dated earlier than most of the surrounding graves and may well have been constructed before 2000 BCE whilst the construction of Mycenae occurred after 1400 BCE and had nothing to do with Stonehenge and perhaps little to do with the origins of Piggott's Wessex Culture (Renfrew 1968).

The shift in chronologies had arisen from the increasingly widespread application of radiocarbon dating to the prehistoric materials of temperate Europe, and we have to be clear as to the implications that were brought about by these changes (Renfrew 1973a). All archaeologists confront two problems: how to date their materials and how to best understand the changing patterns that are recognizable in the sequences of those materials. The original solution to the first of these problems impacted upon the approaches that were taken to the second. Before the advent of radiocarbon dating, along with other methods that were dependent upon the isotopic decay of radioactive materials, the only secure option for European prehistory was to establish links between European finds and the calendar-dated archaeological sequences from ancient Mesopotamia and Egypt. Establishing such links was far from easy and depended upon finding a bridge between the eastern chronologies and those of temperate Europe by way of the Aegean sequence of materials, which could be dated by actual imports to the Egyptian calendar. By this means similarities between European materials and those from the Aegean and eastern Mediterranean formed the basis for the European chronological schemes. The security of these schemes was often slight and seemed to be held in place more by the conventions of academic authority than by the evidence itself. Moreover, this approach to dating was obviously tied to the attempts to explain changes in the prehistoric sequences in Europe by reference to the influences that were assumed to have emanated from the eastern Mediterranean.

The scientific dating of dead organic material developed in the 1950s involved measuring the surviving ratio of the atomically unstable to the atomically stable isotopes of carbon. By knowing the rate of decay of the former, and by being able to evaluate the ratios of the carbon isotopes that had originally been taken up by the living material, it was assumed that a possible age for the death of the material could then be calculated. The first adoption of radiocarbon dating provided for both an independent chronology for archaeologically recovered materials and for a shock, because the dates for early agriculture in Europe began to migrate earlier than had previously been expected. That shock was then compounded by a correction in the technique, which showed these dates lay even earlier on the absolute calendar. This shift in dating arose because the naturally occurring level of the radioactive isotope of carbon found in the atmosphere, and therefore available to be incorporated in living organic matter, proved not to have remained constant through time. Consequently, radiocarbon determinations did not provide accurate dates and the results had to be calibrated, an exercise initially achieved by using reference data derived from the dating of the annual growth rings of the long-lived bristlecone pine (Renfrew 1973a). These shifts were first identified and formalized in Renfrew's seminal 1968 paper 'Wessex without Mycenae'.

Radiocarbon dating meant that it was finally possible, not only to evaluate previously established chronological estimates for monuments, such as the tombs built along the Atlantic margins of Europe by the first agriculturalists, and for major technological developments, such as the beginnings of European metallurgy, but also to assess the claimed links by which such innovations were explained (Renfrew 1973a). If Gordon Childe had indeed been correct to suggest that the major developments that occurred in the Neolithic and Bronze Age of Europe were driven by influences that had emanated from the civilizations of the Orient, then the dating should reflect such a sequence of European dependency. Thus, for example, if a Mycenaean architect had indeed designed Stonehenge as Atkinson had suggested, then Stonehenge must post-date the construction of the Mycenaean citadel, and the radiocarbon dates indicated that this was not the case.

The major consequence of the new chronologies was that the conventional dating for the prehistory of Europe, beyond the immediate area of the Aegean, was shown to have been set too late. To take a single example, the synthesis of what was then known of the stone age agriculturalists of Neolithic Britain that Piggott had published in 1954, suggested that this period of agriculture had begun in Britain after 2000 BCE and ended at least by 1500 BCE in southern Britain with the establishment of the Bronze Age Wessex Culture graves. The arrival of the 'beaker people' was given to have occurred in the final stages of Piggott's Neolithic, and only the first phase of Stonehenge was assigned to the British Neolithic. A single early fourth millennium BCE radiocarbon date that had by then been obtained for Neolithic material from Ehenside Tarn in Cumbria was regarded as 'so high, it is difficult to do more than reserve judgement' (Piggott 1954, 380). Piggott was however less inclined to reserve his judgement when confronted by a date in the early third millennium BCE for the construction of the great late-Neolithic henge enclosure at Durrington Walls in Wiltshire, brusquely dismissing the date as 'archaeologically inacceptable' (Piggott 1959, 289).

A Neolithic period in Britain lasting a mere 500 years, followed by an apparently longer-lasting British Bronze Age, which in southern Britain was set to occur between 1500–550 BCE (Hawkes 1959), was not only far too late but also impossibly short to encompass a history of the Neolithic and Bronze Age that ran from the first agriculturalists to the beginnings of iron-working. Such brevity for a period that we would now regard as being twice as long and extending from about 4000 BCE to about 800 BCE had implications for the kinds of narratives that attempted to account for the various changes in material culture and monument types. In these narratives periods of change were not instigated by any cumulative and internally generated processes that might have given rise to horizons of social, economic and cultural transformation, but by waves of external influences and migrations, including of course Bronze Age warriors supposedly migrating from Brittany to southern Britain and architects supposedly arriving there from Mycenae.

Until the 1960s the changing sequences of European prehistory were accounted for as the product of either cultural influences or the movement of peoples from elsewhere. The various lines of influence, at least for the European Neolithic and Bronze Age, always seemed to run from the east to the west, and to originate ultimately in the Orient. Piggott offered a general distinction in which:

> we can perceive, even in remote antiquity ... a broad classification between *innovating* and *conserving* societies. In the one group, technological developments in the arts of peace and war must have been socially acceptable and therefore encouraged; in the other, once a satisfactory *modus vivendi* for the community within its natural surroundings had been achieved, there seems to have been no need felt to alter the situation.
>
> Piggott 1965, 17 emphasis original

Childe's own desire had been to understand why:

> Four to five thousand years ago the natives of Europe were on precisely the same level, as far as equipment and economic organization are concerned, as the natives of eastern North America – a very similar environment – were only 400 years ago and as some native tribes in New Guinea are today. Why then did they not remain illiterate barbarians . . .?
>
> Childe 1958, 7

In Childe's view European societies were prompted to change due to their proximity to the economically productive and politically organized systems of the Nile valley and the Tigris–Euphrates delta. In the case of metalworking we have seen the way that Childe suggested only a managed food surplus that had arisen from the irrigation systems of agriculture in the Old World could support the specialist producers who were necessary to develop metallurgy. Those skills were then carried into Europe by itinerant traders, smiths and colonizers in search of the metal ores found in the Alps, Iberia, Britain and Ireland (Childe 1957a). The widespread distribution of beaker ceramics and the association of beakers with the earliest metalworking in many (but not all) areas of central and western Europe resulted in the general acceptance that the itinerant metalworker found archaeological representation as the beaker people (Childe 1957b, 222).

The construction of dated sequences of cultural change was no longer a central purpose of archaeology and the comparisons that had once, by the necessity of building a European chronology, linked together the sequences of European and eastern Mediterranean cultural materials became open to, and indeed collapsed because of, the independent evaluation resulting from the radiometric methods of dating. The adoption of radiocarbon dating therefore required the writing of a new kind of European and indeed world prehistory. The innovatory nature of cultures that Childe had argued as having originated with the itinerant smiths of the European Bronze Age now had to be sought to explain monument building in Neolithic Europe and the origins of European metallurgy: but what were these innovative processes that drove these developments?

Colin Renfrew quickly sought to address the challenge facing archaeology. He characterized the new dating technology as necessitating a revolution in archaeological thinking. Associations in the Aegean Bronze Age with Egyptian imports ensured that the Aegean chronology remained tied to the well-established calendric dating of the Egyptian sequence, but to the north and west of this Renfrew saw that the chronologies of the European cultural assemblages had now moved earlier than their assumed eastern antecedents. Renfrew characterized this as resulting in a chronological fault line that had moved the chronologies of temperate and northern Europe earlier than those of the Aegean (Renfrew 1973a).

In 1968 Renfrew published his 'Wessex without Mycenae' essay, written when very few radiocarbon dates were available (Renfrew 1968). Nonetheless he sought to establish that the central and western European Bronze Age that had arisen from earlier traditions of indigenous copper-working, was in existence by 2100 BCE, and predated the development of Mycenaean culture in the Aegean. Given the comparisons that Piggott had made between his Wessex Culture assemblage and the central European Early Bronze Age it was reasonable to suppose that the sequence of Wessex graves had begun to be deposited soon after 2100 BCE, a proposition that has now been confirmed by the determination of a single date for an early Wessex grave assemblage of

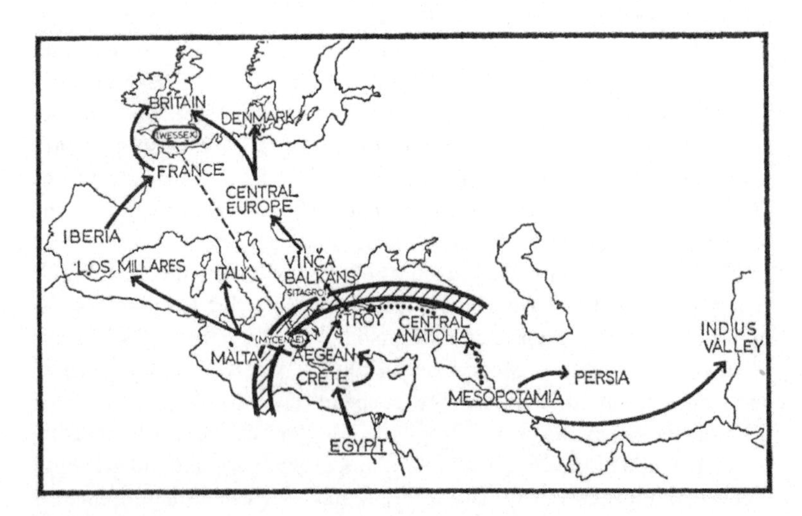

Fig. 1.3 Renfrew's 1973 model of a chronological fault line in prehistoric Europe. Courtesy Colin Renfrew.

between 2020–1770 BCE (Needham et al. 2010). Whilst Renfrew also noted the dates that were available at the time from Stonehenge, it is now also clear that the upright stones with their lintels, the Stonehenge that we see today, were erected earlier than even Renfrew supposed, at around 2620–2480 BCE, and that they were a product of the southern British Late Neolithic and clearly predated the round-barrow graves from the surrounding landscape (Darvill et al. 2012; Parker Pearson et al. 2015a). The development of Stonehenge was therefore neither the product of a Mycenaean architect nor of a supposed Wessex Culture aristocracy. This was followed by the case for a Balkan chalcolithic ('copper age') that should be treated as an autonomous development that did not develop as a product of influences deriving from the Aegean early Bonze Age (Renfrew 1969a).

In both these publications Renfrew used the new chronologies for the European sequences to disentangle them from those of the Aegean and the eastern Mediterranean upon which they had previously been aligned. By this means he sought to argue that, in the case of metallurgy, the European sequences developed independently of any influences from the east. The problem that Renfrew faced, however, was the comparable lack of information for the early development of copper and gold working in the region of the Aegean itself. Throughout these discussions, Renfrew acknowledged that Childe had himself recognized the vulnerabilities that were inherent in his own chronological scheme for the origins of the European Bronze Age (Childe 1957a). There are however three issues that were in danger of being conflated in Renfrew's argument. First is the need to establish a competent chronology for the regional developments across Europe and the eastern Mediterranean. The second concerns the degree to which, if any, the different regions were in contact one with another and the mechanisms by which such contacts might have operated. Third is the nature of the historical processes that gave rise to these sequences, and the extent to which those processes operated at either a level of regional autonomy or at a much larger scale. The latter point is made without necessarily returning to models in which the developments of 'innovating' systems were diffused into 'conserving' systems, although whether this model is accepted or rejected clearly depends upon the kinds of historical process that are regarded as having been at work in these periods. Indeed, of the three issues listed above, the first is clearly of a different order than the latter two. Questions of chronology are now addressed through laboratory analysis and statistical modelling, displaying what archaeologists would accept as a degree of objectivity, whereas questions concerning the mechanisms of inter-regional contacts and historical processes are matters of judgement and reasoned argument that refer to the available material, but upon which differences of opinion are always likely to exist.

Considerable quantities of new data are available fifty or so years since Renfrew initiated the demand that archaeology should write narratives of indigenous developments in Europe that had travelled from the Neolithic to the Bronze Age seemingly without an impetus deriving from the urbanized centres of Egypt and Mesopotamia. Those data have revealed a vastly more complex and diverse sequence of archaeological patterns than were available to either Childe or indeed to Renfrew. These data have not simplified the task of writing a synthesis of 'what happened in history' and we might wonder upon what basis narratives that make these histories understandable might be written. Renfrew argued that:

> European prehistory has for long had a preoccupation with *origins* and with the way in which ideas and cultural traits were transmitted. Today it seems more fruitful to consider *processes* and the way in which such features were *invented.*
>
> Renfrew 1969a, 15 emphasis original

But what were these processes that, after 2500 BCE, drove the widespread use of copper and gold technologies across Europe and followed these with the adoption of the copper/tin alloy of bronze before 2000 BCE? As the full Bronze Age developed, the Wessex Culture graves of southern Britain, with broadly comparable deposits from graves elsewhere in western and central Europe, have been treated as if indicating the emergence of ranked societies and chiefdoms, whilst the 'palaces' of firstly Crete and then of Mycenaean southern Greece, the latter with their archival scripts and associated tomb architecture, have been treated as if witnessing the development of redistributive economies administered from centres of elite residences. Are such social models justified and do they bring us any closer to understanding the dynamics of these periods?

We have indicated that it is by establishing a historical context for the periods under investigation that the processes that operated in those periods should become understandable, and that the material conditions of each context must obviously be constructed from archaeological data. This construction involves, in our view, rather more than the traditional treatment of archaeological material as if it were a record of various kinds of social, economic or political organization. Indeed, we suggest that it is because the steady accumulation of archaeological data has been treated as if it were an increasingly detailed record of such conditions that the archaeology of the periods with which we are concerned has either become increasingly incomprehensible or subject to largely speculative interpretations. Instead we will suggest that archaeology might more effectively treat the material conditions that it describes as the conditions that made certain ways of living possible. We will explore this theme as an understanding of the ways people might once have understood their place in the world by reference to the things that they could use, the places that they could occupy and their relation to their dead.

2

The Emergence of an Aegean Civilization

The controversy that surrounded the first radiocarbon dates obtained for European prehistory, where those dates were much earlier than had been anticipated, is now past. We accept that the plants, animals and probably the people of the early communities of agriculturalists that had originated in south-western Asia colonized Europe, with early agriculture being introduced into south-eastern Europe by around 7000 BCE. But we no longer explain the origins of the first stone-built monumental tombs constructed in western Europe by settled agricultural communities as either indicating an arrival of additional peoples or as the result of religious influences deriving from the eastern Mediterranean, as was once the case (Daniel 1958). Instead this architecture was the indigenous innovation of European agriculturalists, and no one else. Nor do we accept that gold, copper and bronze metal-working was introduced by colonizing smiths arriving from Egypt or Mesopotamia as Gordon Childe had suggested (Childe 1957a), but we treat it instead as an indigenous European development (though see Roberts et al. 2009). And we accept that the major development of the stone architecture of Stonehenge was begun in the mid-third millennium BCE, in the Late Neolithic, and without any motivation derived from Mycenae.

Archaeology has traditionally worked by treating the surviving deposits, objects and monuments from the past as if they described a record of earlier events, where the archaeological concern was with the ways that those events related to various kinds of human behaviour. The new chronology for the histories of the third and second millennia BCE in Europe posed a significant challenge to the ways that those events might be interpreted. The methods of analysis and the languages of description therefore changed as new ways were sought to understand the historical processes that had affected human behaviour without reliance upon the external influences of what Piggott had characterized as 'innovating' societies. Thus, the history of human behaviour in prehistoric Europe was no longer assumed to have changed as responses to cultural influences emanating from the east, and change was instead treated as if it had been self-generated. Central to these new approaches was the idea that the divergent aspects of human behaviour, such as economic, religious, technological and social behaviour, could be characterized as comprising a system, the organization of which was maintained, and at times transformed, as the result of processes that operated within the system itself.

By adopting the position that archaeological finds represent a system of behaviours, the material, whether it be Stonehenge, the Mycenaean shaft graves or sherds of pottery, was no longer treated as if it represented how people had followed the rules of their culture. Instead the various classes of material were treated as if they resulted from the workings of different kinds of behaviour, such that the shaft graves represented the execution of behaviour relating to ritual observation and to the social distinctions between both the participants and the dead. The analytical challenge was therefore to select which parts of the system needed to be analysed and to establish how that analysis could be achieved with reference to the surviving categories of material. One important consequence was that archaeology appeared now to have set itself the task of describing a sequence of past organizations as a prerequisite for any attempt to explain how those organizations had emerged and were subsequently transformed. Less than twenty years after claiming that the radiocarbon chronology had established the autonomy of the European Bronze Age Colin Renfrew argued that a recurrent concern was for:

> archaeology to go beyond the mere reconstruction and description of the past and to seek insight enabling us to explain how that past came about.
>
> Renfrew 1982, 5

How was archaeology going to move from a description of past conditions to an understanding of how those conditions had come about? The problem was that archaeological material (the patterns and the sequences of finds) was used to describe the past in terms of its formation processes. How might that same material reveal both the causes of those processes as well as the historical reasons for systems to which those processes belonged?

Rethinking European prehistory

In the case of Stonehenge, Richard Atkinson had clearly recognized the considerable levels of labour organization demanded by its construction. He believed that this organization of labour resulted from the coercion of a chiefly elite who were represented by the rich Bronze Age burials of the Wessex Culture (Atkinson 1960, 166). However, as we have noted, he also assumed that this level of organized coercion required the further direction of a Mycenaean architect if it was to execute the architectural complexity of Stonehenge. By placing the development of Stonehenge in the Neolithic, and thus before the burials of Piggott's Wessex Culture, and indeed before Mycenae, the challenge posed by the radiocarbon chronology was to establish the conditions that could give rise to the building of Stonehenge.

An initial attempt towards this goal was made by Colin Renfrew (1973b). He situated the building of Stonehenge in an indigenous historical development, and he began by assuming that human populations divided themselves into 'modular' social units, that the organization of each social module tended to be territorial, and that the territorial pattern was visible

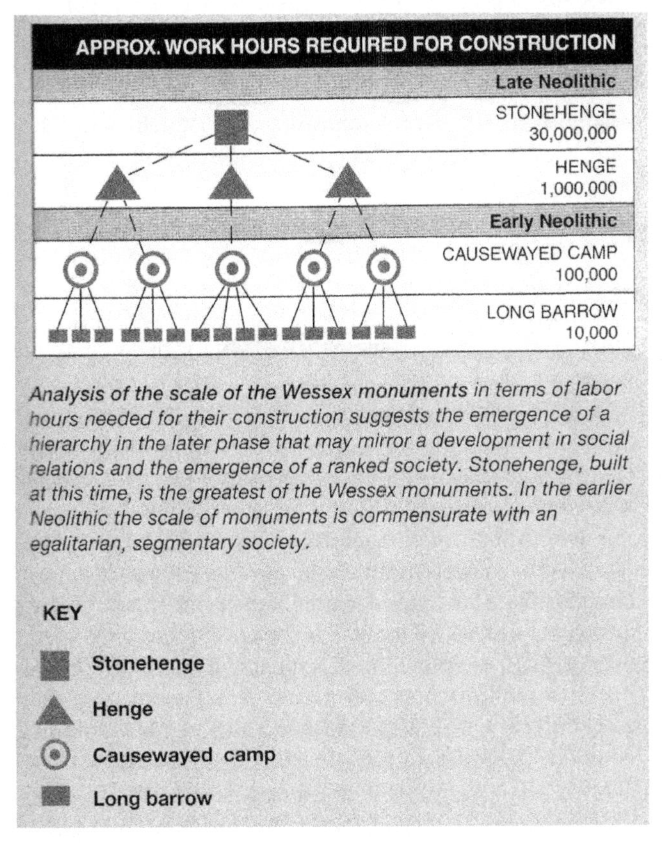

Fig. 2.1 Renfrew's model for a hierarchy of labour in the construction of Wessex monuments. Courtesy Colin Renfrew.

archaeologically by the distribution of residues that had been generated by these kinds of organization (Renfrew 1977). In the case of the British Neolithic, Renfrew proposed that the period originated with the founding of similarly sized territorial 'modules' of agricultural organization, where each module represented a relatively egalitarian level of social organization. In northern Britain, he selected examples where this pattern appeared to be given by the near regular distribution of tombs containing some of a community's dead (Renfrew 1976), whereas in southern Britain clusters of earthwork tombs seemed to be distributed around a single larger 'causewayed enclosure'. Renfrew argued that the distribution pattern of monuments in southern Britain, the hierarchy of labour demands required for building the enclosures compared with that of the tombs, and the widely accepted function of the enclosures as centres or rallying points for populations, implied the archaeology of primary territorial units of population coalescing into larger and more hierarchal levels of organization. Thus, Renfrew attempted to trace the history of social development in the Late Neolithic as having metamorphosed archaeologically into a sequence of ever-larger earthwork constructions, culminating with the building of Atkinson's Stonehenge III. Renfrew therefore read the record of the various monuments' dates, distributions and the scales of their construction as if they represented an internally generated sequence of increasingly centralized labour organization. But why should this sequence have occurred? Why might egalitarian agricultural systems transform themselves into ranked systems that culminated, at least in southern Britain, with the enormous level of labour organization required to build a very elaborate stone circle?

Renfrew approached this question by reducing the unique form of the Wessex monuments to a measure of both the scale of the work that their construction represented and to the structure of their geographical distribution, to reveal the working of a historical context that was defined by a particular kind of social organization. From this perspective he was able to draw upon analogies with the kinds of social organizations which were also attested for by the general anthropological categories of 'tribes' and 'chiefdoms' (Sahlins 1968; Service 1962). Indeed, in the case of his Wessex study, Renfrew offered a checklist of variables, derived from the work of Service and Sahlins, that he took to contribute to the definition of chiefdom levels of organization, claiming that these variables were matched in the archaeological record of Late Neolithic Wessex (Renfrew 1973b, 543). In this way he could argue that he was tracing the indigenous rise of a chiefdom-type organization in the Late Neolithic of Wessex, with the additional benefit that such chiefdoms would be expected to share the same functional qualities as chiefdoms that are attested anthropologically. To this end Renfrew quoted Service (1962, 43 emphasis original) who had claimed that: 'Chiefdoms are particularly distinguished from tribes by the presence of centres which coordinate economic, social and religious activities' and that '[c]hiefdoms are *redistributional* societies with a permanent central agency of coordination.'

Assigning a general role, such as redistribution, to a particular kind of social or economic organization proved hugely seductive for an archaeology that was attempting to explain why various kinds of organization had come into existence. If, for example, chiefdoms have the role of redistributing material through their population then it was but a short step to the claim that the reason that chiefdoms arose was to satisfy the population's need for a system of redistribution. This argument is circular and fails to recognize that the consequences of a period of social and economic change can be quite unpredictable given the conditions that gave rise to that change. Nonetheless, the suggested function of chiefdoms was then linked by Renfrew and others (particularly in the case of the Aegean Bronze Age – as we shall see) with the suggestion that the chiefly redistribution of goods and services resulted from the need to redistribute the products of localized specialized producers (Renfrew 1973b, 554–556). Chiefs thus appeared to be managerially concerned to integrate the products of regionally diverse resources and, in the European Bronze Age, this kind of specialized production seemed to be attested for by the complex products of such production that were found in some of the period's grave assemblages. However, the redistribution model for chiefdoms was rejected in the light of anthropological evidence almost as soon as it had been adopted (Earle 1977), and it was replaced by the image of chiefdoms as systems of political coercion and economic exploitation (Earle 1997; Gilman 1981).

Renfrew's claim to have identified the rise of chiefdoms in the British Neolithic was questioned at the time (Leach 1973; cf. Fleming 2004), and the function, as well as the identification, of chiefdoms remains highly contentious. Nonetheless the principle that was being established was in many ways more important: namely that archaeology should move away from the analysis of historical particularities (such as the design of this or that monument or artefact assemblage at this or that moment of history) and explain the general trajectories in the development of the kind of organization that the particularities supposedly represented. It followed that the explanations that were sought for the kinds of material patterning recorded archaeologically were expressed as the products of these more general processes. This move enabled analogies to be drawn, from anthropology in particular, for the processes of cultural change which archaeology had such difficulty establishing solely with reference to its own data. It also encouraged the view that explanations for cultural change were likely to be expressed in terms of theoretical abstraction in contrast to descriptions of the past that were built out of empirical detail.

Renfrew's approach throughout this and other studies at the time was in line with the principles that defined the birth of the 'New Archaeology', a movement later renamed 'Processual Archaeology'. This approach was expressed by a methodology that read the archaeological record of the materials that had been deposited under specific historical circumstances as if they represented the operation of general kinds of processes. This meant that specific things, like Stonehenge, had to be read as if they represented the type of centre which perhaps coordinated 'social and religious as well as economic activity' (Renfrew 1973b, 543). This could then lead to the claim that the *function* of Stonehenge, for example, was comparable with the ahu and moai of Rapa Nui (the platforms and stone heads of Easter Island; cf. Renfrew 1984, 200–224). These functional comparisons that were made between specific patterns of material were expected to result from a common range of processes (such as those associated with a 'chiefdom', for example). It was these processes that had supposedly mobilized the necessary labour force for monument building. Archaeology was being designed to become a generalizing discipline that, it was hoped, would eventually establish general explanations for the mechanisms governing the social and economic development of human populations.

The one substantial study that best exemplifies the application of this approach to the archaeology of Early Europe was that offered by Renfrew for the 'emergence of civilisation' in the southern Aegean from the late fourth and through the third millennium BCE (Renfrew 1972).

The emergence of civilization

In his study of the Aegean Renfrew was concerned to follow the cultural development that was attested archaeologically for the Cyclades, Crete and mainland Greece over the period that saw the establishment of metallurgy, complex burial rituals and early use of texts, as well as the construction of the dense building complexes in Crete and the southern Greek mainland that included the so-called palaces of the second millennium BCE. The full development of this assemblage of material appeared to herald the birth of a European civilization. The term 'civilization' is obviously ensnared by contemporary assumptions that feed off a wide range of cultural values, prejudices and political judgements (Wengrow 2010), and other archaeologists have sought the greater neutrality that appears to be offered when referring

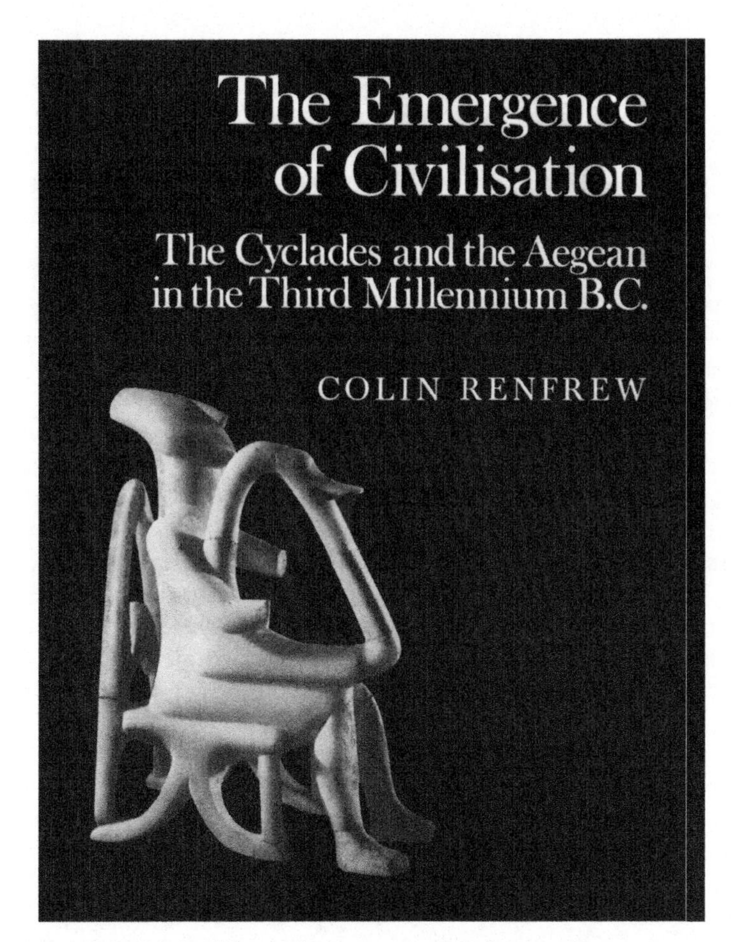

Fig. 2.2 Colin Renfrew's book *The Emergence of Civilisation*. Courtesy Colin Renfrew.

to 'complex' societies (Smith 2012). Both terms are however difficult to define with any precision and, as such, they might hint that more confusion than clarification is gained when we attempt to group very different fields of human existence under the title of a single kind of organization. However, if we are to pursue the claim that archaeology should be a generalizing discipline, and this is certainly the claim that Renfrew was concerned to establish, then that claim necessarily concerns itself with general explanations for the emergence of general categories of existence, and this is the language that we must use.

Renfrew was clear from the outset as to the aim of his study:

> [I]t is widely felt that these first civilisations of Europe were an offshoot of Oriental civilisation, by which they were inspired, and without which they would not have existed.... I have come to believe that this widely held diffusionist view... is inadequate.
>
> Renfrew 1972, xxv

The alternative that Renfrew sought to build required an understanding of the ways that the Aegean contained the mechanisms necessary for its own historical transformation, leading to the question of how these mechanisms might be identified.

The procedure that Renfrew followed was to treat human culture (with the obvious archaeological emphasis upon material culture) as the context that had been constructed to sustain various kinds of human existence. Renfrew concurred with the argument that had been set out in Lewis Binford's 1962 paper (which is widely accepted as a founding text of the New Archaeology) which called for ancient cultural residues to be analysed as if they resulted from the different components of coherently functioning systems. It was the internal arrangement of these systems that defined the various kinds of human organization, ranging from egalitarian systems to states. The histories of these systems, represented by sequences of archaeological finds, thus described the ways that they had provided for the contexts that supplied various human subsistence, social and religious requirements. It was assumed that for most of the time, such systems would tend towards states of stability or 'homeostasis', requiring that any change in the circumstances of one part of the system, or in the environment within which the system had operated, was accommodated by the dampening mechanism of 'negative feedback' between the internal subsystems. What was more to the point was that systems did change at certain moments, and that these changes gave rise, in one example, to the 'palace economies' and civilization of the Bronze Age Aegean. Renfrew emphasized that these changes were structural (although he did not use the word), leading to new levels of organization, and could not therefore be explained simply by the growth in any one subsystem but required instead a positive feedback cycle in which change in one subsystem generated change in other subsystems that in turn amplified the original change. Renfrew referred to this feedback process as the 'multiplier effect' (Renfrew 1972, 27–44). In the case of both negative and positive feedback processes the problem was that the nature of the communicating channels between subsystems was never adequately defined (Clarke 1968, 46).

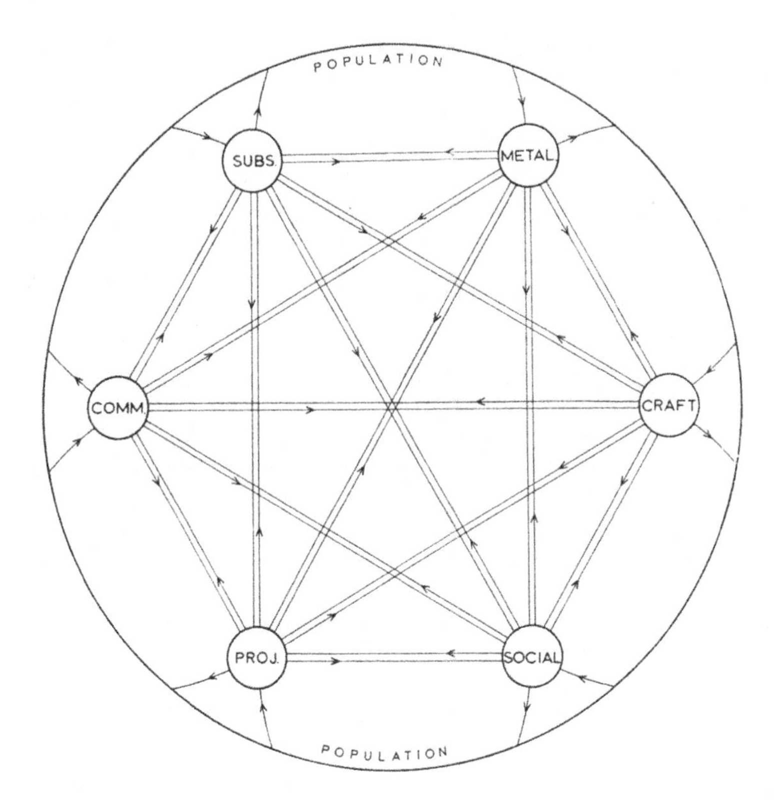

Fig. 2.3 The multiplier effect, as modelled by Colin Renfrew (1972, Fig. 21.1). Courtesy Colin Renfrew.

Renfrew's archaeological analysis of the Aegean treated it as if it had functioned as a single system. The archaeological evidence represented the residues produced by the subsystems that had maintained the regional system. The subsystems, six in all, covered subsistence, metallurgy, other craft production, the social world (conceived of as the immaterial relationships between persons), symbolic and projective systems (language and other symbolic forms of communication, music, dance and religion) and trade (see Fig. 2.3). Any given series of human actions, or any assemblage of material, might easily relate to more than one subsystem, but this was not in itself regarded as problematic, as the model was simply a window onto particular questions concerning a dataset acknowledged as being extremely complex. Using these subsystems as an organizing principle, Renfrew was able to describe the series of changes and innovations of the third millennium that together went to make up his 'emergence of civilisation'. Hence, within the subsistence subsystem he describes the innovation of olive and vine cultivation leading to the production of oil and wine; within the metallurgical subsystem the invention of the dagger in combination with the introduction of tin bronze alloying was seen to drive the sudden increase in production despite the technology having been available for many generations; within the trade subsystem, a move from reciprocal to redistributive exchange reflected centralization of storage and resources in developing political systems.

Renfrew's historical narrative began by establishing what, at that time, was known of the material sequences for the Late Neolithic and Bronze Age of the Cyclades, Crete and southern Greece. These sequences were then correlated to bring them within the ambit of a single southern Aegean cultural sequence. A tentative, absolute, chronology was then established for this sequence using the few radiocarbon dates that were available and by reference to what Renfrew described as 'true cross dating' with the Near East and Egypt (Renfrew 1972, 212). Renfrew's aim was to establish the material sequence of a relatively autonomous Aegean cultural system for the Neolithic and Bronze Age as a secure database which could then populate the theoretical model he proposed to use in offering explanations for cultural change.

Renfrew's claim to the explanatory force of his approach rested first on his notion that changes within subsystems were expected to be exceptional, rather than routine, because of what he saw as the innate conservatism of the human condition, commenting that 'this conservative nature of culture cannot too strongly be stressed' (Renfrew 1972, 487). Most innovation would therefore be met with systemic opposition strongly reducing its effectiveness. When innovation co-occurred within two or more of the subsystems, however, the opposite effect supposedly occurred: the 'multiplier effect' led to the mutual reinforcement or amplification of change, expansion of the system and often to the expansion of the population. Hence the innovative development of the metal dagger was coincident with the introduction of longboats, crucial for the movement of metals; increased supplies of raw materials coincided with increased production; increased production fostered technological innovation: 'trade and metallurgy grew together as neither could have done without the other' (Renfrew 1972, 488).

The growth of any civilization, Renfrew argued, could be explained by reference to a series of coincident innovations that cut across subsystems and were sustained by the multiplier effect. This was the general model and its application to the third millennium Aegean produced a table of forty-five specific coincident innovations, such as 'visible wealth provoking competition and war' (the social, metallurgical and craft production subsystems) or 'Craft specialisation necessitating exchange and hence the formulation of concepts of equivalence, of weights and measures' (the craft production and symbolic and projective subsystems). Out of these, two more general explanations for the emergence of Aegean civilization were offered: one, that the redistributive system, inherent in many of the innovations, was the principal explanation for the range of social changes noted; the other, that wealth and competition was the main factor in the increased stratification of society. In closing, Renfrew emphasized that it was 'the uniquely human ability to find symbolic means to relate' technological and social innovation through symbolic systems of equivalences that made sustained change in human culture possible (Renfrew 1972, 504).

The breadth and scope of Renfrew's project was vast, and it is perhaps not surprising that few have undertaken the sustained research required to employ his general model with other datasets. Concerning its specific application to the Aegean, however, the book was remarkable in coherently offering a rich vision for what archaeology could and should be for. In a discipline that was at that time mired in typological catalogues and pseudo-historical syntheses, Renfrew offered a bold vision connecting different strands of evidence at a detailed level to produce cogent and seemingly causal explanations for major questions in Aegean prehistory. Much in this vision has stood the test of time, such as the importance of the cultivation of the vine and the olive, in truth barely evidenced in 1972, but now richly documented for the third millennium and indeed even earlier (Margaritis 2013a); the central importance of metal in the third millennium remains the subject of much discussion and theorizing, as will indeed be seen in Chapter 4. However, seen from outside the prism of the developing New Archaeology of the time, some of the approaches championed in the book do merit further consideration.

Toward a social archaeology

The original importation of systems analysis into archaeology was relatively short lived, and Renfrew's 1972 *The Emergence of Civilisation* remains the one full length application of these ideas to European prehistory. We have already hinted at one methodological problem that faced such an archaeology, namely that entities such as artefacts, assemblages or monuments could not be related directly to any single subsystem. Individual entities were obviously likely to have functioned in more than one subsystem, as in the way that the Bronze Age palaces of Crete and the southern Greek mainland operated not only with subsistence and social functions, as Renfrew accepted, but were also likely to have functioned within all the other subsystems that Renfrew had identified. It was therefore not straightforward to map archaeological entities on the organization of subsystems. Moreover, not only might archaeological entities act within more than one subsystem, but also subsystems overlapped, so that all the elements of one could also be present within another. This created the potential for over emphasis on cross-subsystem feedback and amplification when in fact the process in question was itself simply part of two subsystems. Renfrew acknowledged both of these points, but he did not consider them significantly to undermine the approach.

It was perhaps the result of this methodological uncertainty within the New Archaeology project generally that individual cultural systems came to be thought of as functioning principally as either subsistence and economic systems on the one hand, or as social systems on the other. Indeed, Renfrew suggested that 'systems thinking' was the analytical procedure that was subsumed within the larger programme of social archaeology (Renfrew 1984, 12). The proposed analytical distinction between archaeologies of subsistence systems and those of social systems (as if these two aspects of any human system were not themselves intimately entwined) was really a distinction about whether the changes that were recognized archaeologically were best explained by reference to subsistence needs or to social motivations. In the former case, explanations for systemic change tended to look towards changes in the wider environment to which the system was assumed to adapt. Eric Higgs and M.R. Jarman, who fronted the British Academy's major research project into the early history of agriculture during the 1970s, took the economy to be '[t]he primary human adaptation to the environment' and therefore the obvious focus for archaeological concern (Higgs and Jarman 1975, 4). Similarly, Lewis Binford, whose work was almost entirely concerned with developing an archaeological methodology for the analysis of hunter-gatherers, and whose stated aim was to avoid explanations for the form of cultural systems that were expressed in terms of a simple environmental determinism, treated the environment instead as having provided a set of possible options within which the system could adapt. Binford assumed that these options were constrained by the technologies that were available to the system and the scale of its population, and he commented that, in his view, the wider range of cultural practices always seemed to depend upon the ways that subsistence processes were organized, writing that:

> when I think about all of the factors that contribute to variability among hunter-gatherer groups, I am impressed with how much the character of the subsistence base has contributed to my explanations.
>
> Binford 2001, 433

In 1978 Redman and his colleagues had applied a 'primitivist' logic when asserting that whilst an archaeological concern with the 'mundane' topics of chronology, the history of technology and subsistence had made major contributions to the understanding of hunting and gathering societies 'where other sources of information are limited', the recognition of a richer database along with the use of theoretically informed model building, aspects of what they heralded as a 'social archaeology', became applicable in the analysis of more complex forms of social organization, thus moving the study 'from hunting and gathering to state societies' (Redman et al. 1978, 2). Renfrew also allowed that the adoption of a social archaeology became unavoidable when dealing with more 'complex' cultural systems, where these material systems tended to buffer the communities concerned from the immediate effects of their environments. In short, hunter-gatherers appeared only to have the cultural resources necessary for adaptation to their environments, and the development of those resources therefore tended to be driven by subsistence concerns and directed by environmental change. By developing more varied cultural conditions within which to operate, complex societies had been able to employ a wider range of socially driven and goal-directed options for their own development. The establishment of a social archaeology was therefore an important part of Renfrew's concern to build a European archaeology that recognized the internal dynamics that had operated to provide for cultural change (Renfrew 1973c; 1984). In considering some of the basic questions that archaeologists needed to address in building a social archaeology, Renfrew identified 'the size of the social unit, its political organization, its relations with its neighbours, and the range of roles and status held within it' as being 'matters of urgent concern' (Renfrew 1984, 10). It was these concerns that structured the kind of systemic analysis that Renfrew offered for the development of the Neolithic and Bronze Age of Wessex and of the southern Aegean.

3

Living with Things: The Politics of Identity

The archaeology of representations

One of the most famous academic book reviews published in the latter half of the twentieth century was Noam Chomsky's review of B.F. Skinner's *Verbal Behaviour* (Chomsky 1959). It is famous not because Chomsky didn't much like the book (he didn't), but because he used his review to undermine the basis of the philosophy of *Behaviourism*. Chomsky carefully exposed the emptiness of Skinner's case in which the explanation that Skinner had offered for the development of human verbal behaviour depended upon the ways the individual responded to externally derived stimuli (other people talking), and to the ways those stimuli – and the individual's responses to them – were reinforced over time. The alternative that Chomsky began to introduce in his review, and which he went on to develop in his later work, was the theory of a *Transformational Grammar* (Chomsky 1972). Why should a debate that was concerned with theories of language matter in a book that is concerned with the archaeology of things?

Whilst archaeologists study a wide range of material residues, and where ideas as to how such residues should be understood vary more than you might expect, most archaeologists do assume that the form of those residues is, to a large part, the result of earlier human activity. This leads us to the working assumption – a taken for granted within archaeology that now requires a more critical handling – that the patterns recognized in archaeological materials should be treated as if they were an eroded pattern of things that *represented* human activity. This characterization of archaeological data is expressed by references that are made to the evidence as if it were an 'archaeological record'. This implies that the differently organized, but now extinct, traditions of human behaviour are recorded by diverse patterns in the surviving materials.

The problem that this kind of archaeology has encountered is how it might move from simply describing the diversity of archaeological finds, and thus identifying the physical mechanisms of deposition and erosion resulting in their formation, to an understanding of why people once acted in a particular way, and the reasons why those various kinds of behaviour might have changed. This move from describing *what* had happened to understanding *why* it might have happened is clearly contentious. However, it is surely necessary for archaeology to do more than merely catalogue the mechanical processes that resulted in the accumulation of archaeological residues. After all, the frustration that many felt with Atkinson's approach to Stonehenge was that he seemed content to describe the mechanisms by which the stones had been hauled into place and then erected, but less concerned to understand why this had happened. And for us to fall back upon the vague assertions that writers like Stuart Piggott offered when referring to the differences between 'innovating and conserving' societies adds nothing either to our understanding of the diverse historical process that supposedly resulted in these different kinds of society (if such existed), or to our understanding of the histories of human variability. Colin Renfrew, on the other hand, attempted to understand why civilization emerged during the Bronze Age of the Aegean, and he did this by arguing that human communities had exploited the environmental potential to utilize a wider range of soils (by means of olive and vine cultivation), had used the products of those new subsistence procedures for storage (centralized redistribution), and had also competed for items of prestige to drive forward technological change (the origins of metallurgy). Each strand of Renfrew's argument made an assumption about the ways that humans were likely to have responded to certain material conditions. For example, in Renfrew's model olive and vine cultivation appear the necessary response to that particular environment, and it is accepted that humans would necessarily have competed for access to the exotic products of an early metallurgy, using those exotics to signify status differences between themselves, both in life and in death. A great deal more material has now been collected from the southern Aegean than was available at the time that Renfrew was writing, and more analytical procedures have also become available, but whilst this more recent work might challenge the detail of the case that Renfrew made, each amendment and each challenge has tended to assume that the human responses necessarily arose as the result of particular environmental stimuli. The obvious problem remains: why these responses and not others?

If we continue to adhere to a methodology that requires us to accept that archaeological remains represent the processes that were both the stimuli for cultural behaviour and the products of that behaviour, and that the former explain the latter, then this places considerable limitations on the kinds of historical knowledge that we are going to be able to establish. Such knowledge will be dominated by a catalogue of all those earlier processes that reliably account for the available debris, and whilst this seems obvious enough, it is an approach that denies us an understanding of how the choices and intentions that are expressed by those actions came to be formulated. Human behaviour is a way of living intentionally towards – and thus of understanding – and coping with existing conditions. Such behaviour is not determined by the conditions themselves but arises from the particular ways in which people might have seen and have understood the world.

Archaeologists have tended to treat human intentionality as a problem because they have assumed that intentionality has always arisen cognitively and that cognitive understandings are not represented in any direct way by the archaeological record. The claim that cognitive planning precedes the execution of any action was captured by Marx when he wrote that:

> many a human architect is put to shame by the skill with which a bee constructs her cell. But what from the very first distinguishes the most incompetent architect from the best of bees, is that the architect has built a cell in his head before he constructs it in wax.
>
> Marx 1930, 169

If Atkinson's presumed 'Mycenaean architect' had built Stonehenge in his or her head, as Marx had implied, before organizing its construction on the ground, then to ask why such a plan might have been formulated and then executed would lead us towards pointless speculation. This lies at the heart of Atkinson's refusal to consider why Stonehenge had been built. Archaeologists have avoided this problem by the simple expedient of adopting the principle that human actions should be understood, not as working from the 'internal' mental formulation of an idea to its execution, but as the responses to 'external' material stimuli that are represented relatively unambiguously by the archaeological record. Thus the continuing adherence to the behavioural premise, that it was the stimuli that explain why a line of action was followed and that both the stimuli and its consequences are available for archaeological analysis.

The 'New Archaeology', that developed across North America, Britain and parts of northern Europe in the 1960s and 1970s and to which Colin Renfrew's work was a major contributor, provided an important approach towards explaining the changing patterns of behaviour that were witnessed archaeologically. This approach recognized that all human actions had to be understood not as the single expression of a cultural idea but as the workings of a system of institutions. This accepted the point that human beings have always operated in relationship with other humans, other forms of life, and a wide range of other material conditions and that all these constituted the social conditions within which human life was lived. Changes in human behaviour must therefore be understood from the perspective of the systemic context within which those changes had occurred.

The Behaviourism that Skinner had championed proposed that an individual's behaviour resulted from the conditions that had stimulated that behaviour, along with the ways that the individual's repeated responses to those same or similar stimuli were subsequently reinforced. This argument, applied to communities of individuals and concerning a wider range of behaviour than verbal expression, continued to find favour amongst archaeologists in the middle years of the twentieth century. From Renfrew's own work it would be possible to argue that olive and vine cultivation was the response that had been stimulated by the thinner soils of the southern Greek mainland which were experienced as having been inadequate to support the fertility and drainage demanded by a sufficiently productive programme of cereal cultivation. The response to these conditions could then have been reinforced by the success of olive and vine cultivation. One problem with such an argument is that both olive and vine harvesting involve the products of mature plants, and the demands of mature growth are hardly the basis for the rapid reinforcement of behavioural change that Behaviourism seems to require. A wider problem is that the argument does not explain what it in fact claims to explain: it does not explain the specific form of the economic response. To take another example: it is very unlikely that any stimulus could be identified that adequately explained the architectural form and decoration of the complex 'palatial' structures that were built in southern Greece and Crete during the Bronze Age. Chomsky's dismissal of Behaviourism drew in part upon this simple point: that verbal responses were always richer and more complex than could be explained by any possible stimulus. Chomsky continued to develop his 'poverty of stimulus' argument by reference to the childhood ability to learn a language (Chomsky 1972). The argument remains contentious, but Chomsky noted that children learn the language of their peers, partly through the external input of being spoken to which, whilst this provides them with a vocabulary and demonstrates the practice of speaking, cannot explain the rapid development of their linguistic abilities. The latter can only be explained, according to Chomsky, by the existence of an innate grammatical capability which enables the learnt vocabulary to be used in ways that make sense syntactically.

Chomsky therefore claimed that whilst languages vary in their vocabulary, and that the range of an individual's vocabulary will increase with age and experience, it is the ability to learn and deploy the grammatical rules of language that define the linguistic skills that are innate to each individual. The important point that needs stressing is that when we refer to innate skills this does not mean that the rules of grammar are somehow 'hard wired' into the brain of each individual child. Instead what is innate is the *ability* to begin to mobilize and to develop the skills that define the grammar necessary for comprehensible language use, and it is this development that is integral to the individual's own development in which biological and cultural developments come as one. The early achievement of these skills is therefore a mark in the growth towards the bio-cultural maturity of an individual. It is perhaps for this reason that the linguistic skill of language learning appears to be fully developed amongst young children, whereas adults, at a different stage of their development, find it that much harder to learn a foreign language.

We must conclude therefore that Chomsky's 'transformational grammar' has evolved as a developmental skill that is employed each time we say, or write, anything original (which we do all the time). It is one of the skills that creates the individual as a social being. Behaviourism had assumed that it was 'external' stimuli that explained why people were able to say certain things and behave in certain ways that were comprehensible, whereas Chomsky proposed that those external experiences were processed via an ability that was somehow innate to the embodied growth of the biological individual.

If the ability to learn grammar is innate in all human beings, in a similar way the ability to learn the rules and etiquette of cultural behaviour in varying contexts is also innate: neither external stimuli nor internal cognitive planning are sufficient in themselves to explain this ability. Individuals learn and develop in the company of others, it is the social and material context that facilitates the development of the individual such that to act comprehensibly is to act in ways that others will understand. How might this understanding be extended to an archaeological understanding of the generation of different kinds of material order?

Cultural understanding

If archaeological data were simply to be treated as if they were the eroded products of human behaviour, then it would seem to follow that any understanding of the historical significance of that behaviour depends upon an understanding of what had guided, determined or had otherwise motivated that behaviour. The conflicting models provided by Skinner and by Chomsky for the competent creation of verbal performances have both found parallels in the ways that archaeology has understood the wider performance of human material production. Skinner's Behaviourism, in which an individual learnt how to behave verbally from their exposure to external stimuli, certainly dominated archaeological reasoning for the first half of the twentieth century by treating the stylistic aspects of human behaviour (such as the production of decoration on pottery vessels, or indeed the design of Stonehenge itself) as the cumulative result of numerous individuals being exposed to, and thus learning to adopt, the cultural norms of the society or the community to which they belonged. It was these external influences of the cultural tradition into which a person had been born that were assumed to have contributed to the geographical and chronological spread of certain styles of material residue. However, the view developed in the middle years of the twentieth century was that such explanations were too general and therefore inadequate for the task of explaining the complexity of archaeological deposits. This meant that the Behavioural principle was reworked to analyse stimuli as impacting upon a system of behavioural institutions, where the responses to these stimuli were worked through those different institutions. The histories of institutions such as those that demarcated social, political and economic behaviour, and which were treated as being represented by different categories of archaeological data, were assumed to have been designed (by some unspecified means) to ensure the continuing adaptation and functioning of the entire system. It was in this way, for example, that Johnson and Earle proposed that chiefdom levels of organization had originated because:

> when population density is sufficiently high to put a population at risk during a shortfall, risk management requires the production of a surplus and its storage can be handled by individual families: when it is centralized under a leader's control, however, risk is averaged across more subsistence producers and the necessary per capita surplus (which we may think of as a kind of insurance premium) is less. The stored surplus also provides the chief with the means to invest in other political and economic ways, on his own behalf or his polity's.
>
> Johnson and Earle 1987, 209

Antonio Gilman (1991, 147) dismissed this model as offering a 'managerial account' of social evolution, one that treated the emergent power of chiefs as if it resulted merely from the redesign of social and political institutions to resolve the impact of certain ecological constraints upon a growing population. Under Johnson's and Earle's model the population had supposedly responded by re-organizing itself in ways that managed those constraints. The implication is that institutions evolved to solve problems that had arisen from the adaptation of the system to a particular set of changing environmental conditions. We have already seen that arguments such as this ultimately fail in their goals because they do not tell us why one kind of adaptive re-organization, such as centralized distribution under chiefly control, had arisen rather than any other. At best the correlation between an assumed stimulus and the institutional response might be treated as if it

Fig. 3.1 Linear B tablet recording the distribution of oil at Mycenae. MY Fo 101. EAM7667. National Archaeological Museum, Athens/Department of Collection of Prehistoric, Egyptian, Cypriot and Near Eastern Antiquities. Copyright © Hellenic Ministry of Culture and Sports/Archaeological Receipts Fund.

described the relationship between a necessary, but not sufficient, condition and the emergence of a particular kind of organization. In the example offered here, we could argue that chiefdoms might only have emerged within systems that had achieved a certain population density, without then assuming any causal relationship between population density and type of political organization.

Chomsky's ideas concerning a transformational grammar, by which humans can employ a finite and learnt vocabulary and an innate ability to employ the necessary syntactical rules to make endlessly original and meaningful statements is, to a certain extent, analogous to an alternative way that archaeology has attempted to establish the ways human agents were once involved in the order of those things that are represented by archaeological materials. Instead of explaining the material patterns as if they included the representations of human responses to 'external' stimuli, human behaviour might be regarded as if it exercised a prejudice as to the ways people might relate to things, and the ways that those things might relate to each other, but in the context of a particular cultural repertoire of things. The adoption of this position assumes that the logic that structured the patterns observable in archaeological residues is comprehensible to us, despite the foreignness of its cultural expression. This assumption implies that the interpretability of the material hinges upon the logic that all human behaviour is the expression of prejudices that are open to understanding by virtue of our common humanity. This seems reasonable, for no other reason than otherwise it would be difficult to see how any people's actions could be understood if they were expressed within a cultural repertoire other than our own. Indeed, how else might cross-cultural studies of humanity operate?

An understanding of others has always been based upon the ways that they expressed themselves, a performance that has taken place within, and in response to, a material context, the residues of which survive archaeologically. Others have therefore become social beings by virtue of actions that have implied a common understanding, but not necessarily a common acceptance, of the world as it was encountered. It has been a commonplace, however, for archaeologists to treat the actions that they claim to observe as if they were the expressions of some mentally formulated belief, with the misleading consequence of treating those actions as if they were the expression of cognitively derived schemes of order. This has occasionally found archaeological expression in the claim that archaeology engages, albeit indirectly, with the ideas that were once 'in people's heads' (Hodder 1984). Following the work and examples offered by Descombes (1986), Artur Ribeiro has shown that archaeology is not a form of palaeopsychology. He has shown that all actions are intentional, meaning that they are directed towards an external object rather than being determined by some mental representation of that object. He comments that:

> Central to the notion of intentionality was the idea that mental acts are external, that is, that fear, hate, love, etc. had to be directed to an external object and not to their internal representation; for example, we fear wolves, not the idea of a wolf, and the Eiffel Tower is visible in the Champs-de-Mars, not its representation.
>
> Ribeiro 2018, 109

This captures the kind of archaeological analysis that we intend to follow here. We make the fundamental assumption that humans experience, and respond to, the world as if it were composed of individual entities, each with their own properties, and whilst the archaeology of things appears to record the order of things, the point is not as much to explain *why* those orders were created but to understand *how* such orders made different forms of life possible. Thus, the order of things does not record a cognitively derived scheme that had been imposed upon an otherwise unordered world, it was not the symbolic representation of an idea. Instead the order of things arose as a testimony to the ways that humans have acted towards the world in ways that expected to find, and to employ, an order that was inherent in those things themselves. Colin Renfrew (2001) has made the point that the qualities of materials are the qualities of embodied experience such as the experience of those things that are dense and heavy, or bright and warm. The residues that are recovered archaeologically were therefore the contexts within which those orders were recognized and towards which the performances of life were directed.

The archaeological project

Peter Winch once wrote that:

> What we may learn by studying other cultures are not merely possibilities of different ways of doing things, other techniques. More importantly we may learn *different possibilities of making sense of human life*, different ideas about the possible importance that the carrying out of certain activities may take on for a man [*sic*], trying to contemplate the sense of his life as a whole.
>
> Winch 1964, 321 our emphasis

From this anthropological perspective, Winch went on to propose that all human life necessitated making sense of certain 'fundamental notions' such as birth, death and sexual relations. It was upon this basis that Winch suggested that:

> The specific forms which these concepts take, the particular institutions in which they are expressed, vary very considerably from one society to another; but their central position within a society's institutions is and must be a constant factor.
>
> Winch 1964, 322

The reality that people's lives confront has always been found to reside in their engagement with others in the context of things, and thus in the shared ways that the qualities that were recognized in those things made an understandable form of life possible. Archaeology must therefore extend beyond the study of patterns of material, and beyond an understanding of the physical process that created those patterns: archaeology is more than the detailed description of the building sequence of a monument such as Stonehenge or an understanding of the mechanics by which the stones were erected. Instead archaeology recovers the remains of the material contexts within which forms of life, quite unlike our own, had become possible. This approach moves us away from treating archaeological data as if they were the representations of various processes and towards their treatment as the mechanisms that had made these other forms of life possible.

Archaeology has long maintained a methodological concern with reconstructing an absent past by reference to a surviving material residue (Lucas 2012), a concern that is haunted by the apparent biases that arise from the fragmentary and partial nature of that residue. The more recent recognition that all life has been lived by finding a place for itself within the particular material assemblages that once existed (Fowler 2013), and of which the residues studied by archaeologists were a part (Olsen et al. 2012), means two things. First that material conditions have always been active (Shanks and Tilley 1987; Bennett 2010), in as much as they have always constrained and facilitated the forms of life that were possible within those contexts. Second that archaeology can contribute significantly to an understanding of those lives because we have available to us some of the material realities that made those lives possible. For us, therefore, archaeology is not a 'discipline of things' but rather a discipline of the possibilities of life as lived amongst things.

In the next three chapters we will explore three different aspects of the contexts that framed and that were colonized by different forms of life in different parts of Europe between the late fourth and the late second millennia BCE. The exchange of materials has tended to dominate the archaeology of this period, particularly in regard to the origins of metallurgy. This emphasis is understandable given the restricted distribution of metal ores against the widening distribution in the production, use and deposition of early metal products. The exchange mechanisms have regularly been described as a process of trade, evoked as the work of merchants, and situated in the social context of value, prestige and display. Our aim is to offer an understanding of the way certain identities are created and the way in which cross-cultural identities can be negotiated. The second aspect of our enquiry will involve an examination of how people's actions and movements towards and within the developing architectural form of place expressed the shared understanding of people's goals. The approaches developed in these two studies are then employed to see how the ongoing recreation of identity required the dead to perform certain roles. In all these cases a social archaeology is being practised. This is not, however, a social archaeology in which the material is treated either as if it recorded the cultural notions shared by the members of a society, nor is the material treated as if it recorded the systemic order of either social statuses or social institutions. Instead forms of life emerged as the material world participated in the bio-cultural development of individuals.

We would stress that we do not regard human identities as simply being 'badged' by certain material symbols, as cultural symbols were once understood to function. For us identity was, and indeed is, something that both the self and others recognize as being a particular kind of human and this is constructed through the ways that materials were used and obligations to others were understood and met or disregarded. Identity is therefore practised as the recognition of others within a given material structural condition. Identity is an ongoing construct, recognized as a product of development and of interpretation, always vulnerable and never a given. What is important about the period which we review here is the ways that the face-to-face construction of knowing the self in the view of others was stretched and extended by the movement of people and the exchange of things under the changing technologies of the third and early second millennia BCE.

The history of various 'forms of life' is therefore the history of the extent and means by which people had been able to find the intentions of each other's actions as intelligible (cf. Ribeiro 2018). This was only possible through their varied access to, and a practical reference towards, a shared understanding of some part of the wider material assemblage. It was those assemblages that provided the conditions of possibility for a social existence and it is the residues of those assemblages that survive archaeologically. By gaining access to some portion of the material assemblage people will have gained access to a context in which notions of moral convention, and deviancy from those conventions, could be monitored. A form of life is and was a way of following a rule, which means an ability to take the next step beyond that which had been taught or learnt. To follow a rule was therefore to be empowered by experience, to move forward pragmatically and imaginatively, to know how to go on, to understand the options that are available, to foresee the effect of behaving in an unexpected manner, and to know when and how a mistake might have been made. In this way the conventions of how to proceed were maintained and evolved whilst the material assemblages that were occupied changed through their decay, elaboration or abandonment.

The ground work that Colin Renfrew laid to enable the archaeology of the fourth, third and second millennia in Europe to be re-thought was based firstly upon a methodology in which archaeological residues represented different kinds of social organization, secondly a social theory that treated the processes at work within any system in terms of their functional roles in sustaining that system, and thirdly an enquiry that assumed that systemic change resulted from feedback between two or more processes internal to the system, rather than a cultural input derived from external sources. The problem with this kind of analysis, that it should deliver causal explanations to the question 'Why did such and such a condition arise?' is that it tended to assume that answers would come in the form of a relatively limited set of antecedent conditions, such as the prior development of regionally specialist production resulting in the need for a system to develop that redistributed those products. Such an assumed simplicity can be questioned, given that a considerable range of causal conditions (cf. Botterill 2010), many lying beyond the means of archaeological representation, are likely to have been active in any such process. By treating archaeological data as residues of the material conditions that had made forms of life possible we are able to consider not *Why* questions concerning the causes of certain material patterns but *How* might different forms of life have arisen within the complex networks that existed between people, other life forms and things.

4

Things that Mattered: Identity in the Production, Exchange and Use of Materials

Introduction

Before the critique that was offered of it by the 'New' or 'Processual Archaeology' in the 1960s, the basic unit of archaeological analysis was taken to be that of a 'culture' (Roberts and Vander Linden 2011). Cultures were mapped geographically and they were defined by the similarities that were observed in the form of the archaeological remains that could be assigned to any one period of time. These similarities in the design of materials were assumed to represent the work of people who had once shared common ways of doing things like making pots, building houses and burying their dead (Childe 1929, v–vi). Consequently, all the material variation observed archaeologically was assigned to a particular cultural group, and this restricted the archaeological analysis of material variability to one of simply tracing cultural sequences in which any change in those sequences was seen to be the consequence of different degrees of externally derived cultural influence.

With the rejection of the assumption that all material variation was merely the representation of the socially established rules of human behaviour, and the adoption in its place of the view that material variability reflected various functional demands, then the study of categories of bounded groups, such as 'cultures' or 'cultural areas', was rejected. This was replaced by the desire to use material variability to identify adaptive and functioning systems that comprised different kinds of behaviour. For example, where variation in burial deposits had been interpreted as representing cultural variation, Processual Archaeology treated burial practices as a kind of behaviour that represented the treatment in death of different social categories of person (Brown 1971).

Processual Archaeology never denied that cultural variation must have existed between people, it was simply that it treated such variation as if it were no more than the human tendency to conform with existing patterns of behaviour (cf. Renfrew 1977, 92–97), rather than assuming that such behaviour was ever actively employed to maintain or transform historic conditions. Nonetheless, long-term and regionally coherent patterns of both organizational *and* cultural development are in fact witnessed in the European Bronze Age, a period which necessarily required the widespread exchange of materials as well as the seemingly extensive movement of people (Kristiansen 1998).

All artefacts have been variously 'entangled' in different kinds of behaviour: those involved in identifying and procuring the raw material, of crafting and production, and of exchange, use and deposition. Each of these demand different rights of access to resources as well as a different set of skills, and the embodied performance of these skills may identify different kinds of people. Cultural archaeology tended to treat the identity of people as if it had in some way preceded its cultural representation. Our emphasis will be different, inasmuch as we treat identity to be something that is constructed, partly by biological development but also by the granting or claiming of rights of access and by the developing skills of performance. The ability to act is facilitated by the technologies of the materials that are available to each performer. This means that different kinds of performance, and thus different kinds of identity, are possible depending upon differential access to resources which may be under the control of others. In this way we begin to recognize the active role of material culture in the making of different kinds of humanness, and that there is always a politics involved in these processes.

The politics of the eastern Mediterranean

In 1982 Mehmet Çakır, a Turkish sponge diver from the village of Yalıkavak, brought his sketches of the copper objects that he had seen on the seabed just off the south-western coast of Turkey to the attention of the director of the Museum of Nautical Archaeology at Bodrum Castle. The follow-up investigation by divers from both the Bodrum Museum and from the American-based Institute of Nautical Archaeology recovered what remained of the cargo of a vessel that had foundered against the rocks of the Uluburun promontory sometime around 1300 BCE. A second Bronze Age cargo had been observed by another sponge diver, Kemal Aras, in 1954, resulting in the excavation in 1960 of a vessel that had foundered around 1200 BCE at Cape Gelidonya, to the east of the Uluburun wreck (Pulak 1998; Bass et al. 1967).

Some twenty years before the disaster that had overtaken the Uluburun vessel, the Pharaoh Tutankhamun was laid to rest in the Valley of the Kings. The discovery of Tutankhamun's tomb in 1922 ranks amongst the most famous of all archaeological discoveries, but the excavation of the Uluburun cargo might be regarded as just as remarkable a find. Whilst the richness of

Tutankhamun's tomb is what we might have expected for the tomb contents of an Egyptian Pharaoh of the New Kingdom, the scale of the Uluburun cargo was entirely unexpected, and it is its range and sheer quantity of material that continues to pose a significant challenge for our understanding of the eastern Mediterranean in the mid- to late-second millennium.

The discovery by Howard Carter and Lord Carnarvon of the tomb of Tutankhamun produced a burial assemblage of objects that display the highest levels of skills employed in their production, whilst the Uluburun wreck yielded a cargo that was dominated, at least in weight, by raw materials, including ten tons of copper ingots and about one ton of tin, 175 ingots of glass, storage jars which had contained around one ton of terebinth resin (which might have been intended to burn as incense) and some ivory. But the cargo also included an assemblage of finely produced objects including jewellery (both complete and scrap material), drinking cups (four in faience and one in gold) and an assemblage of tools and weapons (Pulak 2008). Along with the bulk cargo of raw materials, the Uluburun assemblage might therefore have included some personal possessions of the crew, such as weaponry, although other things, like the gold drinking cup, are perhaps unlikely to have lain amongst the crew's possessions. The Uluburun cargo was therefore diverse, ranging from raw materials, fine items including both useable and scrap gold jewellery, some personal equipment and, as if emphasizing the commercial role of the venture, a collection of pan-balance weights. The Cape Gelidonya wreck site also produced copper and tin ingots, although far fewer than those from the Uluburun cargo, along with a wide range of bronze tools, fittings and scrap bronze, stone weights, mortars, glass beads, scarabs and a cylinder seal along with some Mycenaean pottery and weaponry (Mee 2008, 365; Bass et al. 1967, 52–133). Clearly the two cargos differ in more than their scale. The Cape Gelidonya cargo included more in the way bronze tools and scrap metal, whilst lacking the jewellery found amongst the Uluburun cargo.

The relationship between the Pharaoh's tomb assemblage and these wreck finds seems understandable, at least from one perspective, given that the economies of the eastern Mediterranean would clearly have required the procurement and trans-shipment of raw materials. The strict religious and social conventions that operated in the kingdom of Egypt may be enough to explain the ways that a Pharaoh, such as Tutankhamun, could have been expected to be entombed along with a wealth of precious materials and finely produced artefacts. Our challenge, however, is try to understand the place of southern Greece and Crete in an eastern Mediterranean political and economic system of production, exchange and consumption that is represented archaeologically by, among other things, these cargos.

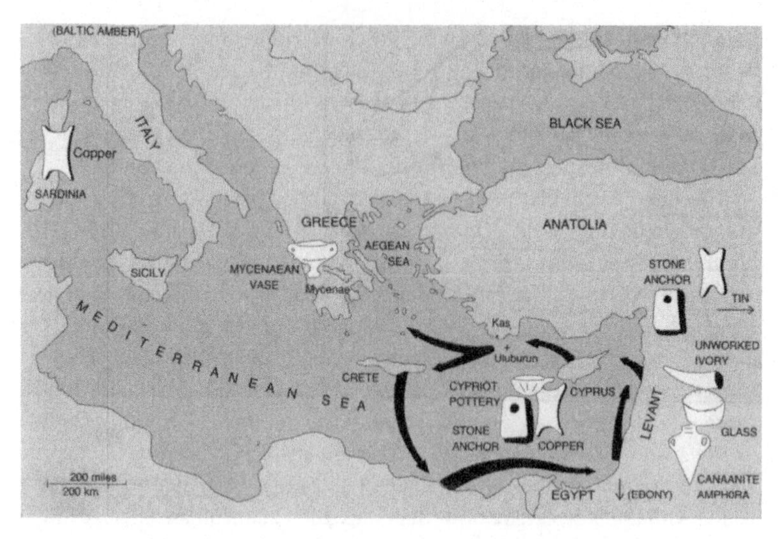

Fig. 4.1 Possible routes of the Uluburun vessel, and likely sources of the materials carried as cargo. Courtesy Colin Renfrew.

It is widely accepted that both the Uluburun and the Gelidonya vessels were exploiting the prevailing currents and winds to sail in a westerly direction around the Turkish coast (Pulak 2008), and analytical techniques are now well-enough developed to provide a relatively secure understanding of the geological, and thus geographical sources, of some of the chemical constituents of the metals, clays and vitreous materials amongst the cargos (Fig. 4.1). It is in this way that the Near Eastern origins of much of the cargos can be mapped, whilst the apparently mixed nationality of the crew has been claimed to be indicated by the style of the personal possessions recovered from the sea floor at Uluburun. The direction of travel towards the Aegean islands and perhaps the Greek mainland, and the possible mixed ethnicity of the crew, would certainly indicate that the Uluburun vessel was moving between different political worlds at the end of the second millennium BCE and that these worlds could have included that of the citadel at Mycenae. Whilst it is therefore possible to map the original sources of some of the raw materials, and to extend that distribution to include the wider pattern of objects produced from this source material, and whilst we know of the available technologies for the transportation of bulk materials (Harding 2013b), these data alone do not provide us with an understanding of the historical contexts within which the trans-shipments had been attempted.

The problem that archaeology continues to face is captured by these deposits. Archaeologists can see that things were moved, sometimes over considerable distances, and that these movements were of both raw materials, including ingots, cut wood and ivory, jars of resin, and perhaps also scrapped metal artefacts that could then be reworked, and also complete artefacts produced in locally distinctive forms, such as ceramics, and things produced in exotic materials, such as the jewellery and drinking cups found amongst the Uluburun cargo. Archaeology can also say something about the technologies by which such movements occur, such as the shipping that is attested by the two wreck finds and is represented by Egyptian temple and tomb wall paintings. Indeed, we can also describe the changing density of finds with distance from source, where those sources are known, as Renfrew, amongst others, has demonstrated (Renfrew 1975). However, all these factors are simply different ways of describing the patterns that have been recovered and the mechanisms that brought them about. The problem seems to be to establish the historical processes that generated those mechanisms and that can account for the changing strategies of trade and exchange between communities. The nature of this archaeological problem was captured by Lewis Binford (1987, 392) when he asked how archaeologists might move from the statics of material patterns that they recognize to an understanding of the dynamics of the historical processes that brought those patterns into existence.

One possible solution might be to compare the distribution patterns of things with different models that describe the ways that exchange systems could have been organized, and to evaluate which of those models best explain the distribution patterns (Renfrew 1975). This would simply result in the static distribution patterns of things assigned to one period being equated with a model of organized exchange, but historical understanding surely requires more than this. Archaeologists glimpse something of the material conditions through which people lived their lives, and this leads us to assume that a historical understanding is able to suggest how such exchange systems gave those lives a renewed sense of reality. This shifts our focus from the material itself to the ways in which those materials could have been used to construct peoples' understanding of who they were and their place in the world. It is from this perspective that we confront the contentious problem of deciding what motivated the development and the transformation of exchange relations and to enquire as to why these things might have changed.

Processes of material production, circulation and consumption in the ancient world have been described as if they had operated either according to a commercial logic (formalist models) or according to a logic dominated by social and political obligations (substantivist models). Both these views accept that the production, circulation and consumption of things functioned to satisfy the consumer's demands, whilst treating the human relationships involved as either those of commercial transaction or of social and political obligations. This simple distinction has encouraged assumptions that all ancient exchange mechanisms either followed a commercial logic or were more likely to have been embedded in various social institutions. This bald distinction has now lost much of its force as the sheer complexity of the processes of exchange that were likely to have operated in the pre-modern world have come to be accepted (cf. Oka and Kusimba 2008). It is unlikely, given the diverse kinds of political organizations that were operating across Egypt, Mesopotamia, the Hittite Empire and Mycenaean Greece in the second millennium of the eastern Mediterranean, let alone those of the western Mediterranean, central and northern Europe, that a single model is applicable for these economic processes.

Something of the likely complexity of exchange processes is exemplified by the Uluburun finds. If the Uluburun vessel was a merchant ship engaged in seeking commercial exchange for its cargo, then a very high risk and speculative investment will have been required to fund the vessel, its cargo and its crew before any commercial return could have been secured. The cost required would have been substantial. Christopher Monroe (2010) has calculated that the loss of the ship and cargo might be accounted as equivalent to the cost of feeding the population of a city the size of the port of Ugarit, on the Levantine coast of the eastern Mediterranean (in the north of modern-day Syria), for a year, and he asks 'who could amass such capital and also assume the risks for sending it overseas' (Monroe 2010, 29). Wealthy merchants are certainly known from around this time in the city of Ugarit where they are attested by texts in the trade archives (Monroe 2009). Engaged in both maritime and overland trade they dealt, amongst other things, in both copper and tin. Of the four merchants considered by Carol Bell (2012), who compares the status of these individuals to the oligarchs of post-communist Russia, each performed a number of roles, including that of administrator for the Ugarit state. Their handling of produce was taxed, and they will also have transported produce on behalf of others, including the ruler of Ugarit whose need to transport materials would have been one of the obligations of diplomacy.

The ability of the rulers of the early empires around the eastern Mediterranean to procure considerable quantities of objects and raw materials, either as loot resulting from warfare or as tribute from subservient communities, is exemplified by the power of the Egyptian Pharaoh and is illustrated, for example, by the limestone relief dated to around 1450 BCE from the Karnak temple of Amon-Re which depicts that part of the war booty dedicated to the temple by the Pharaoh Tuthmosis III (Sherratt and Sherratt 1991, Fig. 2). The political domination achieved by such rulers would have been exercised through the extraction of tribute, which we should remember comprised both the labour required for the processes of extraction and production, as well as the procurement of the materials that such labour had extracted and produced. It was presumably in the context of such tributary demands exercised by the Pharaoh that the extensive bronze casting installation at Qantir – Pi-Ramesse had operated (Rehren and Pusch 2012). This substantial production facility (Fig. 4.2) must have been sustained by the ability to procure not only labour but also ingots of copper, presumably from Cyprus, and tin from Anatolia and Central Asia. The tributary presentation of ingots and materials is well-represented in Egyptian tomb paintings, whilst the archive of correspondence discovered at the Pharaoh Akhenaten's capital at modern-day Tell el-Amarna provides

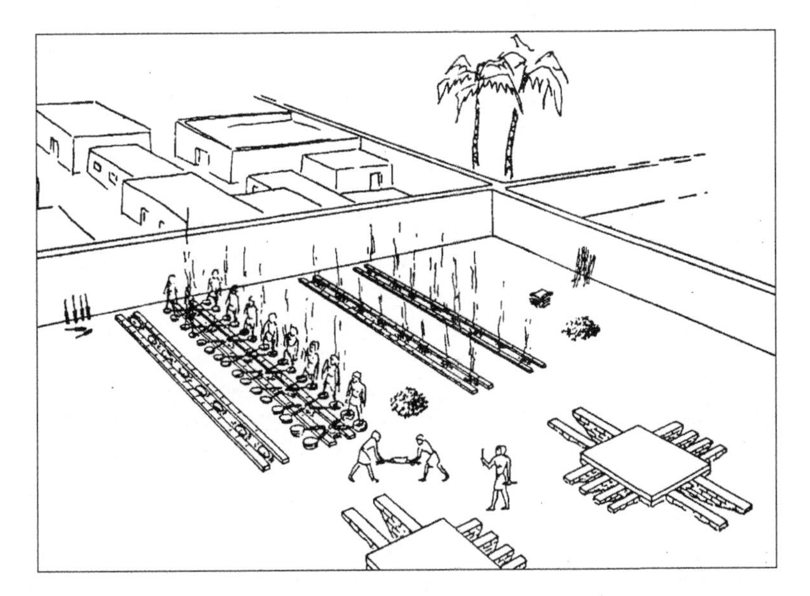

Fig. 4.2 Reconstruction of the bronze casting installations from Qantir – Pi-Ramesse in use. After Rehren and Pusch 2012, Fig. 22.1. Design E. Pusch and A. Herold, drawing J. Klang. Copyright Grabung Qantir-Piramesse, Roemer-Pelizaeus-Museum, Hildesheim. With permission.

us with an understanding of the ways in which raw materials, as well as finished articles, moved between royal households by means of diplomatic presentations, face-saving gifts and the demands of friendship, presentations in other words that both achieved and demonstrated political status and authority. The reach of kingly power was therefore demonstrated by its ability to move both people and things, and it would have been facilitated by the recruitment of merchant vessels and caravans. It is from this perspective that the Uluburun vessel with the bulk cargo of ceramics, resin, wood, glass and metals, and the finished articles of jewellery and drinking vessels, might best be understood.

Cycles of raw material extraction, production and consumption have defined the archaeology of regional economic systems, and the eastern Mediterranean has been treated as one such system. However, we emphasize that by tracing the changing structure of economic relations we also trace the likely history of political obligations and alliances across the same region. For example, whilst the second millennium cessation of the exploitation of local copper sources in the Aegean is attributed by Yannis Bassiakos and Thomas Tselios (2012) to the exhaustion of the local ore sources, it also marked the reorientation of exchange relations for the Cretan settlements, away from the north and the isles of the Cyclades and eastwards towards copper ingot supplies from Cyprus (Betancourt 2012) and thus to Egypt. It would be naïve to explain this reorientation as if it were driven simply by the requirement to maintain metal supplies, without recognizing that such a change would have also involved a shift in the axis of political alliances.

As we have already indicated, formalist and substantivist models no longer seem to provide the basis necessary for an understanding of the complexities involved in the economic development of the eastern Mediterranean in the third and second millennia. This development did more than identify new resources and move materials along new routes and between new political centres, the ways in which the trace of its history is described archaeologically. It was a development that provided for changing conditions in which different forms of life could be created, and it is from this perspective, as an understanding of the mechanisms by which the various interdependent identities of peoples and things were brought into existence, that archaeology might create the history of the period.

If forms of life are brought into existence by performances through which individuals grew and by which they created and demonstrated their place within the material conditions of life, then the effectiveness of such performances required the recognition of particular qualities and values invoked in their material contexts. Societies cannot be treated either as the units requiring historical analysis nor can they be treated as if they were the determining actors in the historical narrative. Societies did not 'do' anything, instead history was made in the evolving matrix of things, plants, animals and people. The performances of those who sought to extend their influence and thus their control over the lives of others in ways that defined, for example, the geographically bounded regions of a state or of an empire would be understood within this same matrix as would the performances of those others subject to them. The way that such people might have gained something of their political legitimacy was by both claiming and being treated as if they were the embodiment of the life forces that sustained their subjects, perhaps as gods, just as the slave owed their place in the world to their labour that was controlled by others.

By performance being the expression of the desire to become a particular kind of being, it expressed the values that defined existence as a place in the world. It should come as no surprise therefore that the material conditions that enabled such desires to be expressed were sought after and, as Andrew and Susan Sherratt recognized, this means that the growth in exchange systems was driven by the demands of consumption rather than by the growth in their productive potential (Sherratt and Sherratt 1991). This argument carries the further implication, that those who could facilitate the satisfaction of those demands, exemplified by the Pharaoh's ability to offer the materials he might procure as booty or as tribute, had the ability to achieve the politically dominant role of patron. Is this the context within which the Uluburun vessel was operating? The arrival of bulk raw materials in that vessel's cargo, including metals, glass, wood and resins, into the Aegean would have required the availability of artisan labour to convert those materials into useable things. The archives of clay incised scripts of Linear B (Fig. 3.1) that are known from the destruction levels of some Mycenaean 'palaces' might indicate the attempt to both account for and administer the development of various specialized practices of artisan production required to work the new flow of materials in ways that lay beyond the traditional, orally transmitted rules and well understood routines of traditional agrarian labour (Nosch 2006; Killen 2006).

Connectivity, identity and metallurgy

Let us now return to the third millennium and the working of materials within the particular regional context of the Aegean. The performances of those who worked on the metal ingots were performances that created the performers as artisans, as well as creating the objects of their labours. Roger

Doonan, Peter Day and Nota Dimopoulou-Rethemiotaki comment, with reference to metalworking in the third millennium on Crete, that:

> Metallurgy is a dramatic process that unfolds through time. A technological liturgy where certain acts, for instance bellows being pumped, minerals being transformed by fire, and metals being poured, need precise choreography in order to be successful.... Metallurgical performances are surrounded with a sense of anticipation towards the emergence of the final object and completion is itself uncertain, and hence adorned in risk.
>
> Doonan et al. 2007, 115

These authors allow that there is 'no compelling reason' why the different stages of the process, from the mining of ores to the casting of objects, were undertaken by different persons, before noting, in the case of early Aegean metalworking, the evidence that 'smelters favoured isolated windy promontories whilst artefact production ... takes place in more public locations' (Doonan et al. 2007, 116). This 'combination of isolation and advertisement' might in fact indicate, contrary to their own assessment, that during the third millennium the spatial and visual rupture in the passage that they identify as running from mining to smelting and on to casting of metals had provided for the emergence of a complex network of political identities and their relationships. By the second millennium such networks could ultimately have extended across the eastern Mediterranean.

By the beginning of the third millennium, living with metals had been part of the material conditions of life in the Aegean for countless generations (the first metal appearing in the fifth millennium). Encounters with metal were, if not necessarily common, certainly not alien. However, speaking of encounters with metal in such generic terms masks the specificity of the particular practices in which we are interested. The question is how the practices associated with a particular material form in one creation of personhood might be recognized, adopted and adapted in other expressions of identity. If we perceive a change, or even a revolution, surrounding the generic concept of 'metal' sometime in the third millennium BC, the challenge must be to identify new forms of practice and how certain kinds of interactions led to the adoption of versions of these practices more widely.

One particular form that has become emblematic of the first half of the third millennium is the dagger (Renfrew 1972, 319–323; Nakou 1995; Broodbank 2000, 253, Fig. 4.3). These are first seen in Early Bronze I (3100–2700 BCE) in the Cyclades and Crete, but most examples come from Early Bronze II contexts (2700–2200 BCE). Stylistically and technologically, the

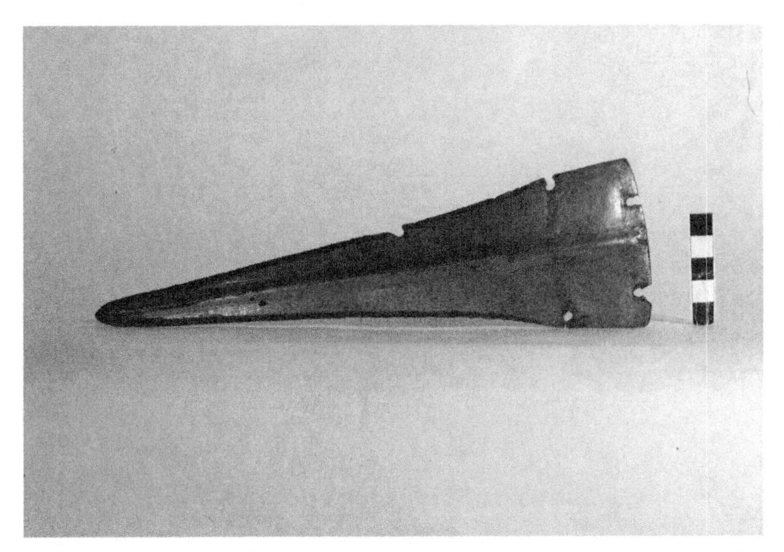

Fig. 4.3 A Cycladic dagger. Naxos Museum. Copyright © Hellenic Ministry of Culture and Sports/Archaeological Receipts Fund.

Cretan and Cycladic forms differ, but production converged upon the same kind of object. The importance of this particular material culture artefact and its associated sets of practices is that they do not merely represent some generic process of intensification of metal use. With the daggers, more complex chains of communication are clearly involved than we will encounter with some other artefact categories. Away from the limited ore sources of the Aegean in the western Cyclades or Attica, all metal was imported, whether in finished artefact form, metal ingots, or even as ore for smelting. Acts of communication would be essential for the adoption of the dagger form, but these were only part of an ongoing, long-term, changeable and multifaceted set of engagements.

Smelting and casting are often envisaged as taking place near, or at, ore sources (Georgakopoulou 2016; Fig. 4.4), though there can be exceptions where ore is transported over long distances (as at Keros in the Cyclades, or Chrysokamino on Crete, both of which most likely used ores imported from western Cycladic islands: Georgakopoulou 2016, 55). There is limited clear-cut evidence for production before Early Bronze II: at Final Neolithic (4500–3100 BCE) Kephala on Kea (Coleman 1977), Final Neolithic Chrysokamino (Betancourt 2006, although the evidence for the early date is not clear-cut),

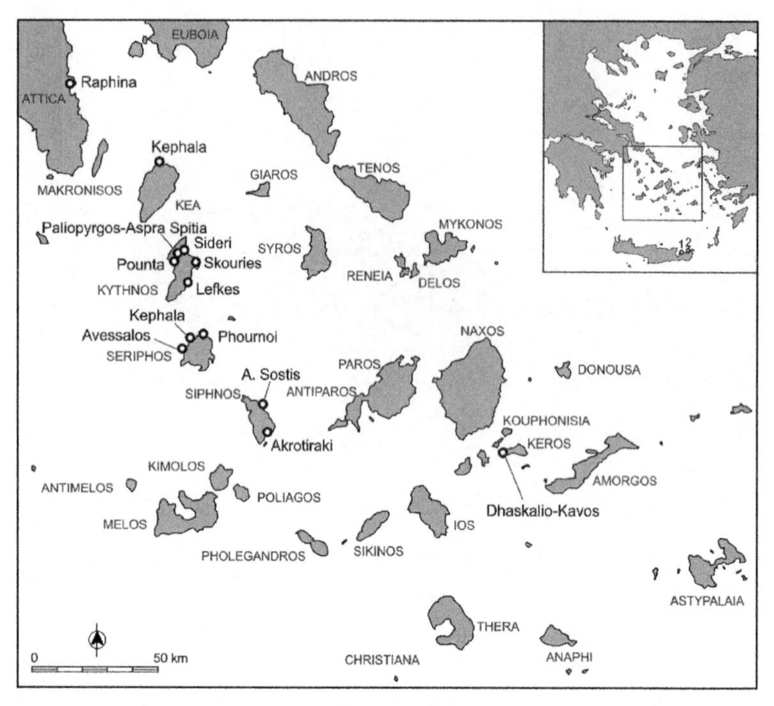

Fig. 4.4 Smelting sites in the Early Bronze Age Cyclades. After Georgakopoulou 2016, Fig. 4.2.

Final Neolithic–Early Bronze I Kephala Petras (Papadatos 2007) on Crete, and at Early Bronze I Çukuriçi Höyük (Horejs 2017), Liman Tepe and Bakla Tepe (Keskin 2016) in coastal Anatolia, all in the region near Izmir. The evidence for primary production (smelting) before Early Bronze II is therefore limited, perhaps supporting the suggestion of a real increase in production in Early Bronze II. However, Çukuriçi Höyük has recently presented evidence of an advanced, complex and highly-organized metalworking centre in Early Bronze I (Horejs et al. 2017; Mehofer 2014). Here a series of buildings has been excavated, each containing its own metalworking furnace, maintained during the life-history of each building. The evidence is for primary production of arsenical copper, organized at the scale of the settlement, with some tin bronze working also close to the end of the site's use period. The very large quantities of Melian obsidian at the site place it within Aegean networks, although it also functioned within a local, Anatolian context, utilizing local ore sources, and the smelting technology used does not match that known from elsewhere in the Aegean.

Çukuriçi Höyük presents evidence not only for smelting but also for the production (casting and finishing) of artefacts. There seems little doubt that these artefacts were not merely intended for local use: this highly-organized site was producing artefacts and some ingots that were destined for other locales (Mehofer 2014). While there is evidence for artefact production at other nearby sites, the evidence from Çukuriçi Höyük is for a specialized production centre, operating at a scale far above nearby sites where the evidence is much more limited, presenting the full spectrum of metallurgical activity from primary production to the production of finished artefacts. The artefacts produced, as indicated by finds of the artefacts themselves and from moulds, were a full set of tools and weapons. These include daggers, though not, it seems, of types common in the Aegean. This may indicate that although Çukuriçi Höyük was fully implicated in Aegean political networks involving obsidian procurement, the circulation of metals operated differently, and in a western Anatolian context only.

By contrast, elsewhere in the Aegean smelting and the production of artefacts seem usually to be separate as Doonan et al. imply (2007, quoted above), and sites operating on the scale of production seen at Çukuriçi Höyük are not yet known. As noted, primary production usually takes place near ore sources; the reshaping of metals into artefacts takes place in settlements. More particularly, smelting seems to be an outdoor activity, while it is argued below that artefact production in fact takes place behind closed doors. In the Aegean, smelting sites are located mainly in the vicinity of ore sources on islands such as Kythnos and Seriphos (Georgakopoulou 2016, Fig. 4.2 and Table 4.1), usually situated away from settlements; an important exception is Keros, discussed further in Chapter 5. These smelting locations appear to be open-air, and in that sense public; however, Doonan et al. (2007, 114–117) emphasize the need to travel away from settlements in order to procure ore and then smelt it, in an act effectively shared only by voyagers, hidden from the putative 'home base' and where, they suggest, the more public acts of metallurgy would normally be those of secondary production, i.e. casting. However, the evidence is that although artefact production does seem normally to take place within settlements, it also takes place in closed and cramped environments. Evidence for artefact production is not in fact widespread; important evidence comes from Early Bronze I–II Poros on Crete, located just to the north of Knossos, and the sites of Dhaskalio (Keros), Kastri on Syros, and Ayia Irini on Kea, and further north at Poliochni on Lemnos. At Dhaskalio, now the site with the best evidence for metalworking in the Aegean, the remarkable result seems to be that metalworking was almost ubiquitous throughout the settlement (Georgakopoulou 2013). This contrasts with Kastri, where metalworking seems to have been more localized, although the evidence is ambiguous (Tsountas 1899; Bossert 1967; Georgakopoulou 2007), and Ayia Irini, where metalworking evidence is present but limited (Wilson 1999; Georgakopoulou 2007).

Doonan et al. (2007, 116) depict all metalworkers as 'ambiguous figures merging in and out of isolation and publicity'. Their isolation is seen to occur during voyages and during mining and smelting. Conversely, arriving at stopping points on voyages or at the destination makes them public figures who brought with them news of the wider world. Back at the settlement after the voyage, their return with smelted metal is seen as very public, and while the acts of production themselves may be hidden behind closed doors, the products might have been displayed triumphantly.

It is important to compare this model of spatial distinctions with what we can learn from Dhaskalio. Despite being the largest built-up area in the Cyclades at the time (see Chapter 5), it is difficult to see the site as a simple 'settlement', from which metalworking voyagers might have set off in search of ore, and to which they might have returned with metal. It is not only metal that was imported to Dhaskalio: everything was imported (Renfrew 2013b). There is no locally produced pottery (Hilditch 2013; Sotirakopoulou 2016); ground and chipped stone were all imported (Rowan et al. 2013; Carter and Milić 2013; Boyd and Dixon 2013), as were marble (Renfrew 2013c; Gavalas 2013; Renfrew and Lebegyev 2013) and everything else, including food. However, there is evidence for production at Dhaskalio, albeit using imported materials: most importantly metals, but also obsidian, and some limited evidence for marble working (Georgakopoulou 2013; Carter and Milić 2013; Gavalas 2013). Consequently Dhaskalio may have come to form a very central node in Aegean networks, clearly drawing in far more than it was actually producing, but performing a role as a metalworking centre. This means that, rather than the image of groups of local metalworkers voyaging to procure materials, as implied by Doonan et al. (2007, 114–117) and described above, Dhaskalio was a centre drawing in people, skills and resources from throughout the Cyclades (and perhaps the mainland too). The buildings of Dhaskalio seem less like domestic houses and more like the workshops of artisans, and the storehouses needed for the materials brought in. The smiths of Dhaskalio may in fact have been from multiple locations in the Cyclades, but something was drawing them to Dhaskalio in order to produce their artefacts. Indeed, it is possible that the identity of the artisan, constructed in part through locations of practice, was changing quite rapidly in the opening centuries of the Bronze Age as the systems of political authority evolved. Hence, rather than multiple voyages of local smiths from a home base to an ore source and back again, a better model might be that of coalescing groups of smiths coming together both at ore sources and at production centres, of which the only clear-cut examples at the moment are Dhaskalio on Keros and most likely Poros on Crete. It was here at these production centres that objects such as daggers were produced, and from these production centres the objects were procured or obtained. The dagger itself may have come to be understood as the material result of a particular kind of life event, a development that was displayed on the body in such a way as to imply that the identity and experience of the wearer involved voyaging, contact and involvement in complex networks centred on places such as Dhaskalio. The rise of this framework was sustained by an emergent and changing political authority, and how Dhaskalio came to host it is discussed in Chapter 5.

The evidence from the Cyclades enables us to conceive that during the third millennium we may have witnessed a development in a network of labour and tribute obligations, diplomatic alliances and political authority by which different human identities were created in the performances that ensured the passage from the identification of sources of raw material to its working and consumption. We have chosen to emphasize the drama of the 'techno-liturgy' of metallurgical processes because they leave something of a recognizable archaeological trace in the eastern Mediterranean whilst often being less easy to follow elsewhere in Europe. The unevenness of the evidence results, in part, from the character of the processes, with the potential for the recycling of material and the fragility of some materials, such as tin ingots, to chemical and mechanical weathering, and from archaeological methodologies that have been more concerned to establish the chemical sourcing of ores and the typological characterization of objects than to consider the material as contributing to the contexts in which these lives were lived.

The politics of northern European metallurgy

Exotic materials that derived from contacts between different political and cultural systems could only be incorporated into the indigenous system of materials and traditions of behaviour by gaining a value and a significance within some part of the indigenous tradition. This assimilation of the exotic is therefore a form of translation by which aspects of other worlds became understandable and useable, at least to some. Contact between cultural systems is more than a simple search for materials, it involves a complex negotiation of perceptions and prejudices.

The role of contact has long been noted as a salient aspect of Early Cycladic culture (Renfrew 1972). Broodbank defined voyaging, concomitant of contact, as a central aspect of the period (Broodbank 2000). The distribution of Melian obsidian has long been seen as a proxy for contact and voyaging in the Aegean, from Palaeolithic to Bronze Age times. Voyaging was essential for the initiation and maintenance of contact, and so the movement of people was the mechanism by which aspects of a Cycladic identity could be propagated or contested.

Obsidian in the Aegean and the distribution of jade axes across Europe in the fifth and fourth millennia are both indicators of the distribution of some materials resulting from the complex motivations of desire and the obligations of politics. However with no third- and early second-millennium wreck and accompanying cargo deposits known from around its Atlantic and Baltic coasts (the wreck find reported in 2010 lying off the Devon coast dates to *c*. 1000 BCE), and lacking any inscribed textual evidence, the archaeology of the third and early second millennium of Europe north of the Mediterranean has relied upon the formal comparisons of artefact typologies, a detailed analysis of local sequences of artefact development, and the chemical analysis of metal artefacts in relation to potential ore sources to trace the flows of material that brought metal objects into those regions that lacked any native ores. The problem is that, detailed as both the narratives of artefact sequences and typological and chemical comparisons might be, they do not reveal the nature of the political networks that had once activated either the exchange of material or the movements of people, but they might enable us to understand how forms of identity were constructed over this period.

Southern Scandinavia is one region across which a long-term coherency is implied by the character of the surviving archaeological materials. Scandinavian copper technology originated sometime around the mid-third millennium BCE, and seems likely to have depended upon copper deriving from Alpine ores. This is confirmed by the few Swedish artefacts analysed by Ling and his colleagues (Ling et al. 2014), with artefact matches to ores from North Tyrol including the so-called Ösenring copper which supplied, in central Europe, the production of the Ösenringbarren, which are assumed to be ingots that were cast and then hammered into the distinctive shape of rings with looped terminals (Junk et al. 2001). In addition, copper sources from Iberia and Sardinia are indicated by lead isotope analysis for the production by the early second millennium of bronzes in southern Sweden, along with the possibility of some metal contribution from Greece and Cyprus (Ling et al. 2014, 121–124). British and Irish copper and tin from south-western Britain are also component contributors to Nordic metal production (Vandkilde 2017).

Copper artefacts are therefore in use in the region from just after 2400 BCE (Vandkilde 1996) whilst the working and alloying of bronze had originated here by about 1700 BCE, implying that political relations had been established by then to ensure the procurement of metal ingots, along with some metal artefacts, from elsewhere in Europe. Ling and his colleagues have demonstrated by geochemical and isotopic analysis of Swedish material that throughout the period of the Nordic Bronze Age the metals for these artefacts came from the south and did not originate from any exploitation of the ores that were available to the north, in Sweden itself (Ling et al. 2013). These particular relations of supply and consumption map a political geography rather than one of economic expediency. It is important to recognize that if metal supply, exchange and the politics of identity and obligation sustain each other, then we should expect fluctuations over time as the politics of supply shift. Ling et al. have noted that 'every single Bronze Age period has its own metal distribution pattern' (Ling et al. 2013, 299). This would imply that every typological change in the design of objects, which is used to define an archaeological period, is the product of a change in the politics of production and identity. We must also bear in mind that the likely recasting of scrap metal will, over time, mix metals that were likely to have different ore signatures and thus mix those signatures (cf. Ling et al. 2014, 117–119).

These analyses raise the intriguing question of whether the portfolio of source material that supported Nordic metallurgy prior to 1500 BCE is indicative of direct trans-shipment along the coasts or over land and waterways to Scandinavia from diverse southern sources. A similar question occurs with the earliest metallurgy of the British Isles which is almost entirely supported by the copper mined at Ross Island, Co. Kerry, in south-western Ireland (Bray and Pollard 2012; O'Brien 2004). The archaeological literature on this matter is redolent with references to trade and to traders, supported with maps confidently representing assumed trade routes, but is any of this likely? We have already commented on the speculative investments that any trader had to meet before any return could have been gained. The levels of complexity by which these trading networks could be established do not seem to have existed at this time in northern Europe.

In many communities, whether in the Aegean or in northern Europe, metal casting converted a material that derived from distant sources, procured through various forms of political alliances and patronage, and employed that material to sustain the practices of use and deposition that had developed locally. Michael Rowlands and Johan Ling have suggested that regions of sustained identity in prehistory were those regions that utilized the flows of externally derived material and people to produce specific systems of value, in contrast with those of outsiders (Rowlands and Ling 2013). By drawing upon the work of Fredrik Barth (1969) on ethnicity, Rowlands and Ling accept that boundaries persisted because of, and not in spite of, the persons and materials that flowed across them as ethnic groups came into being and existed by 'belonging to a larger field of inter-ethnic contact and interdependence' (Rowlands and Ling 2013, 518).

The continuity of any regional identity was once supposedly revealed in the coherent pattern of an archaeological culture, whilst Processual Archaeology sought to establish the continuity of the regional system of social and economic organization. The archaeological analysis of material culture continues to sustain comparisons between the forms and styles of production, although the significance of these comparisons is often obscure and can, all too easily, encourage archaeological narratives that do little more than speculate upon the motivations of the producers. Indeed, the New Archaeology's rejection of cultural analysis was to a large extent driven by the desire to avoid such speculative accounts. Nonetheless, formal comparisons do exist and some account has to be offered for them. It is perhaps worth remembering that the acts of production had to be publicly accountable both in terms of performance and product, meaning that the objects produced had to be recognizable and useable as objects of a certain kind. Effective production would therefore have been directed towards what was known and what was commonly understood.

The transmission of etiquette and style

No single archaeological methodology exists that can guide us unambiguously towards interpretations of comparisons of form, but some effort must be made to distinguish the likely interpretation from that which is unlikely. This distinction might be achieved by specifying the scales of those experiences that we claim were relevant for an understanding of the patterns of production under investigation (cf. Jones 2002, 83). An example of the problems that attend upon such analyses is given by some of the ceramic material from early to mid-third millennium Britain and Ireland. This was material in use at the time that the sarsen stones were being erected at Stonehenge. The archaeological perception of this cultural assemblage provides for a geographical coherency that is described by reference to the distribution of the Grooved Ware ceramic styles. The Grooved Ware tradition (Fig. 4.5) of the Late Neolithic of Britain and Ireland has long been taken to be indicative of an indigenous cultural identity that extended across these islands but did not extend into continental Europe (Thomas 2010). The earliest occurrence of the Grooved Ware tradition is attested amongst the third millennium

Fig. 4.5 Reconstructed Grooved Ware vessels. After Thomas 1991, Fig. 5.3. Courtesy of Thomas and Cambridge University Press.

settlements and ceremonial sites of Orkney, whilst by the middle of that millennium the distribution of this material extended across Britain and Ireland, including the substantial assemblage recovered from the great enclosure at Durrington Walls, within 4 km of Stonehenge itself (Wainwright and Longworth 1971).

The distribution of Grooved Ware makes sense in two ways. The Orcadian material was the domestic assemblage of agricultural communities, and its intimate relationship to the working practices of people is not only indicated by the common size range of vessels found amongst the debris associated with each of the houses in the Barnhouse settlement on Orkney Mainland (Richards 2005). The remarkable evidence is that the production strategies at Barnhouse drew upon claybeds that were geologically specific to each household. These geographically distinct claybeds were therefore part of traditional patterns of household rights over different landscape resources (Jones 2002, 120–133). The implication of the common vessel form and the shared decorative motifs employed across the Barnhouse settlement, given the dispersed, non-centralized, processes of production, is that the practices associated with production and with vessel use were part of a commonly recognizable kind of performance which sustained not only individual household identity and wider settlement identity, but also an island-wide framework of practice. This re-emphasizes that the human security of belonging to a particular community and material world was a security that was achieved, at least in part, through the production and use of material things.

The distribution of the Grooved Ware ceramic tradition more widely across the British Isles by the mid-third millennium is attributable to a more complex process than simply the migration of a 'grooved ware folk' from the north of Scotland to southern Britain. The building of the massive enclosure and timber circles of Durrington Walls (Wainwright 1971), the labour of the quarrying, transportation and erection marking the construction of the stone structure of Stonehenge, and indeed the slightly later undertaking of digging and building the massive earthwork of Silbury Hill (Leary et al. 2013) would all have necessitated the movement and congregation of considerable numbers of people in the chalklands of Wessex. The recent excavation of the settlement buried beneath the southern portion of the bank of the Durrington enclosure and dated to around 2500 BCE led to the suggestion that food in the form of pig and cattle carcases was also brought from regions beyond the chalkland soils of Wessex (Craig et al. 2015). These communal undertakings, which were directed towards a common purpose, expressed a shared understanding of purpose, however much coercion of the labour forces might have been involved. Such an understanding would hardly have been possible if there had existed strong regional variabilities in everyday practices of domestic life or wider cosmological understandings across the British Isles. The means that created the common design and sustained the common function of the material was also the means by which a coherency and common purpose was constructed that was expressed in the building of the monuments of the period. It was a common understanding that had to be formed, literally, from the ground up: that is, it emerged from the daily practices that finds archaeological expression today in such cultural patterns as the distribution of Grooved Ware ceramics.

It is important to stress two things. First that the construction of a common identity did not arise with the monument building, but was constituted out of the mundane and everyday practices of settlement and agricultural labour, including rights over resources, and it was situated within a shared cosmology. Second the making of such an identity must have drawn in part, and possibly quite pragmatically, upon commonly understood design motifs that may also have been employed in numerous contexts. These contexts include pecked designs on certain stones in late Irish megalithic tombs of the third millennium (Twohig 1981), where design motifs shared with some Grooved Ware ceramics were employed. This occurrence implies a common framework of understanding between populations in Ireland and Britain in the third millennium BCE (cf. Thomas 2010, 6–7). In light of this it is important to note the dependency on Irish copper ore sources for early metallurgical production in Britain which might extend into the early third millennium, providing for the possibility of a metallurgy that might predate the inclusion of metal artefacts in graves from *c*. 2400 BCE onward (Harbison 1969, 70).

By way of contrast, in northern and central Europe in the third millennium, subtly different ceramic styles (Beakers and Corded Ware) fulfilled an emerging requirement for drinking sets, indicating a shared understanding of etiquette. Archaeologically this material is most clearly perceived in grave assemblages (Fig. 4.6) where it forms part of a set that sometimes included,

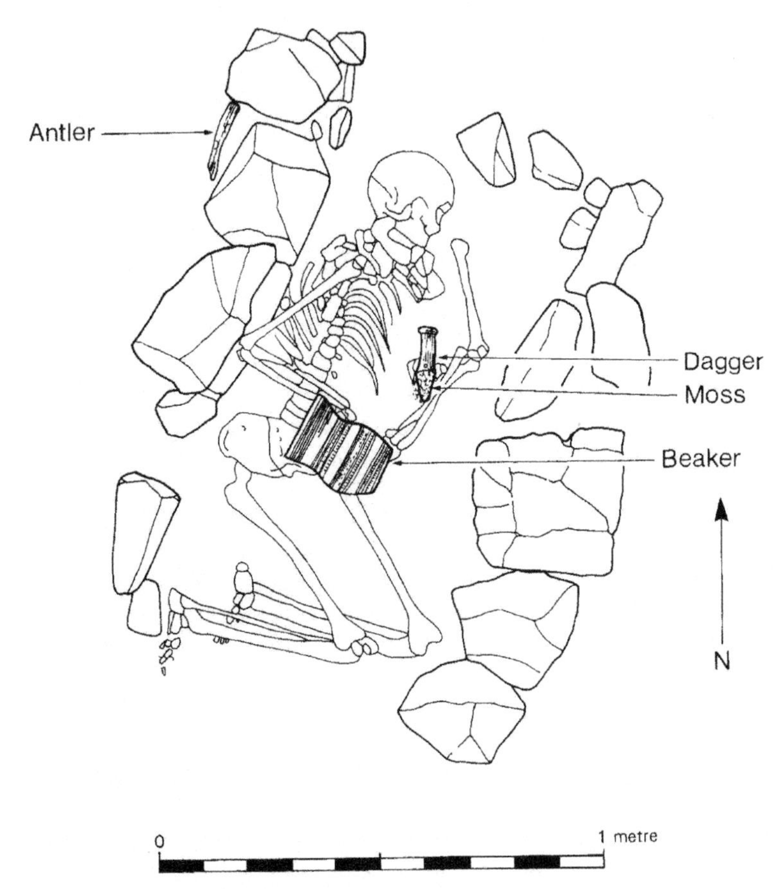

Fig. 4.6 Primary burial at Shrewton 5K. After Green and Rollo-Smith 1984.

in the case of Corded Ware, polished stone artefacts, and in the case of Beakers, copper or bronze artefacts. Sherratt (1997, 376–400) recognized that drinking practices emerged during the Neolithic of Europe and that these were executed through recognizable ceramic forms. This increasingly broad distribution indicates the adoption of a shared cultural framework within which identities were constructed. Gene-flow has recently been highlighted as a factor in this period (see Chapter 6), but this alone did not determine the ways in which people found their place within their material world. Britain and Ireland participated in these cultural practices after *c.* 2400 BCE through the adoption of new burial practices, which entailed inhumation rituals utilizing metalwork and beakers. This broke with the insular patterns of identity formation discussed above.

Comparisons between the British Isles and Europe in ceramics, burial rites and the associations of both with early copper, gold and bronze working have long encouraged the view that the changes associated with metalworking in the latter half of the third millennium were associated with a considerable reorientation in contacts, exchanges and in the movements of people. The likelihood of widespread migrations occurring in this period has been given additional support by the matching of haplogroups recovered as stretches of ancient DNA (aDNA) from human skeletal material in samples taken from across northern and central Europe and into the Eurasian Steppe. These are issues to which we shall return (Chapter 6), and it seems clear that previous attempts to explain the continent-wide distribution of formally similar artefact types purely in terms of exchange relationships between relatively stable populations (cf. Shennan 1986) is no longer satisfactory. However it is equally unsatisfactory to understand the new aDNA evidence as in itself explaining cultural change, in terms of movements of populations with fixed identities. Instead, it is possible to understand material worlds in which human beings were able to find their place and reconstruct their identities by means that sometimes included movement, adoption of new practices focusing upon the exchange and working of new materials, and adapting to the consequent changes perceived in the world around them.

Instead of treating the late third and early second millennium distribution of Beaker ceramics as if it mapped a migrating population and thus as if it were some kind of 'cultural badge' for the identity of those migrants, we should consider the goal towards which the use of Beaker ceramics was directed. This recognizes that contact, travel and migrations involving individuals or groups are subtle and complex cultural practices aimed at bringing about a change in the cultural horizon. In order to investigate the complexities of scale in questions of contact and movement, let us now consider the implications of

Fig. 4.7 Sauceboat from the Cyclades. EAM6107. National Archaeological Museum, Athens/Department of Collection of Prehistoric, Egyptian, Cypriot and Near Eastern Antiquities. Copyright © Hellenic Ministry of Culture and Sports/Archaeological Receipts Fund.

the appearance and use of one particular ceramic form of the early third millennium in the Aegean, the so-called sauceboat (Fig. 4.7).

This is an unusual vessel, the mechanics and etiquette of whose use cannot be deduced simply by examining a specimen. The spout seemingly connects it with pouring or drinking, although the handle is too small for effective manipulation when full, suggesting a two-handed use. The spout could also have been used as a handle, conceivably making the vessel able to function as ladle, transport and delivery mechanism for small (individual) portions of liquid (Rutter 2017). However, how such vessels might be used in different contexts could only have been understood by direct observation or by description.

The importance of sauceboats was highlighted by Renfrew (1972, 284), who associated them with new serving and drinking sets for wine consumption. Some sort of ritualized use has been widely assumed, and more recently a cogent case has been made for their use in commensality or, more specifically, feasting (e.g. Peperaki 2007, 116–117; Pullen 2013). In the Early Bronze II assemblages of mainland Greece and the Aegean they are found widely; 'one of the most common' shapes on the mainland (Rutter 2017, 4), but perhaps originating in the Cyclades (Rutter 2017, 5), where there is greater variation in shape and decoration, with some examples in marble (two gold sauceboats are thought to originate in Arcadia, and a similar gold vessel was found at Troy). On the other hand, on the Anatolian coast they are rare, with imported examples at Troy and Liman Tepe (Şahoğlu 2011); they appear on Crete only as limited Cycladic imports (e.g. Wilson 2007).

The locations of sauceboat production centres are unknown as their fineware fabrics make them less amenable to provenancing by petrography. Chemical analysis of a small number from the island of Keros, south of Naxos, suggests a range of provenances, including a significant number perhaps from the mainland (Hilditch 2018; Hein and Kilikoglou 2018). However, the very large numbers found at Keros (discussed further below) suggest that, as noted by Sotirakopoulou (2018), some production within the Cyclades is likely.

In 1972 Colin Renfrew identified the sauceboat as one component of what he called the 'international spirit' of the third millennium (Renfrew 1972, 451–455). He suggested that the basis of the international spirit was peaceful contact, and the movement of goods regulated as commercial trade. Metals were the primary example of traded goods, whose value appeared incontestable. But sauceboats were also part of the 'package': what was the value of the sauceboat? Or, for that matter, marble folded-arm figurines (Chapter 5)? Renfrew's view of trade requires a shared notion of value, but we have to ask how that notion of value ever came to be shared in the third millennium BCE.

Regardless of whether sauceboats were locally made or imported at any given site, prior to such import or local manufacture the form itself needed to be seen in use and understood as something other than merely an obscure, exotic object, but rather as a technology of practice. It therefore requires meaningful contact between some people who were comfortable performing part of their identity through their use of these objects and others for whom its use was unknown, or perhaps known only by repute. Such contact alone, however, does not explain adoption. Contact reveals new aspects of material life, many of which are not selected for adoption. But contact may have led to a desire for the material practices of others, when viewed through the lens of a more favourable and expanded identity within the newly enlarged horizons of the world. Adoption always means adaptation, as the new practices and their accompanying materials come to be understood alongside existing notions of practice.

The locale where the interaction takes place is important. Except in cases where groups of travellers meet at an intermediate location (exemplified by the case of Keros, as described below), most meaningful contact takes place between one group who are 'at home', acting within the familiar conditions of everyday life, and another group who are outside the comfort of the routine:

the voyagers (cf. Broodbank 2000). This creates an imbalance in information exchange between the two groups. The travellers are able to absorb some understanding of the material structural conditions within which materials might be used and understood. But those at home perceive the travellers as being out of context. Thus a feast held at Lerna in the Peloponnese, for example, might impress visitors with the use of sauceboats amid a wide array of paraphernalia, all playing its part in the stage management of the event. But travellers stepping off a boat, sauceboat in hand, would face a much more difficult task in making themselves, their practices and their materials understood.

In the case of the sauceboat, adoption means primarily the transformation of specific practices into the general concept of 'how we do things'. Once adopted, this new material form, and the social practices adopted and adapted with it, formed a specific, referable point of identity between the groups concerned. Renfrew's 'international spirit' perhaps had more to do with increased contact and the transformation of other groups' cultural practices, rather than with the mechanics of trade in raw materials and 'valuables'.

This assimilation of practice applies most obviously to the uses and perhaps specific etiquette of this unusual vessel. But it also applies to the practice of vessel manufacture. Manufacturing techniques for these complex and often very thin-walled vessels may have been difficult to copy merely from inspection of an example, and it seems less likely they could have been manufactured based on description alone. The direct contact between potters seems the most likely means by which the requisite skills were transferred. Although not nearly enough is yet known about the extent of locally manufactured versus imported vessels in the different areas where sauceboats were used, several centres of manufacture seem likely in the Peloponnese, Attica and the Cyclades, and in many cases local manufacture of at least some vessels is indicated. So the processes of adoption of the sauceboat must be imagined in many cases to include the manufacture as well as the use of the vessel.

Sauceboats are found in quantities at some sites, such as Lerna in the Argolid, or at Keros in the Cyclades. But at other major sites such as Phylakopi on Melos or at Geraki in Laconia they are less common. If the sauceboat does not appear in great quantities at all sites, this perhaps confirms the restricted range of its use, which was already suggested by its obscure shape. At Lerna (Fig. 4.8), sauceboats are found in the same assemblage as seal impressions (clay used to close doors or objects such as vessels or baskets bearing impressions made by pressing carved stone seals on the wet clay, subsequently fired in the burnt destruction of the site; Peperaki 2007; 2016). Partly because of these seal impressions, along with its impressive architecture, the site of

Fig. 4.8 Plan of Lerna IIIC (above) and IIID (below). Courtesy American School of Classical Studies at Athens.

Lerna was for long heralded as a precursor of later palaces: its excavator, Caskey, described it exactly in such terms (Caskey 1959, 203), and Renfrew noted the central building and fortifications as indicating central authority, with the sealings demonstrating redistribution (Renfrew 1972, 390). Recent analyses have not sustained this vision of an incipient palatial system (Pullen 2011) and, as we shall see, understandings of how different later palatial systems may have worked have become more nuanced in recent years. In particular the notion of centralized redistribution as the backbone of palatial economies has undergone sustained criticism (e.g. Nakassis et al. 2011; Lupack 2011; Nakassis et al. 2016).

At Lerna, much of the attention has focused on the public building known as the House of the Tiles, and the open area immediately in front of it (Fig. 4.8). Weiberg (2007, 52–57) argued that the building and its surroundings should be seen as multifunctional public space, rather than the residence of a ruler. The sealings, along with six to eight sauceboats and 55–62 saucers (but no other vessels) were found in a storage room on the building's south side. These, and the remains of pithoi nearby, have been interpreted as the remains of a feasting assemblage (Pullen 2013), perhaps made together (Wiencke 2000, 235–236) for a single event (Peperaki 2004, 223–226) where the sealings record contributions to the feast (Peperaki 2004; 2016). The pithoi, sauceboats and saucers represent a limited repertoire of foodstuffs, and a specific etiquette for service and consumption (Peperaki 2004, 225). The location defines the maximum number of participants and allows for some hierarchy in terms of position within the spaces of the building and its external space. The six to eight sauceboats that formed part of this context are significantly fewer than the 55–62 bowls found with them, suggesting here at least that sauceboats are either related to service, or to consumption by select participants, rather than consumption by all participants.

However, these few vessels tell a limited story. What is interesting about the sauceboats of Lerna is that they are present in significant numbers: in Lerna III Phase D, the period to which the context above is assigned, 100 examples are found throughout the site, and a further 134 examples are found in less well-dated contexts of this phase or the preceding one; and the total for all periods is 833 sherds. So a focus on the vessels found in the House of the Tiles destruction assemblage may be misleading. A study of the better dated contexts of the preceding Lerna III Phase C, just before the construction of the House of the Tiles, shows 179 sauceboats distributed over eleven contexts. In every case bar one they are the second most numerous shape, the saucer being the most common. These two shapes count on average for 62 per cent of the pottery from these contexts (ranging from 85 per cent at most to 45 per cent at least); no other shape is remotely as common (it should be borne in mind that these data are based on retained pottery: these 1950s excavations discarded pottery judged less useful at that time, so the frequencies of shapes discussed here will be weighted more heavily because of that to finer vessels). Hence it would appear that at Lerna the sauceboat and saucer were a set, the latter accompanying the former at a ratio around 2:1, and this seems to be the case in all the deposits of this period. The areas under investigation (the 'fortifications' and associated rooms CA and DM: Fig. 4.8, top) do not seem to be domestic, and the whole complex appears 'special' in nature; so the consistent presence of what may be a 'feasting' assemblage makes sense in this context. Hence the unusual nature of Lerna's architecture is complemented by the prevalence of this material form, one which is plentiful here but rarer at other contemporary sites.

The regional role of the contemporary site at Keros in the central Cyclades is examined in Chapter 5. The two 'special deposits' that form the core of the site consist of deliberately deposited broken materials such as marble figurine fragments, marble vessels, pottery and obsidian. The inclusion of large numbers of figurine fragments has focused attention on the site and its unusual character since the first excavations in the 1960s. However, the composition of the pottery assemblage is also of interest. In the Special Deposit South no less than 5,122 sauceboat sherds have been recovered (Renfrew and Boyd 2018; Sotirakopoulou 2018), with thousands more coming from the (looted) Special Deposit North (Sotirakopoulou 2004). Keros is therefore by some margin the site with the largest number of known sauceboat fragments. None of these were locally made but were imported from other Cycladic islands and from the mainland (Sotirakopoulou 2018; Hilditch 2018; Hein and Kilikoglou 2018).

The 5,122 sherds from the Special Deposit South form 41 per cent of the diagnostic ceramic material from that location. While a large range of other shapes makes up the remaining 59 per cent of sherds, one shape stands out: the conical necked jar accounts for 25 per cent of the diagnostic material, while the many other shapes account for no more than 5 per cent of the diagnostic material for any given shape. This points to a highly structured deposit: while the range of shapes represented is large, the sauceboat and conical necked jar far outnumber all the other forms, and must therefore have played an important role in the activities that led to the formation of the deposit. This pairing of the sauceboat with another shape is also reminiscent of the pattern just described at Lerna, although the partner shape is quite different in this case.

However, as we explain in Chapter 5, the ceramic and marble material deposited at Keros was deposited in fragmentary form. The selected deposit of which we speak does not reflect feasts or breakage that took place at Keros:

the breakage took place elsewhere, most likely in local rituals on other Cycladic islands before a sample of the material was selected for transport to and deposit on Keros in gatherings of participants from all over the Cyclades and perhaps beyond (Renfrew 2013a). Recognizing the sauceboat and the conical necked jar as the two main ceramic shapes implies that these two forms were utilized in repeated practices, perhaps involving feasting. After breakage the sauceboat and jar fragments were preferentially selected for transport to Keros (but usually only one or perhaps two fragments of each vessel: most of the other fragments were retained and deposited elsewhere). It is remarkable that these practices were widely repeated through the Cyclades, the initiation of each such event on disparate islands implying an end point at some later time in a different geographical location. Each feasting event carried with it the implication of future voyages and of contact with other islanders at the focal place (now defined as a sanctuary: Renfrew et al. 2012; Renfrew 2013a) where the depositions would take place.

Although many gaps remain in our knowledge of the production, use and deposition of sauceboats, these examples have shown us that these idiosyncratic vessels were differentially adopted over a very wide geographical area. Their use seems never to have been routine, but rather to have involved different local customs and rituals. The specifics of their use will have varied from place to place, but their idiosyncratic form perhaps ensured that some aspects of their etiquette of use were maintained over a wide area. Their adoption, starting in the Early Bronze II period, is just one example among many of the building of personal and group identities that tended to assimilate and foreground non-local cultural practices. These types of exchange – even where materials are exported and imported – do not fit any classical model of commercial trade. The vessels themselves, where transported, did not contain stored goods, and were not themselves obviously intrinsically valuable, but they clearly had a value to the practitioner. They celebrated and cemented the participation of those involved in networks at different scales. These networks were not brought into existence in order to satisfy some fundamental need for imported raw materials. Instead, the entanglement of persons and things across space and time was an endlessly reworked condition pertaining to the engagement of agencies and material conditions across physical and scalar boundaries.

This perspective supplied by the example of the sauceboat, and its position in ever-changing nexus of contacts and engagements, allows us to return to the apparently more basic and fundamental question of the use of metals. The importance accorded to metal in our understanding of prehistory is so deeply embedded its use gives us our period names in most regions of the world: Chalcolithic (or Copper Age), Bronze Age, Iron Age – all stages described technological progress from the preceding Neolithic (Rowley-Conwy 2007). In the Aegean, Renfrew in 1972 made metal the driving force behind his 'international spirit', the great increase and contact in trade in the Early Bronze Age. Trade was facilitated by the invention of the longboat and driven by the 'first ... commodity really worth trading' – metal, now seen as a necessity (Renfrew 1972, 455). Both Renfrew and Branigan (1974) highlight an apparent great increase in metals in the Early Bronze II period, although it has been suggested that this might in part be explained by a change in depositional practices from curation to conspicuous consumption in graves (Nakou 1995). However, the sauceboat was also part of that 'international spirit'.

With the sauceboats, we envisaged the augmentation of people's perception of personal and group identity through the adoption of a material culture form and its associated practices. These, from the moment of adoption, did not require further dependency on distant resources or restricted technologies. However, we have also seen that, as the third millennium progressed, only limited metalworking was seen at many sites: its prevalence at the two regional centres of Poros and Keros indicates that strategies of production and circulation quite different from those of sauceboats were in effect. Finished metal products, such as daggers, travelled widely, and were more likely to be longer used than sauceboats, with distinctive biographies, and clear curation strategies; sauceboats, on the other hand, were deposited in some locations in large quantities, and may sometimes have been manufactured for single events. Hence, although the sauceboats and the daggers do indeed form part of a pan-Aegean social phenomenon that we may still wish to call an 'international spirit', it is now possible through the detailed evidence available to us to envisage different networks and the roles these objects played in their articulation.

Mutable and entangled conditions that existed across the eastern Mediterranean in the third and early second millennia enabled people to construct identities for themselves. Those entanglements varied in their scale, and they sometimes included, for example, the exercise of divine and political power by which subjects recognized the authorities of those who ruled over them, performed the practices of enslaved and corvée labour, and sustained the material flows of tribute. Political alliances and acts of patronage were serviced by gifts, trade and marriage, and these appear to have extended at least as far as to link the kingdom of Egypt with the Mycenaean world (Cline 2014, 44–54). At the more local scale, these entanglements created identities that succumbed to traditions of local etiquette that were expressed through styles of personal appearance and in the practices employed in the service of food and drink. It was through the inhabitation of such entanglements that we can understand the ways that 'self-ascribed identities whether individual or collective, [were] not primordial and fixed, but emerge[d] and change[d] in diverse circumstances: socio-political, historical, economic, contextual and . . . geographical' (Knapp and van Dommelen 2010, 4).

Materializing personal identity in the second millennium

Given the possibility, granted by the analysis of artefact source materials, of identifying the possible contacts between the different parts of Europe through which different materials passed, we might better consider the developing mechanisms by which the communication between different regions might have been achieved, whilst also maintaining the long-term identities active in each region. In other words: how did people communicate an understanding between each other, a negotiation across identities?

Renfrew has commented that 'no material, not even gold, has intrinsically high value. "Value" is something which is socially ascribed' (Renfrew 1991, 8 emphases omitted). This might imply that the value of things, arising as a process of social ascription involving a shared response to the thing that is valued, is culturally and socially specific. This would seem to be true when value is a matter of measuring the equivalence between one thing and another, such as in a process of exchange. However, there are things that have often seemed to evoke a cross-cultural and non-socially specific response among people in ways that those things seem to be 'valued' more widely. In materials these things include gold, jade and amber, which appear to have a vibrancy. Amber, like metal ore, is a material that has long been treated as evidence that a trade network linked the Baltic, Britain, Central Europe and the Aegean (Harding 1984, 68–87). Like the early use of metal, which is often related to the projection of self among others, amber does not satisfy mere functional needs. Chemically identifiable (Beck et al. 1964), the so-called Baltic amber might derive from a geographically wide area, extending around the southern North Sea and Baltic coasts but also including possible sources in northern Germany, Poland and Ukraine (Harding 2013b, 375). The finds of this Baltic amber in Italy and Greece demonstrate that amber had achieved an extensive distribution by the Bronze Age, occurring amongst grave assemblages in both Britain and the Aegean. The use of amber varies to include, in Britain, two amber cups (Needham et al. 2006, 96–99), the lost dagger pommel from Hammeldon, Devon (Piggott 1938, 62), and necklace beads (Fig. 4.9), including the complexly-bored 'spacer plates'. The complete amber necklaces in Britain belong to grave assemblages dating to the opening centuries of the second millennium (Woodward and Hunter 2015, 363–388), whilst in the Aegean the distribution of amber seems to occur slightly later

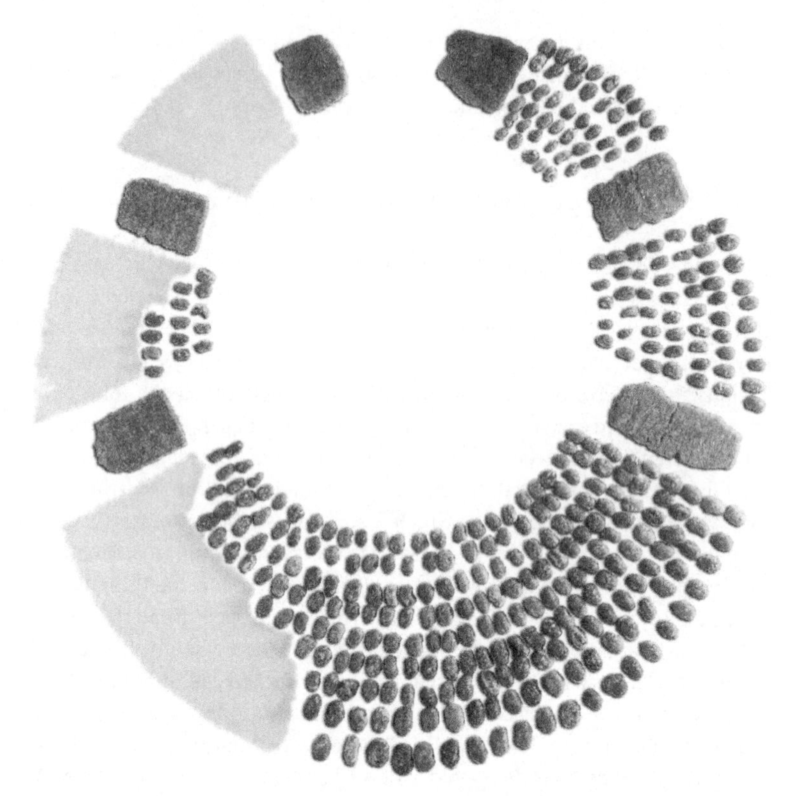

Fig. 4.9 Amber necklace from Upton Lovell G2E. Courtesy of Wiltshire Museum, Devizes.

on the Greek mainland and extends to Crete in the Mycenaean period, around the middle of the second millennium (Czebreszuk 2013).

The widespread assumption that these distribution patterns were the result of trade provides little by way of clarity concerning the social and political context that might provide the concept of trade with a more precise definition. It is perhaps also important to note where amber does not occur at this time but where it might have been expected if it was simply the manifestation of such a notion as a 'prestige material'. Piggott noted the 'excessive rarity' of amber from Brittany (Piggott 1938, 63) and none of the northern European amber is known from either end of the Mediterranean, in either Iberia or in Egypt (Lucas and Harris 1962). If the movement of people could have been aided by means of their ability to redesign their identities and obligations, then we should expect material to enter into circulation in those contexts in which it became understandable. That understanding was locally created, it was not carried within the material itself. Joseph Maran has criticized the archaeological assumption that materials that are chemically indistinguishable and objects that look to function in similar ways, at least according to archaeological analysis, must therefore have once evoked the same response by all people, whatever their cultural or political context. He comments that such objects could only have been meaningful relative to the contexts in which they were employed, and he refers to Latour's concept of *translation* as involving the 'negotiation of the meanings of the cultural traits received from the outside through their integration into social practices and discourses within constantly reassembled networks comprising human and non-human actants' (Maran 2013, 147). It is upon this basis that Maran goes on to address what we might call the Mycenaeanization of amber artefacts (cf. Harding 1984, 68–79).

If this entire argument is accepted then we might expect a raw material such as amber, that might have evoked a widespread metaphorical association with, for example, the warmth and the glow of sunlight, to have been worked into specific forms within particular regional and cultural contexts. A common response to amber was that it was worn as a personal adornment with most second millennium finds occurring as beads and necklace plates, although the occurrence of the dagger pommel and cups from Britain also indicate more ambitious use. Nonetheless, more precise regional differences might also be recognized. The necklace arrangements from Britain seem to include the complexly-bored 'spacer plates', mostly found as single pieces in graves but occurring in the seemingly complete necklace arrangement that accompanied the Wessex-type cremation, possibly a secondary deposit, in the barrow of Upton Lovell G2(e) (Woodward 2002, Fig. 2). The stringing of the Upton Lovell beads would provide for a crescent-shaped necklace, possibly paralleling the shape of the golden lunulae found in Britain and Ireland (Taylor 1980, 36–41; Gerloff 1975, 200) whilst Hachmann (1957) reconstructs the necklaces, also with complex spacer plates, from central Europe as being of a collier-type arrangement (but see Harding 1990, 142). It is noticeable, however, that Hachmann also allows for crescent-shaped necklaces amongst the Aegean finds and Harding (1984, 79) has also noted the comparable use of amber between Wessex and Mycenae such as in the binding of amber discs with gold.

Amber appears in the Mycenaean world a little after 1700 BCE in the shaft graves at Mycenae, and in other burials in impressive built structures elsewhere (tholos tombs: Chapter 6). Although most of the amber known is concentrated in just a few large deposits, it is also sufficiently widespread in time and space to indicate that it always had a place in an understanding of 'exotic jewellery' (Harding and Hughes Brock 1974). By far most of the amber comes from early Mycenaean contexts, such as the 1,290 objects recovered from shaft grave IV at Mycenae, or the *c.* 500 objects found in Kakovatos tholos A in the south-west Peloponnese (Maran 2013). The forms these objects took are so similar to their Wessex equivalents that they are widely cited as indicating that the Mycenaean material somehow made its way from manufacture in Wessex to the Aegean; nonetheless there is disagreement that this material might indicate direct exchange, since Aegean objects are not found in Wessex (though see Maran 2013). Maran also notes the similarities in context: found in graves, associated with gold. However, the Mycenaean finds are found in a distinct historical context: one where an eclectic mix of materials was being assembled in quite explicit acts of forging new identities.

In the shaft graves (which as a phenomenon are discussed in detail in Chapter 6), amber, found only in a few graves, is associated with a range of materials seemingly emphasizing expanded networks of contact and awareness: ostrich eggs, ivory, alabaster, lapis lazuli and faience. Some of these are finished objects with a distant provenance, such as the silver stag rhyton from Anatolia, and indeed the possibility of Wessex amber; but most of the objects made with Egyptian or western Asian materials seem to have been crafted or partly reworked on Crete (Burns 2010, 94), and it is also Crete that provides most of the imported material, as well as many of the motifs adapted on locally produced materials. The suddenly expanded horizons in Peloponnesian societies *c.* 1700 BCE were initially at least mediated through a much greater degree of interactivity with Crete. If, as many have suggested, long-distance exchange was a source of political standing and social authority (Bradley 1984; Beck and Shennan 1991, 138) then the origins of the exotic material carried by that exchange had, presumably, to be appreciated by those who accepted the authority that came from it. Otherwise perhaps amber 'as bright as the sun' was simply treated, like gold, as if it were the appropriate adornment for those whose authority arose from other, more traditional principles.

The new identities being forged in these burials reflected a new scale of engagement. This engagement represented neither a sudden Mycenaean pan-Mediterranean trade network, nor merely restricted interactions between a new Mycenaean elite and the 'palace' institutions of Crete. Instead, communities throughout the Peloponnese were beginning to find their places within networks of communication that already linked Crete, the Aegean islands and western Anatolia. The first widespread manifestation of this new engagement was the creation of a new pottery style, based initially on Minoan dark-on-light fineware. In its first century or so of use, this pottery was found in fairly restricted contexts and quantities, but subsequently became much more common, and came to be found, and manufactured, throughout the southern Aegean, then distributed widely through the central and eastern Mediterranean. It became an instantly recognizable declaration of an Aegean identity which individual communities could easily assimilate by producing for themselves – and which could, as already seen with third millennium examples, be implicated differently in the generation and projection of identity in different places and at different times. The Mycenaean-style pottery which became an Aegean material culture *lingua franca* in fact replaced earlier styles of pottery based on Minoan forms (Broodbank 2004) performing similar roles: a means around which participation in wider networks could be mediated. Since the Mycenaean pottery was itself derived from earlier Minoan forms, this replacement need not have seemed very dramatic, but it reflected shifting axes of power in what was by this time, around 1400–1200 BCE, a highly interconnected world.

We have already seen that this world was implicated in even wider-flung networks of communication and exchange, evidenced by the Uluburun shipwreck where this chapter began. At the highest level, this was a world of literate communication between kings and leaders, such as those preserved in the Amarna letters, documenting the exchange of gifts and tribute between Pharaohs and kings (Cline 2014). However we have no preserved letters to or from individuals in the Aegean. Writing technologies did develop in Crete a little after 2000 BCE and were used on the mainland from about 1400 BCE, both disappearing around 1150 BCE. Almost all the evidence is for the use of these technologies in accounting systems, although some short, possibly ritual, inscriptions are preserved on artefacts in Crete (in undeciphered scripts) and some types of jar are inscribed with personal and place names written in Linear B, a script used to write the Mycenaean Greek language (the language or languages used on Crete, and hidden in undeciphered scripts, are not known). The available evidence does not document the use of these scripts for high-level communication within the Aegean, and communication further afield would have required the use of a diplomatic language such as Akkadian, for which there is no evidence at all. The accident of preservation may obscure a more complex picture, but at present it appears that the upper echelons of Aegean communities did not contain the 'brother' monarchs, addressed in such terms in communications between other potentates.

One possible reason for this was that it seems most unlikely that the Aegean was ever united under a single ruler during the Bronze Age. The scales of infrastructure seen, even during the heyday of Mycenae, do not match anything seen in the Egyptian or western Asian polities. The Aegean was nonetheless part of the networks of relationships of the eastern Mediterranean, indicated by the eventual widespread distribution of its material culture, by depictions of Aegean peoples in Egyptian frescos, and by finds of imports in Crete and at the Mycenaean 'palaces'. One remarkable inscription in Egypt from the reign of Amenhotep III (ruled 1391–1353 BCE) lists a series of place names in the Aegean, including Knossos, Phaistos and Kydonia on Crete, and Mycenae on the mainland, with another (perhaps to be equated with Amyklai) perhaps indicating the important, newly discovered Mycenaean site at Ayos Stephanos, Lakonia. The other place names are very tentatively identified (Cline and Stannish 2011; Burns 2010). These have been interpreted as an itinerary and correlated with discoveries of possible diplomatic gifts bearing Amenhotep's (or his wife's) name, especially at Mycenae. This list is of great interest, as it depicts an interest in the Aegean, but not one that led to a more sustained interaction; and its list of place names, presented equally, suggests that there was no single centre of power, at least from the Pharaoh's point of view, at this time.

The means by which human identities were created had developed out of the European Neolithic and into the European Bronze Age through an increasingly complex range of technologies that focused upon the body itself. The range of performances that bodies undertook was extended, not only by the requirements of a developing metal technology but also by the demands of the etiquettes of the service, and consumption, of food and drink, and by the occupancy of increasingly complex forms of architecture. In addition, the appearance of the body was enhanced by new forms of dress and decoration. All these forms of performance depended upon access to an increasingly wide range of material conditions and, as we have argued here, that access depended upon submission to, or the extension of, political alliances and obligations. By considering material culture, not simply in terms of source materials, distribution patterns and form but in terms of practice, and by avoiding the common assumption that stylistic comparisons represent the previous existence of cultural identities, we have traced the development of the third into the second millennium in two regions of Europe as a process in which populations made the material conditions of their own existence, but not necessarily under conditions of their own choosing.

We have attempted to develop these points with reference to the eastern Mediterranean from the third and into the second millennium BCE, an argument that treats a form of life as the ability to live (that is to perform) amongst things in ways that were recognizable to, and whose effectiveness could be judged by, others. Archaeologically attested forms of life are therefore the practical ways in which intentions might once have been enacted and understood in the direction that they took towards archaeologically observable material conditions. In these conditions identities were constructed, both as

commonly held understandings of how to live and as a contra
and these identities were contrasted with those whose liv
expressed alternative systems of value and where such comparisons
been enacted in terms of relations of political obligation and conflict. It was
this way that a Mycenaean world had emerged by the second millennium BCE.

We thus see, in the material culture traces of the second millennium, an interconnected world in which different actors and communities could endlessly remake their place through differing scales of participation, where identity became something beyond the personal or local, its construction sometimes implicating the most far-flung connections. The dramatic cessation of these interconnections during the Bronze Age led to a complete reconfiguration of how the world might be understood and lives led within it.

5

Places that Mattered: Movement and Belonging

If, as Richard Atkinson suggested, a Mycenaean architect really had turned up in southern Britain to propose how Stonehenge might be constructed, why would anyone have listened? Despite its concern with the specific ways that human behaviour had done things, earlier archaeology was remarkably reticent when it came to explaining why those people had done those things in those particular ways. The assumption was always that influences flowed from what was regarded as the 'higher' or more 'advanced' culture to those who were somehow less advanced, or as Atkinson had put it, from those who practised architecture to those who merely constructed.

As we have seen, the tracing of particular cultural influences was abandoned and replaced by the arguments of the 'New' or 'Processual Archaeology' in the 1960s. These made the case that the behaviour that was represented by archaeological finds should be treated not in the particularities of its motivations but as having had clearly defined but general kinds of consequences. This meant, for example, that certain finds could be treated as if they represented behaviour that had economic consequences, or religious consequences, or social consequences, and so on. What motivated such behaviours was, apparently, the search for greater effectiveness. We have traced some of the ways that this new approach impacted upon possible explanations for the changes in the material residues that were recovered archaeologically. Change was no longer explained by the influences that might have been exerted by one set of cultural ideas upon another, but instead by the interaction of the different kinds of behavioural consequences that had operated in the context of changing environmental circumstances. It was in this way that various systems of human behaviours were traced as if they had been organized both with reference to various environmental conditions and, as Renfrew's 1984 emphasis upon a social archaeology made clear, with reference to processes of internal social and political competition.

One methodological problem with this 'new' reasoning was that different traditions of behaviour could obviously have had more than one kind of material consequence. Take Childe's 1957 model for the origins of metallurgy as an example. In that model the elite religious and social institutions of the ancient orient were claimed to have had the economic power to support specialist producers. Thus, the temple and the palace might be taken as representing both religious and social behaviour, but they might also be treated as if they represented an important aspect of economic behaviour. Or, to take another example, should the materials that were recovered from a seemingly ritual deposit, such as the early metal hoard from Pile in Sweden (Vandkilde 2017) be treated as if it represented religious, social or economic behaviour?

In this book we argue that archaeology needs to consider the ways that humans might have been able to live amongst, and thus to have made sense of, the inherited and accumulated mass of the material conditions that are attested for archaeologically. We are therefore also concerned with the ways that local traditions of understanding the world might have drawn upon and used things that originated in other worlds and with other people. In the historical processes that we are attempting to understand we recognize a similarity with Ian Hodder's recent observation (Hodder 2012) that relations of an 'entangled' dependency link together all things, such that the interdependence that had existed between humans and things, living and non-living, was an interdependence that had enabled certain forms of human life to come into being (Barrett 2014). This was because people have always depended upon the things that were available to them to bring the world into view and to act with reference to the things that were around them. As a consequence, cultural conventions that simply describe particular ways of living, were adopted because those conventions made sense with reference to the things amongst which people were able to live. In this way the building of Stonehenge made sense to those who worked upon it as the result of the particular perspectives that they had upon the world in general and upon that place in particular. This was a perspective which the gradually developing structures of Stonehenge or the citadel at Mycenae will have brought into sharper focus and have clarified, until the historical conditions arose in which those monuments were now only seen as the incomprehensible wonders of the ancient world. What we must demonstrate in this chapter is that archaeology is capable of understanding at least something of the ways that people recognized and identified themselves through their encounters with, and their uses of, particular places, and the ways that the architectural embellishment of those places made sense in these terms.

Having an archaeology that attempts to understand how forms of life made sense of their worlds and, upon that basis, may have lived within the existing material conditions, means that human identity was constructed out of the archaeological contexts that we investigate. Places in archaeology are traditionally treated as if they were the locations at which particular kinds of past activity can be identified. Thus, a place such as Stonehenge was one that had witnessed a particular range of building acts along with the deposition of certain materials, and the 'palaces' of Mycenaean Greece were the locations for acts such as procession and specialist production. Having established the different kinds of activities that might be represented by the finds, archaeology then normally enquires as to why those particular activities might have arisen at that time and at that place. From our alternative perspective, however, places only achieved their historical significance to the extent that they enabled occupants both to understand their worlds and to act in ways that sustained a particular order of things.

Joakim Goldhan has suggested that the cosmological ordering of things that the populations of the northern European Bronze Age might have believed to have existed can be understood from a perspective that accepts that all humans have contemplated a number of fundamental questions 'since the dawn of time', such as 'How and why was the world created?' (Goldhan 2013, 248). It is self-evident that Bronze Age communities were centrally concerned with their cosmologies and with the cosmologies of those with whom they interacted. However we disagree with Goldhan's emphasis in two ways. First, we would argue that the asking of such metaphysical questions as those suggested by Goldhan was not a primary characteristic of the Bronze Age or any other period but has only really been encountered amongst a relatively small portion of populations, such as the elite religious and the secular intellectuals of medieval and modern Europe. The reason we argue this is because we take the orders of the ancient world, including the forces that were deemed to have created and to have held that order in place, to have emerged out of people's direct experience of, and actions with reference to, the order of things. These sustained the empirical taken for granted understandings that the anthropologist Maurice Bloch has characterized as those things that 'go without saying' (Bloch 2012, 143–185). Second, the skills of living and the ability to divine an explicit representation of the orders of things were not equably distributed across all members of a community and may well have been deemed to depend upon experience, age and gender. Thus, knowledge of the order of things emerged through the routine occupancy of places and their associated material conditions. Finally, we note that once a practice has seemed to work it will have resulted in certain material consequences; thus the interdependence of things and practices will have become embedded and will have secured the continuity of human understanding in the physical patterns of things.

We will certainly allow that the orders of the world are likely to have been recognized explicitly in moments of ritual expression (Bloch 1985; Barrett 1991), or in moments of material renewal. We might therefore expect that the landscape of places that can be mapped archaeologically, contained those places that were routinely encountered as the order of things was revealed and came to be accepted, as well as those places where the governing orders of life were made explicit, and that these two kinds of location were not necessarily geographically distinguished one from the other. Thus, the domestic space of the house in which routines were lived and where people grew to maturity was likely to have been the place where schemes of order were learnt through routines of practice, but where those schemes might also, at certain times, have been made explicit. What we will detail here is the ways that journeys to, and the practices at, certain places made the orders of the world explicit. It was at these places and under such circumstances that the question 'How and why was the world created?' might have been asked and indeed answered. Let us now attempt to clarify our argument by means of a brief example from northern Britain.

The Orcadian Late Neolithic

One region in western Europe where this cumulative development in the architectural form of the places occupied can be traced in some detail from the end of the fourth to the end of the third millennium BCE is Orkney (Fig. 5.1). The detailed survival of the material and the work undertaken by Colin Richards and his colleagues at Barnhouse and the more recent excavations at the Ness of Brodgar under the direction of Nick Card does allow us to point to the Orcadian Neolithic as an example of the kinds of processes to which we refer.

The complexity of the sequence of Neolithic activity in the centre of Orkney Mainland, long known from the location of the henge of Stenness, the stone circle of Brodgar and the tomb of Maes Howe, was extended by Richards' excavations of the settlement at Barnhouse and more recently by the discovery and excavation of the remarkable complex of the Ness of Brodgar. The latter lies on the isthmus between the Loch of Harray and the Loch of Stenness, centrally placed between the stones at Stenness and the Ring of Brodgar, and immediately to the north-west of the Barnhouse settlement. Whilst the sequence of building at the Ness is currently uncertain, excavation is ongoing, and it has proved difficult to identify material from amongst the structures to submit for radiocarbon-dating (Card et al. 2018) however it seems clear that the settlement was developing at least by the early part of the third millennium although some structures may have had a relatively short period of use due to subsidence. The occupancy of Ness currently known from excavation was largely contemporary with Barnhouse

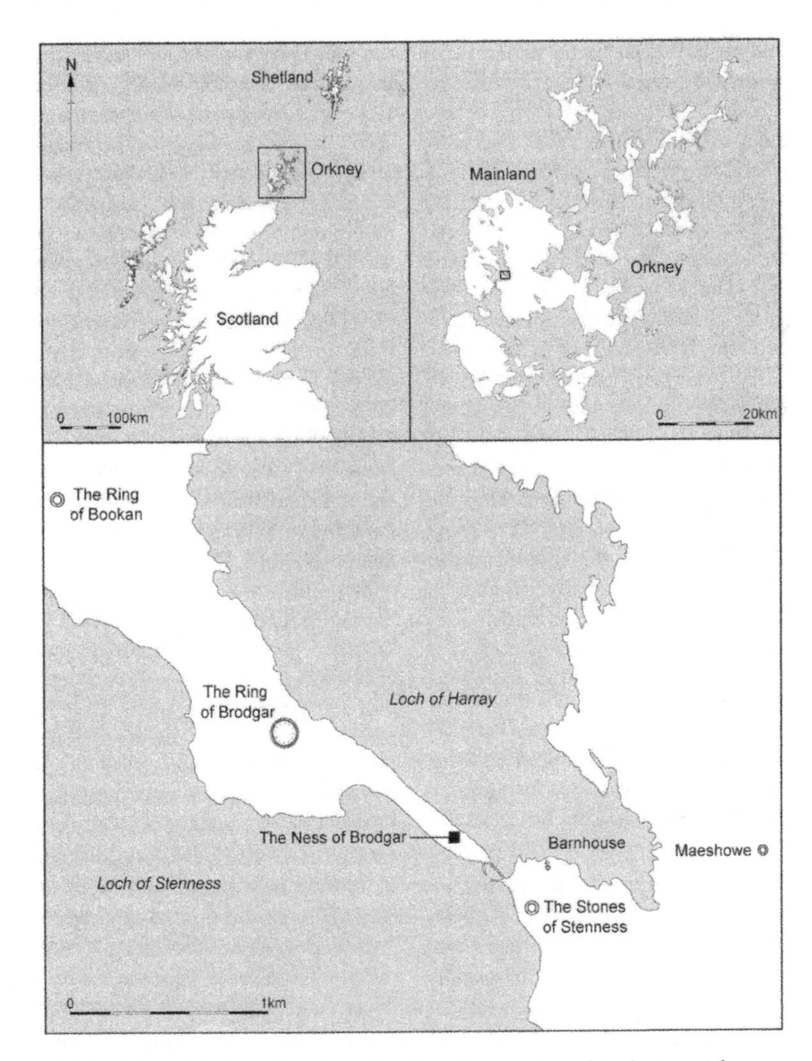

Fig. 5.1 Map of Orkney Mainland showing sites mentioned in the text. After Card et al. 2018, Fig. 1.

and it was a development that culminated in the construction of the large house structure 10. This is comparable in its internal organization, if not in its scale, to the largest structure at Barnhouse. Upon its abandonment after several centuries of use this late structure was infilled with rubble and midden material before a phase of final activity that might have spanned a further

300 years (Card et al. 2018, 247) resulted in the deposition of the slaughtered remains of what are calculated to have been around 400 head of cattle. Depending upon the period over which these events occurred and the numbers of animals involved, then these deposits mark periodic acts of feasting at the centre of Orkney Mainland that might have made quite heavy demands on the available stock of Orcadian cattle. This activity on the Ness is currently believed to have started sometime around 2400 BCE, although activity on the site seems to have continued throughout the third millennium (Card et al. 2018).

The spatial logic of this and the wider Orcadian sequence would tend to be obscured if we were to treat it as a sequence of dated deposits, acts of construction and sequences of monument types. Archaeologists commit considerable effort to the detailing of the sequences and the methods used in such things as wall construction and to the processes of collapse, whereas the occupants of these buildings will have experienced them somewhat differently. Those occupants lived the differences in architectural order as the spatial differences between things, people and activities, and will have linked those areas by means of paths of movement and by visual perspectives, such as the view from Ness to Brodgar, or the path from Barnhouse to Stenness. The point of historical analysis is therefore to recognize that the ongoing processes by which places were modified and thus enhanced by building works, described archaeologically as sequences of building types, are likely to have developed as if they expressed an ongoing spatial order of occupancy and performance. The practical experiencing of that order will have revealed, for the participant, the forces that they believed had brought that order into being and sustained it. This was the empirical confirmation of things operating 'as they should be': life, in other words, made sense. Such an order of experiences may well have been re-examined explicitly at moments of ritual transformation and ceremonial display. However, it was not initially formulated as some kind of mental abstraction, as if it were a design to be imposed upon the material. Instead it emerged pragmatically by the repetition of material practices in ways that worked. Archaeology should therefore resist the temptation of listing the sequence of things as if such lists were the representations of the historical process. Instead we might aim to treat history as a narrative that traces not a sequence of things but the ways that people were able to identify their place amongst a particular order of things, and it is upon such a basis that we aim to understand the ways that places were defined, enhanced and ultimately abandoned. Thus, whilst the order of an entangled life was emergent in the routines of daily and seasonal practice so was the point at which such orders no longer worked or failed to deliver the results that were expected of them.

The scale and concentration of settlement, ceremonial and burial monuments found in central Mainland Orkney, along with the late midden deposits that must have resulted from feasting events that spanned the latter part of the third millennium, imply that this area must have been known and to have attracted voyaging from within and beyond the Orcadian archipelago. The dangers of such voyaging, particularly across the waters of the Pentland Firth, are obvious, and overcoming such dangers presumably enhanced the status of those who undertook these journeys. If this picture of movement and voyaging is accepted then our understanding of the third millennium here and elsewhere shifts from one in which human identities were grounded upon insular origins to one in which those identities arose through journeys taken and places seen.

The suggestion by Richards and others that the Orcadian Neolithic can be understood as belonging within Levi-Strauss's category of 'house' societies (Levi-Strauss 1982, 185; Richards et al. 2016, 226) implies that it was the physical presence of the location of the places of residency that embodied the physical identity and continuity of a particular community, and where the mechanisms of recruitment to that community were openly negotiable, extending beyond the more restrictive demands of lineage descent. From the end of the fourth millennium BCE it is possible to trace something of the physical means by which such communities constructed their identity, and in which the fundamental architectural orientation of the domestic space

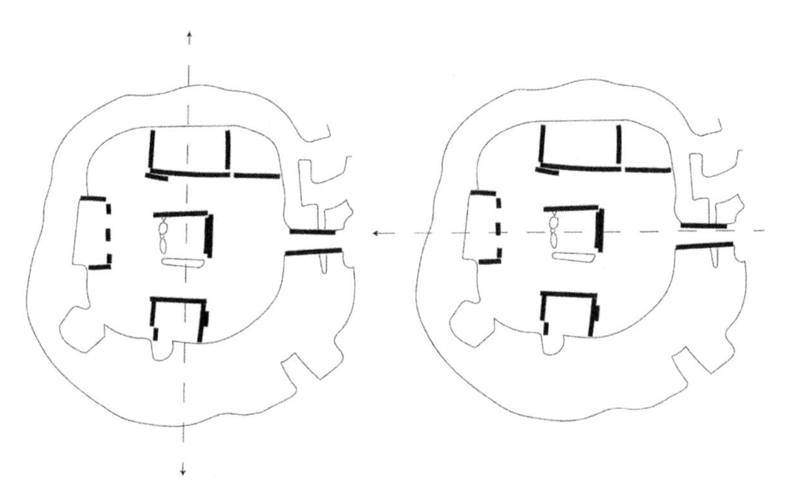

Fig 5.2 Spatial organization of the Late Neolithic house. After Richards et al. 2005, Fig. 4.1.

appears to have been initiated with reference to the position of the hearth that was set centrally in the floor of the house (Fig. 5.2).

The role of the hearth in orientating various patterns of behaviour might explain why in the immediate landscape around Barnhouse the transference of what appears to have been a domestic hearth by the reuse and resetting of the hearth-stones could have orientated the way that the central space of the henge enclosure at Stenness was used (Ritchie 1976). Surely the Stenness case implies that an analogy was being drawn between the occupancy and use of this penannular earthwork enclosure and standing stones of that henge, and of the lived space of the rectilinear house interiors of the adjacent settlement of Barnhouse (Richards 2005, 221). In this way the hearth appears to have drawn together certain activities in the domestic and ritual landscape of the Ness, Barnhouse and the adjacent henges and stone settings, creating a contrast with the further-flung monumental landscape of the dead including the great passage grave of Maes Howe, where no hearth-type structure has been located in its central chamber. Maes Howe was also isolated by means of the cutting of an encircling, and possibly water filled, ditch around the burial mound (Richards 2005, 232–235). If the foundation and maintenance of the hearth and with it the domestic fire did indeed evoke the foundation and reproduction of the living community in contrast with that of the dead, then it might be more accurate to characterize the evolution of the Orcadian Neolithic as the evolution of a 'hearth' society.

Stonehenge

Two observations may now be made with reference to the Orkney data that are of relevance to our understanding of the Stonehenge landscape. First is the remarkable density of buildings that appear to have satisfied different sacred and profane requirements, from settlement through ceremony to burial. The archaeological treatment of these as individual sites might deflect from an understanding of how these different places functioned together as a single field of experience for the occupant. This is a very different organization of space from the model of the Stonehenge landscape offered by Parker Pearson and Ramilisonina (1998) with its clear spatial division between 'domains' of the living and of the ancestors. We should perhaps now expect the Stonehenge landscape to be far busier with a range of activities than the Parker Pearson and Ramilisonina model suggests. The second observation concerns the fundamental way in which the routines of domestic life inculcate the ways that different practices, people and things should be ordered spatially, and the ways that such an ordering is then employed in the

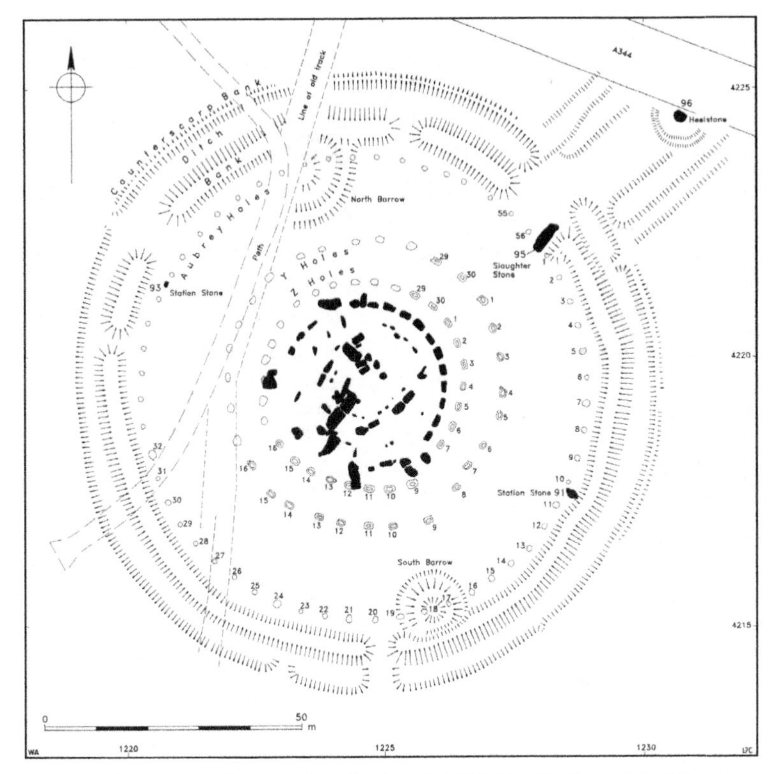

Fig. 5.3 Plan of Stonehenge. After Cleal et al. 1995, Fig. 13. Copyright Historic England.

practices of ceremony and ritual. Upon this basis we should perhaps look again at Darvill's suggestion (Darvill 2016) that a degree of spatial homology should be expected between domestic architecture and the clearly non-domestic site of Stonehenge. It would follow from these two observations that the historical significance of Stonehenge cannot be understood by treating it as the representation of a condition, be that a design in the mind of an architect, or the rise of a chiefdom level of organization, rather than as one place in a field of experience.

The place selected for the erection of the sarsen monument had already been pre-determined in the first half of the third millennium (Darvill et al. 2012) by, among other things, the construction of a large circular enclosure with an inner bank around which were dug fifty-six so-called 'Aubrey Holes' and into which cremated bone had been deposited (Cleal et al. 1995, 94–107;

Parker Pearson et al. 2009; Fig. 5.3). This place, along with an apparent inner timber setting, therefore marked, from one perspective, the end point of a lengthy funerary ritual, the earlier stages of which, such as the preparation of the corpse and of the pyre and its firing, are not currently recognized archaeologically. Parker Pearson has suggested that these deposits were marked by the erection in the 'Aubrey Holes' of so-called blue-stones whose geological origins lay in south-west Wales (Darvill et al. 2012; Parker Pearson et al. 2015b). If this use of the blue-stones were indeed the case then this location on the chalkland of Wessex was clearly the place towards which paths and labour were directed whose origins may have lain at some considerable distance. The implication is that the location was already one that was widely understood to reveal something of the forces that provided for an order to the world.

The enhancement of this location and of the revelation that it facilitated had, by the middle of the third millennium, become a matter of widely shared purpose that involved a massive investment of labour. Recent excavations have indicated that one focus for the gathering from far and wide of this labour force was at Durrington Walls, a gathering which began before the building of the massive earthwork enclosure at that site (Parker Pearson 2012, 109–127). This investment resulted, around the middle of the third millennium, in the construction of a 'horse-shoe' or 'cove' arrangement of five closely-set pairs in lintelled sarsens (the trilithons: Fig. 5.4). This

Fig. 5.4 Trilithons at Stonehenge. Photograph by Elaine Wakefield. Copyright Wessex Archaeology.

substantial project set in place an apparatus within which ceremony and ritual could conform with the solar and seasonal cycle, with the sun setting at the mid-winter solstice behind the central and tallest pair in the trilithon setting and rising in front of the same setting at mid-summer and possibly framed by the heel stone and its now missing partner (stone 97) at the entrance to the earthwork. The cove that was formed by the trilithons remained the functioning apparatus of revelation throughout the rest of the third millennium and was enhanced by further acts of construction on the site.

These enhancements began with the construction of the surrounding ring of sarsen standing stones that survive, at least in part, today. These were capped by the addition of a continuous line of lintels that united at least some of these stones and screened the view towards the inner trilithon setting from the north-east when approached along the line of the avenue, also added around this time. The completeness of the ring of standing stones has been confirmed by the recording of parchmarks in the turf that covers the presumed stone-holes of those stones that are now missing to the south-west, behind the trilithon cove (Banton et al. 2014). However, there is still considerable doubt as to whether the line of lintels was ever completed around the full circuit, not least because some of the remaining standing stones appear to be too short to support lintels (stones 11, 16 and 23) and because, if the supposition is correct, the felling of south-easterly stones 8 and 9 in antiquity would also have brought down any lintels, if present (Pollard et al. 2017, 288–289).

The third millennium embellishment of the location of the trilithon cove continued with the various settings that were dug to take the blue-stones. These stones, quarried in south-west Wales (Parker Pearson et al. 2015b), had themselves, at some point in their histories, been dressed to form a lintelled stone monument (Cleal et al. 1995, 29). However, by the end of the millennium the form of the landscape, and thus the place of Stonehenge within that landscape, had begun to change.

Whilst the erection of the stone monument had begun about a millennium earlier than Atkinson had originally assumed, many writers still suggest that the development that traces a chronological path between the building of the trilithons and the Wessex barrow cemeteries of the early second millennia, and that surround it in the landscape, was one that is marked by a continuity of historical development. Renfrew, for example, regarded such continuous development as one that traced a developing social hierarchy, originating in the fourth millennium and running through into the second millennium. If we maintain our emphasis upon the extent to which 'continuity' should imply

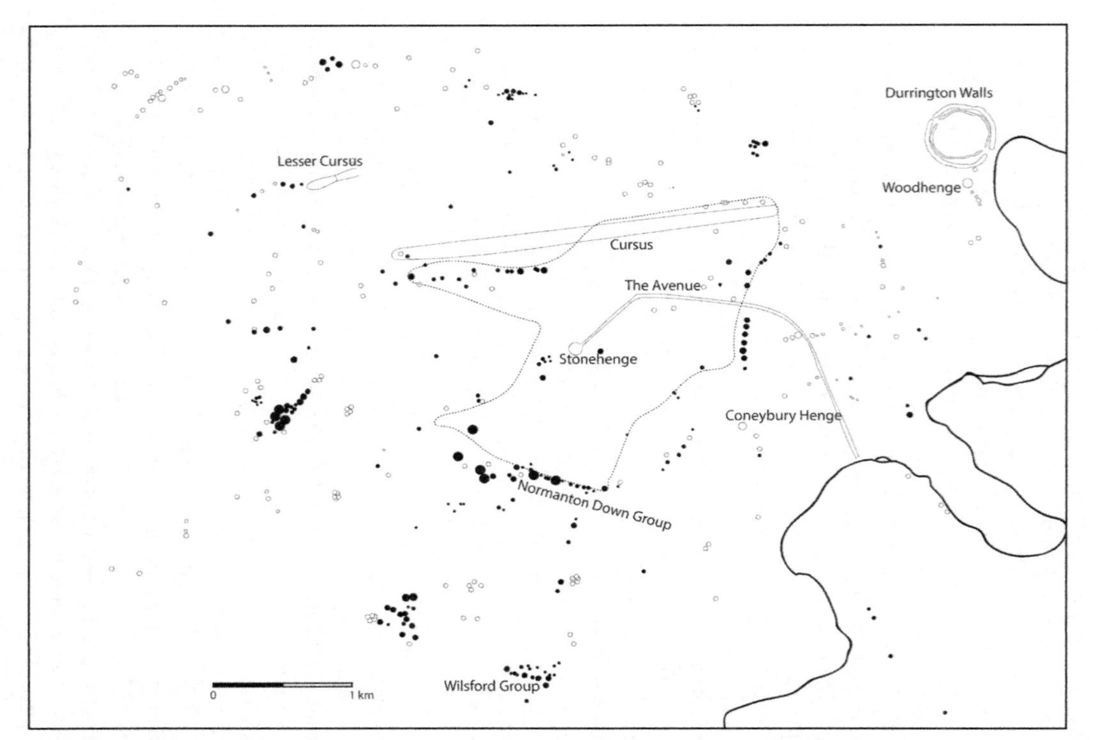

Fig. 5.5 The immediate visual envelope of Stonehenge. Dark Circles indicate barrows, white circles ploughed out barrows or ring ditches. North is to the top. After Cleal et al. 1995, Fig. 21.

the continuing role of the monument in providing a means by which a source for the order of life could be witnessed, then the evidence implies that the opening centuries of the second millennium witnessed a significant change in the ways that locations within the landscape were worked. The result was a more spatially dispersed ritual focus upon mortuary rites, and it was under these circumstances that the focus upon the place of Stonehenge was necessarily re-invented.

The steady embellishment of the trilithon arrangement in the centre of Stonehenge appears to have begun to change in the third quarter of the third millennium with the burial, in the recut ditch around the monument, of an individual who had died as the result of a number of arrow wounds (Evans 1984; Pollard et al. 2017, 284–285). After this time and for the rest of the third millennium, inhumation burials were placed in earth-cut graves in the landscape around Stonehenge, but where the locations selected for these mortuary rites lacked any obvious focus upon, or indeed proximity to, Stonehenge itself (Whittle 1981). This pattern of funerary practices then changed again in the opening decades of the second millennium with the construction of large burial mounds, or barrows, built either of combinations of chalk and turf or of turf alone, that covered the primary deposits; these mounds then became, in some cases, the receptacles for secondary deposits. The building of these mounds of various forms over funerary deposits had the effect of creating a new arrangement in the landscape architecture which involved the clustering of mounds into linear and grouped cemeteries. The contrast between the low mounds covering the earlier, spatially dispersed mortuary deposits and the substantial burial mounds that were built in the opening centuries of the second millennium appears to coincide with the reworking of the visual form of the Stonehenge landscape. In this way the mounds were placed on the skyline to the north, east and south of Stonehenge, whilst the one barrow cemetery to the west lies out of view from Stonehenge. The result is that during the first half of the second millennium Stonehenge was increasingly situated within a 'visual envelope' defined by the monuments of the dead (Cleal 1995, 35–37; Fig 5.5). It was at this time that the representations of axe heads along with a few of hafted daggers were chipped into the surface of two of the standing sarsen stones, one a trilithon (stone 4), and one belonging to the outer ring (stone 53; Pollard et al. 2017, Fig. 18.6).

By the second millennium therefore Stonehenge lay centrally within a visual envelope defined by the barrow cemeteries and where the larger landscape might have brought together the annual ceremonies of the solar year with the rituals associated with at least some mortuary rites. The original trilithon structure of Stonehenge witnessed an ongoing, if at times somewhat ad hoc, embellishment throughout the second half of the third millennium (Darvill et al. 2012). We have noted that it would be wrong to assume that the patterns of later activity, however slight, marked a decline in the monument's importance; instead these modifications further enclosed and enhanced the trilithon setting, attesting to its continuing importance as a place of gathering from near and far throughout the third millennium (Pollard et al. 2017, 282). Nonetheless, the second half of that millennium was clearly a period during which the material world was changing. The continuing material concern with the stone settings is indicated by the digging of the so-called 'X and Y holes' around the outer ring of sarsen stones that occurred towards the middle of the second millennium BCE, but it was also around this time that the linear land division of a palisade, later recut as a ditch, was built to divide the visual envelope within which the stones were set by running to the north-west and, eventually, turning south but out of sight of Stonehenge itself. Perhaps it was with this land division and the re-ordering of activities that included the developing agrarian landscapes of the mid- to late second millennium that the significance of Stonehenge and the truths that it had once revealed began to drift from view. If this was indeed the case then it would emphasize that Stonehenge addressed an understanding of the world that had developed in the third through to the first half of the second millennium, an understanding that perhaps involved movement and even migration across the landscape and that was lost with the establishment of the land divisions and the intensification of agrarian production that rendered a place like Stonehenge a place of incomprehensible wonder rather than one of understanding.

The archaeology of the third to mid-second millennia BCE in Orkney and southern Britain has begun to reveal worlds in which forms of life, lived as routines of understanding, also constructed the means by which those taken for granted orders could have been made explicit and their origins identified. On this basis we can trace the possibility that discontinuities occurred in such histories such as the building of the trilithon core of Stonehenge and the ways that it was enhanced and encountered over the millennium of its further use. In the case of Stonehenge this discontinuity results from an increasing emphasis upon burial rites that were instigated, not by a seasonal routine, but by the death of individuals. This provides us with the image of a fragmentation and dispersal away from the central focus upon solar and lunar cycles and seasonal change. By the early second millennium the two themes could have been held together by the placing of burial mounds with the consequence that their visual reference was established from the vantage point of Stonehenge itself.

Keros

On the other side of Europe, we can also trace the development of certain locales that came to offer much larger groups than previously seen places in which to find their place in an ordered world. This sequence is one that traces a growth in the scale of communities of agreed purpose and of a common understanding, and, in the Aegean, is intimately connected with the growth of that condition that has been referred to as civilization (Renfrew 1972). In tracing this development we will consider three kinds of place that, in their different ways, acted as foci that drew people towards them by facilitating their discovery in both those places and in their journeys to them, of a common identity. None of these places housed, initially, a chief or a ruling household and if such politically dominant institutions were to emerge, and we certainly see little evidence for some form of an emergent ruler in the Bronze Age of the Aegean, then it grew from the seedbed of common values that had been nurtured over the previous millennium.

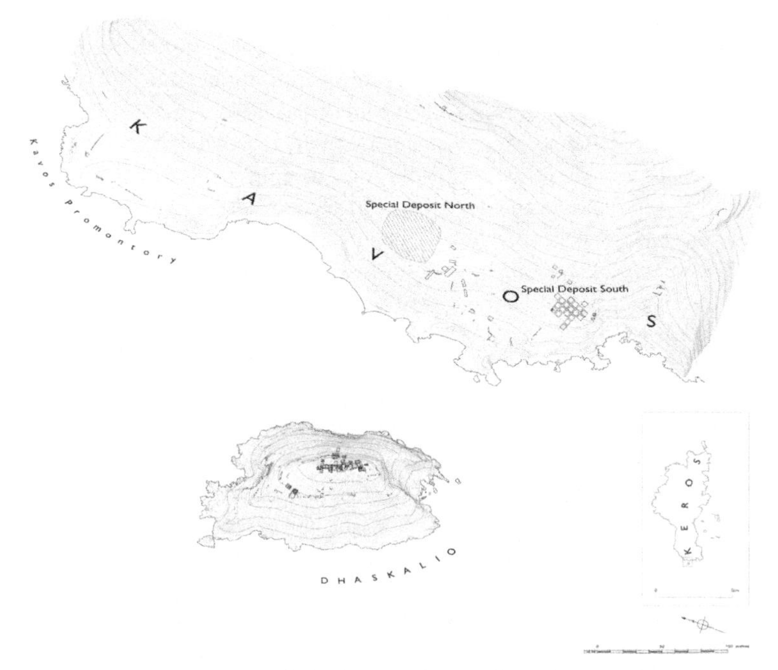

Fig. 5.6 Perspective view of Dhaskalio and Kavos from the west. Contours at 0.5m and 5m intervals. After Renfrew et al. 2015, Fig. 1.1.

Around 2750 BCE the previously uninhabited island of Keros (Fig. 5.6) was host to the opening acts of a sudden, remarkable focus of attention that led to the creation of a pan-Cycladic centre taking part in multiple networks of movement, exchange and contact within the Aegean and beyond. How did this remote spot become central to Cycladic life?

Previous signs of habitation on the island are limited (Renfrew et al. forthcoming) and it may be that no-one resided there permanently when the first activities began to take place at the western end of the island, on an unpretentious slope above the sea in the area now called Kavos. No architecture embellished the place: instead, Kavos became the visually unimpressive yet long-term site of formalized depositional activity. Looting activities in the 1950s in one part of Kavos have caused irreparable damage to one of the two locations of repeated deposition (now referred to as the Special Deposit North). But excavations from 2006–2008 uncovered the second such location (now the Special Deposit South) which was unlooted and apparently undisturbed since the end of the Early Bronze Age (now fully published: Renfrew et al. 2015; 2018, with earlier references).

The Special Deposit South contained a restricted range of material culture, deposited over a two-hundred year period. The material consisted of sculpted marble in the form of vessels in various forms and anthropomorphic shapes ('Cycladic figurines') as well as broken pottery and much obsidian. Elements of domestic life such as ground stone or organic remains, as well as metal, were all but absent. It seems that deposits were made in small batches, perhaps in earlier years exposed on a rock shelf, and later, when an overburden of soil and stone had developed, by digging pits and depositing into them. The series of depositions largely came to an end when a low cairn of stone was placed over the deposit, perhaps around 2400 BCE.

Two aspects of this deposit are remarkable. First, the pottery seems to have come from a wide range of production centres in the Cyclades and perhaps beyond (Hilditch 2015; 2018; Sotirakopoulou 2018; forthcoming). But secondly, everything in the deposit seems to have been broken and fragmented, before deposition, at some location other than at Kavos (Renfrew 2013a; 2015). Careful excavation showed that small marble chips are not part of the makeup of the Special Deposit South, and a search for a potential breakage site elsewhere on Keros was fruitless (Renfrew et al. forthcoming). But more importantly, there are very few joins among the many fragments. Even where joins were located, these fragments did not constitute a complete figurine. The culmination of the journey to Keros was seemingly the deposition of a single fragment of an already broken figurine, and the breakage took place elsewhere, and this before the journey began. This implies a remarkable chain of actions across time and space. Some evidence for broken fragments in graves and other deposits shows that Keros was not the only locale where figurine fragments could be deposited; but the sheer numbers, coupled with the longevity of the site, suggests that breakage of a figurine almost always took place with deposition of one piece on Keros in view. We must now imagine that many figurines had a use-life, perhaps involving multiple episodes of painting (Birtacha 2017; Hoffman 2002; Hendrix 2003), followed in most cases by a breakage ceremony, where they were typically broken into 4–6 fragments (2–3 for schematic figurines, and rather more for complex figurines such as musicians). One or occasionally two of these fragments were brought to Keros for deposition, but most did not reach Keros, perhaps remaining in circulation, some eventually being deposited in graves or other places. The figurine fragments were not the only component of the Keros assemblage: it also included a prodigious quantity of pottery fragments (mainly sauceboats and conical necked jars: Chapter 4), and fragments of broken marble vessels. As with the figurines, the pottery and the marble vessel fragments of the Special Deposit South only rarely joined. It seems that these categories of material were treated in the same way as the figurines, and it therefore seems likely that the rituals of breakage practised elsewhere involved all three categories of material. One way of understanding this action is the concept of 'enchainment' (Chapman 2000) where the different fragments connected people and ideas through the distribution, retention and circulation of those fragments. But equally important is the journey itself: it was not just the materials that were transformed through these sequences of action, the voyagers also were changed by the undertaking of the journey, the congregation on Keros, and the deposition of the chosen fragments, before the journey home.

The two Special Deposits have been together described as a sanctuary (Renfrew et al. 2012), a centre of congregation (Renfrew 2013a) comparable to Stonehenge. But unlike Stonehenge, no physical architecture sets this place apart: the deposits are only defined by their contents, and the actions that brought about their deposition. It seems that the purpose of the voyaging was to bring the fragments to the sanctuary and deposit them, in the case of the better-known Special Deposit South, on a shelf of bedrock, and later as deposits accumulated in pits dug for the purpose. Provenance studies have shown that the pottery came from all over the Cyclades, although most of the stone artefacts were made using Naxian marble. It seems that a long-lived tradition developed of bringing these mixed fragments from other islands and depositing them on Keros, potentially at great meetings of people from diverse groups, congregating for the purpose. If these deposits did indeed occur as part of congregations, then one outcome of them was the creation, maintenance and negotiation of a Cycladic identity and the place of the different participants in that identity, rooted in place and material culture.

Within the basic framework of what material was acceptable for deposition here, the variation that is noted (apart from chronological implications) might play into the definition of different types of identity within the overall Cycladic community being celebrated and, in a real sense, created and recreated here.

The characteristic Cycladic figurines (Fig. 5.7) which form an important part of the deposit were produced in marble in the Cyclades (and sometimes

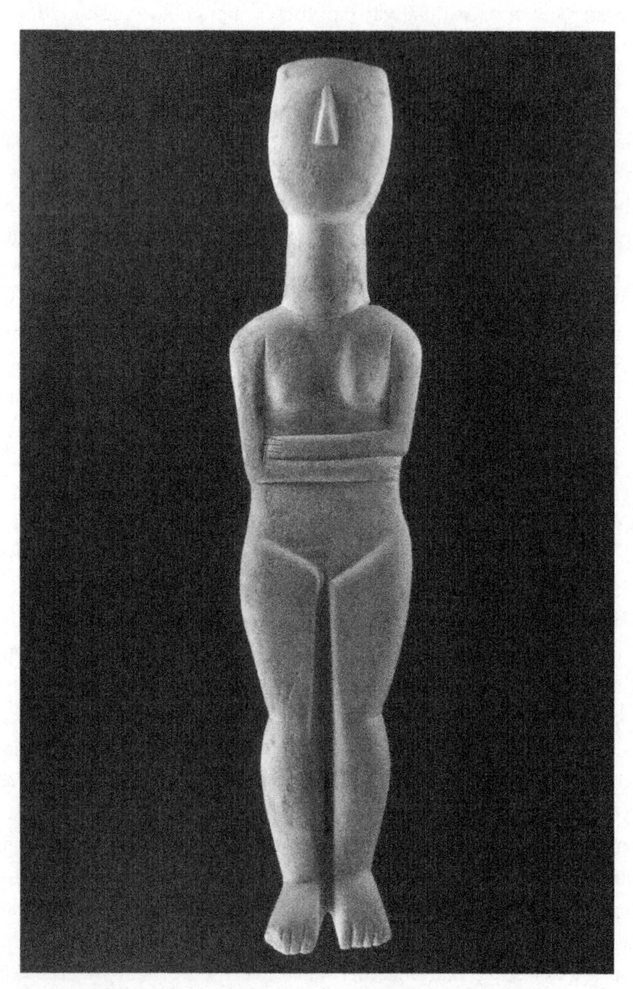

Fig. 5.7 Marble figurine from Keros (Naxos Museum 4181). After Zapheiropoulou 2017, Fig. 22.7.

elsewhere, occasionally in other materials) in the mid-third millennium BC. The object in Fig. 5.7 is the only apparently intact such sculpture recovered by archaeologists from the looted part of Kavos, although it has been claimed many others were found there – an important claim that cannot now securely be assessed (Sotirakopoulou 2005; 2008; Getz-Gentle 2008; Renfrew 2008; Papamichelakis and Renfrew 2010).

With a minimum number of at least 900 figurines represented in their fragmented state in the two Special Deposits at Kavos, and almost certainly far more before the looting of the Special Deposit North, the vexed question of the use and meaning of these objects comes into clearer focus. Previous finds in graves led to speculations on their roles in funerary practices, but the sheer numbers deposited over two centuries on Keros must now make it clear that most such objects were destined to be deposited here, and this factor probably formed part of how they were to be understood from the very moment of production. The breakage of these objects along with sauceboats, conical necked jars and stone vessels as a prelude to deposition on Keros was described in Chapter 4. Their deposition at the Kavos location was the final act in a chain of events that encompassed the voyage to Keros, preceded by the feasting and breakage elsewhere, and the prior use-life and the production of the artefacts. Their afterlife might have included the distribution and eventual deposition or loss of the other fragments elsewhere, and the rediscovery of individual fragments within the Special Deposits during future acts of deposition.

The commonest objects in the Special Deposits, the sauceboats, the stone vessels and the marble figurines, all exhibited in their production and style both a knowledgeable flair and competence in their making and an element of standardization that Renfrew has referred to as iconicity (Renfrew 2013a) and they might have expressed the collective ideal of identity. The components of these identities included not only the common recognition of the form of the objects, their production techniques and the etiquettes of their use, but also specific requirements of movement in the Cyclades. It has long been noted that marine mobility itself is a key feature of Cycladic society (Broodbank 2000), and the gatherings on Keros do indicate cohesion and coordination; whereas the journey from Kouphonisi or Naxos would have been almost routine, journeys made from further afield would have required planning, time and skills. But as we saw in Chapter 4, voyaging, contact and the remaking of identity through the adoption of new practices was the essential arena in which the Cycladic identities expressed in the depositions on Keros could be formed and reformed. While Keros lacked both the longevity and the architectural impact of contemporary Stonehenge, it functioned remarkably similarly in its regional role, drawing in participants from far-flung communities in the creation of shared space in which common expressions of identity could seem to make sense.

In contrast to the depositions of broken material in the deposits, there is also some evidence for productive activity in the environs of the sanctuary. At Kavos Promontory, some 120m to the north, evidence of primary metalworking has been detected (Brodie and Georgakopoulou 2015) in the form of smelting of copper ores. Keros is far from the nearest ore sources on Kythnos or Seriphos – in fact, it is the only securely identified smelting site in the Cyclades not located in the so-called 'metal-rich' area of the western Cyclades and Attica (Georgakopoulou 2016, Table 4.1). The small quantity of slag at Kavos Promontory might mark the practice as short-lived, or small-scale, or both and might be linked to a second craft tradition, also attested at Kavos Promontory, that of obsidian working. Obsidian working also involved long-distance resource procurement: the source material comes from Melos in the south-western Cyclades. The two crafts are linked not just by the need to procure raw materials from distant sources, but also by the highly skilled nature of particular transformative practices: in both cases it has been argued that skillsets were performed to entrance the observer (Carter 2007; Doonan et al. 2007). Like the acts of deposition, they involve specially imported materials, different skills, the physical reality of voyaging and complex, intertwined networks of people, places and material instantiated in the rituals, centred on Kavos, but stretching out across the Aegean and back in time.

Recent survey on Keros itself (Renfrew et al. forthcoming) has not produced convincing ceramic evidence of habitation there before about 2750 BCE, although obsidian pre-dating the sanctuary has been found in several locations. However, an explosion of habitation evidence on Keros thereafter indicates that Keros quite suddenly became a focus of activity when the sanctuary had been established, rather than the sanctuary being founded amidst an existing network of sites. This relatively sudden focus on an island with no resources remains difficult to explain. Settlement of the island was a culturally driven process, and, if not entirely propelled by the inception and growth of the sanctuary, at least it is clear that settlers lived there symbiotically with the sanctuary. Only by establishing this ceremonial site on a previously uninhabited island did that place enter the wider geographical perception of the Cycladic world.

On the adjacent small promontory of Dhaskalio, with an unparalleled view of the south, west and north Aegean on one side, and a panoramic view of the sanctuary on the other, quite different activities may be observed beginning not long after the first use of the Special Deposits. The earliest phase (perhaps around 2650 BCE) saw the first monumental terrace walls ringing the promontory in order to create level spaces for construction. In the subsequent phase (*c.* 2550–2400 BCE) an explosion of construction saw the

Fig 5.8 The north end of Dhaskalio. After Renfrew et al. 2013, pl. 4a.

entire promontory covered in buildings. The last phase (*c.* 2400–2300 BCE or a little later) saw a marked diminution in activity, with many buildings abandoned and collapsing, although occupation continued at the summit, with some substantial complexes.

In its physical aspect, around 2500 BCE, Dhaskalio must have appeared something like a stepped pyramid rising from the sea, towering over the Special Deposits (Fig. 5.8). This, the largest known site of the Cycladic Early Bronze Age and one of the most impressive of the Aegean at that time, was an intricate and planned building complex whose construction involved a massive effort in importing raw materials and demanded considerable architectural foresight and practical skills. Most of the stone used was imported from south-east Naxos, 10 kilometres distant (Dixon 2013). It is of course not clear whether this great quantity of stone, at least 1,000 tons, was mainly imported over a relatively short construction phase, or evenly imported over the lifetime of the site, but either way indicates both determination and organization involving significant work on Naxos, on the sea journey, and at Dhaskalio. It is yet another indication of resilient networks of mobility centred on Keros, and how those networks slowly came to have their focus shift towards Dhaskalio rather than on the Special Deposits.

Although by convention the word 'settlement' is used to describe this place, in reality the broadly domestic range of activities implied by that word are not yet well-evidenced at Dhaskalio (Renfrew 2013b; Margaritis 2013b). Instead, craft production (particularly metals: Chapter 4) forms the main evidence from within the buildings, with some evidence for organized storage, but little evidence – so far – for domesticity. Settlement elsewhere on Keros may have been more directly related to daily agricultural routines. Moreover, the unparalleled architectural ostentation on Dhaskalio would imply daily routines other than those of more modest habitations.

The effort focused on Dhaskalio transformed it from another Aegean rocky outcrop to an entirely built-up environment whose impact on those approaching by sea and then climbing to the summit can only be imagined. The architectural work carried out at Dhaskalio, and then the endless cycles of daily routine embedded within it, and the innumerable interactions involving actors and materials creating all the different networks entangled within its walls, and the remarkable range of the comings and goings of the place, all interacted in the ongoing creation of its sense of place and the projection of itself out into the Aegean and both backward and forward in time. In this way the networks of ideas, people and resources first materialized by the deposits on Keros came to be transformed by the very effort of building Dhaskalio and thereby imagining the routines of life that could be centred there.

In attempting to understand this confluence of networks, materials and people through time, the notion of fields of discourse (Barrett 1988a) or fields of action (Robb 2010) might be useful. The field describes the conditions within which human action takes place: material culture, architecture, the encultured landscape, along with structuring principles such as memory and the understanding of the expectations of others. These fields cross-cut and the site-complex at the western end of Keros provides an intricate knot of interlocking of such fields. The paragraphs above have outlined some of these fields: the rituals in the Kavos sanctuary, the activities on the Kavos Promontory, acts of monumentalization on Dhaskalio, craft practice on Dhaskalio, voyaging and interlocution between locales separated by stretches of sea. In all this we can begin to trace the processes by which Keros became seen as a 'place' in the lives of the Cyclades through incremental changes in the interactions that it hosted, from the ritual centre of the earlier days to a monumentalized centre of production and power.

Knossos

Keros, like Stonehenge, has now been revealed to be a great 'centre of congregation' (Renfrew 2013a). Knowing how and when to move toward and occupy a place like Keros was part of the process by which people became known for who they were to themselves and to others, and in which their identities were recreated through action. Performance, revelation and restricted access are three factors at work here and at the other places that mattered and are discussed in this chapter. The particular forms of locale, architecture and practice may vary but the central qualities are the same.

One other such place that mattered in the Aegean at this time, even if there are significant differences in the particularities, is the site of Knossos, in north-central Crete. Like Mycenae, discussed further below, Knossos lies at the very foundation of Aegean prehistory. Its thorough excavation by Sir Arthur Evans in the early years of the twentieth century, and its very full publication (Evans 1921; 1928; 1930; 1935), combined with the sheer richness of the finds, architecture and iconography uncovered there, made it the defining site of the so-called 'Minoan' period, whose fascination has passed well beyond the confines of academic archaeology.

Evans' Knossos consisted of a multi-phase building that he referred to as a 'palace' essentially of the second millennium BCE, albeit with a rich earlier prehistory. Now we recognize that the history of inhabitation at what is effectively a tell at Knossos stretches back to 7000 BCE (Efstratiou et al. 2004), a history of inhabitation that is essentially unbroken. In recent years many new insights into the third millennium at Knossos offer a much deeper and more satisfying picture of a place that came to regional prominence at that time. Previous debates sought to explain the surprising and relatively sudden development of this very complex architecture at the very end of the third millennium in terms of punctuated equilibrium (Cherry 1983; 1984) and peer polity interaction (Cherry 1986). These models of development involved specific cultural and technological triggers, such as the invention of the sail. However, insights into the history of human practice at Knossos is now allowing for a richer understanding of the remarkable history of that place.

During the long Neolithic occupation of the tell, Knossos was principally a domestic centre. Recent work has shown the Initial and Early Neolithic (*c.* 7000–5300 BCE) site was small and part of a network of (so far undiscovered) other sites (Tomkins 2008). The site expanded in size in the Late Neolithic (*c.* 5300–4500 BCE), but not in the subsequent Final Neolithic (*c.* 4500–3000 BCE: Tomkins 2008). Connections to other regions of Crete and beyond are indicated by imports of ceramics and obsidian; but in general Neolithic Knossos is now seen as a typical, rather than an exceptional, settlement of the period (Tomkins 2008, 41).

It was during the latter stages of the Final Neolithic *c.* 3300–3000 BCE, that a series of walled terracing operations on top of the tell removed earlier strata (Tomkins 2012, 42). This provided a central and open space that has been referred to as a court (Tomkins 2012, 42), in direct analogy with the systems

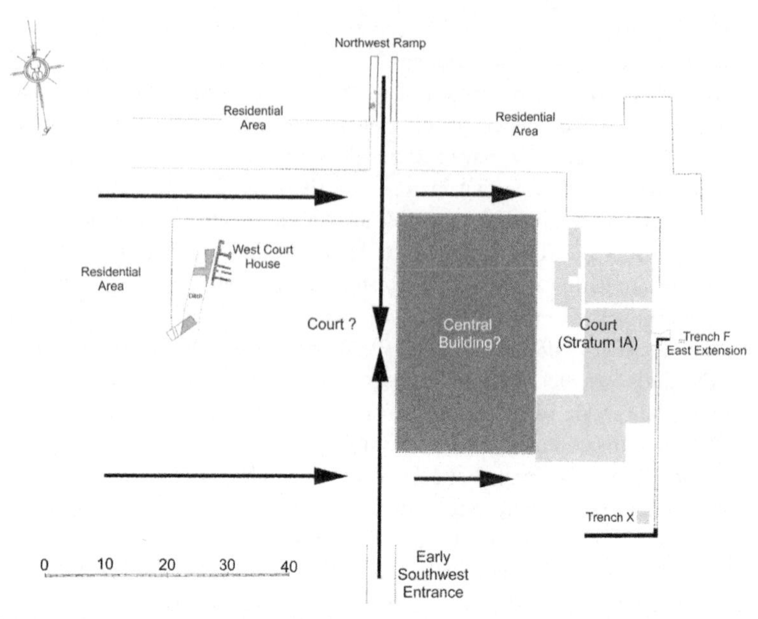

Fig. 5.9 Knossos in the early third millennium. After Tomkins 2012, Fig. 2.

of alternating open and built areas of later Minoan 'palatial' architecture. The court was retained but enlarged in the early third millennium (Early Bronze I; Fig. 5.9), and it may have been a gathering place where the consumption of meat was formalized presumably by cooking on stone hearths. In the middle part of the millennium (Early Bronze II) the court was probably re-laid on the same orientation and close to the dimensions of the later, second millennium central court. A hypothetical 'public building' (or buildings) was reconstructed on its western side and a system of buildings, passageways and retaining walls seems to have been built up and maintained, followed by further buildings clustered around this central open area. Although the evidence is heavily fragmented by the later constructions of the Minoan 'palace', it does now seem that the use of this particular place in Crete for communal gatherings may go back to the later fourth millennium, and that by the first half of the third millennium the court that hosted these gatherings had already reached approximately the size and configuration it was to maintain until well into the next millennium. That configuration included a series of axial routes which terminated at the court and the public buildings around it, all of which were maintained, with much embellishment, for nearly two thousand years.

It is obviously important for us to understand the activities that drew people into this court, and the places from which they came. Frustratingly little direct evidence is preserved for activities in the central court in any period. Indirect evidence for specific practices comes from a number of locations close to the court (Day and Wilson 2002). Day and Wilson identify a drinking set consisting of cup, jug and bowl, which is first seen in Early Bronze I and continues to occur in several deposits in Early Bronze II. The specific pottery shapes change, but are characterized as very fine wares, and their proportions within the assemblages suggest non-domestic, perhaps single-event, deposition after episodes of feasting. A notable change between the Early Bronze I and II deposits is the prevalence of forms employed in communal drinking in the earlier period and individual drinking shapes in the later period. It is also notable that a far higher proportion of this fine ceramic is of non-local origin (Wilson and Day 1994). This implies that by the later period Knossos was drawing in persons and groups from all over Crete to participate in ceremonies in the central court. Despite the fragmentary nature of the evidence, it is possible to imagine that Knossos' place as a regional centre, analogous to the role of Keros in the Cyclades, was established at the same time that those depositions were taking place on Keros around 2700 BCE.

The evidence from Knossos points to non-domestic activity involving gatherings of people to consume food and drink in a space set aside and, over time, embellished for public performances (Schoep 2012), mirroring at least in function the sanctuary at Keros. A similar homology exists between the settlement at Dhaskalio adjacent to the Keros sanctuary and the port area of Poros-Katsambas just north of Knossos (Day and Wilson 2002; Doonan et al. 2007). As noted in Chapter 4, Poros was the site of intensive metalworking and obsidian working. Moreover, large quantities of imported Cycladic pottery were present – of which not a single sherd has been found at Knossos. All of these activities situate the site in the same broad Aegean networks within which Keros was also operating, and they emphasize that the processes that we might identify as incipient urbanization went hand in hand with the Keros sanctuary and in a similar way with the gatherings in the Knossos valley.

The rise of both Keros and Knossos (and, indeed, Stonehenge) as centres to which people and resources were drawn emphasizes their equivalent roles in the significant creation of new congregations and thus new identities. The concentration of resources, skills and labour at these places was in itself new and this was recognized and affirmed as part of the identities being created during the gatherings at these places.

Knossos not only continued as a centre to which people were drawn until well into the Late Bronze Age, it also grew exponentially in size (Whitelaw

2012). It moved from what we might identify as the proto-urban to the truly urban, covering most of the Knossos valley with differing densities of habitation. At the core of this expansion the central court was retained, redesigned and reimagined; it must always have been a space to which people were drawn, and a locale where certain kinds of ways of seeing the world were made manifest.

Mycenae

The places discussed in this chapter – the Stonehenge landscape, Neolithic Orkney, Keros in the Cyclades, Knossos and now Mycenae – are all places which in some ways are defined by great gatherings of people that once were drawn in to them. But what did this process of 'gathering' entail and what transformations did it bring about?

The process of gathering was one which invited the sharing of information, and which demanded mutual recognition. Participants travelled, moving away from the everyday to a specific arena chosen for the purpose of this non-routine engagement. Sometimes the act of travelling must have been a considerable undertaking, as when a sea journey was involved at Orkney and Keros. Bands of travellers may have begun to meet up along the way, perhaps thus emphasizing corporate or kin groupings. Indeed, the very act of travelling beyond known bounds changed a person, as their vistas opened up, and their concept of place in the world changed.

Sometimes the endpoint of such gatherings formalized these acts of engagement with place, with others, and fundamentally with self. Nowhere is this clearer than at the site of Mycenae in the Peloponnese (Fig. 5.10).

The name of Mycenae is well-known to even the most casually interested observer (French 2002; Burns 2010). Made famous first for the excavation of rich graves (see Chapter 6), many years of excavation in the late-nineteenth and twentieth centuries have uncovered a complex and monumental site comprising multiple interlocking elements. Much of its earlier history is obscure; little is known of the configuration of the acropolis itself before the middle of the second millennium, although it seems to have been used during the third millennium. Beyond the acropolis we can see today some of the development of the Mycenae landscape occurred from about 1750 BCE (Middle Helladic III) to the end of the Bronze Age, around 1100 BCE.

Mycenae is situated at a confluence of landscapes and vistas. The acropolis itself is in fact dwarfed by the two peaks of Mount Zara to the east and Profitis Ilias to the north. Mycenae forms a foothill of Zara, projecting into a system of ridges rising above and to the north of the large Argive plain.

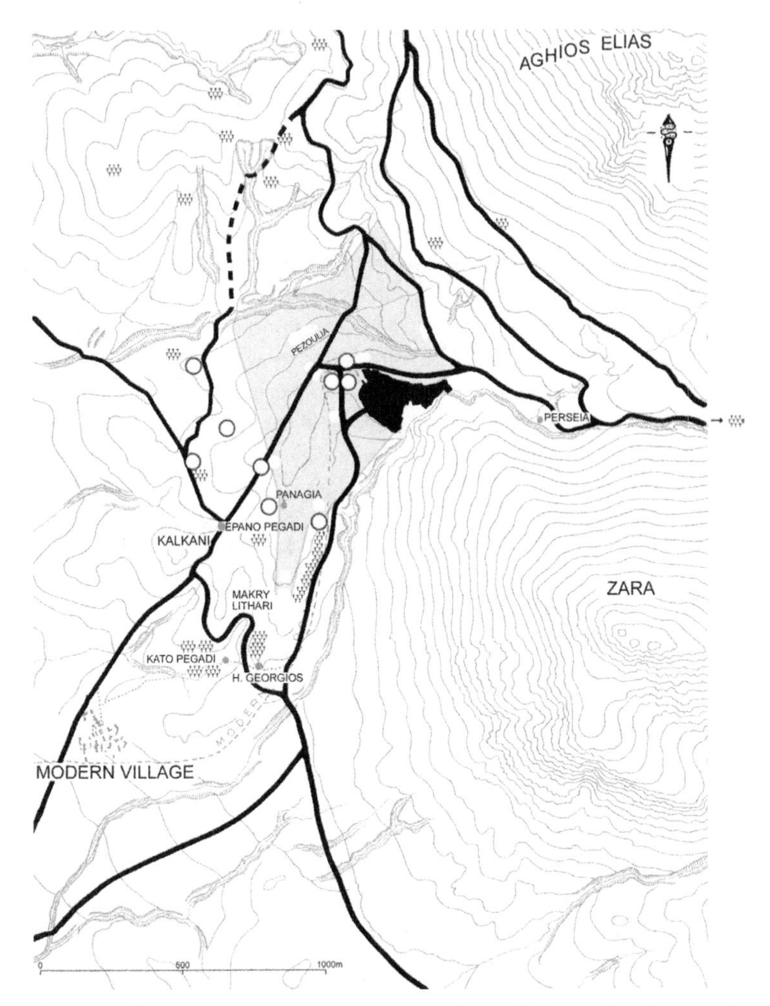

Fig. 5.10 Plan of the area of Mycenae. Circles indicate tholos tombs; clusters of crosses, chamber tomb cemeteries. After French 2002, Fig. 25. Copyright Mycenae Archive.

Mycenae thus sits between pathways north, south and east, and at the point of transition between different land types. Those passing through had likely long used Mycenae as a meeting point on their different ways. The local topography includes a long north-south ridge (the Panayia ridge) lying to the west and marking one of many routes from the plain to the Longaki-Drakonera pass east between Zara and Profitis Ilias. Smaller ridges run west from the Panayia ridge to the northern tip of the plain, and to routes north and west.

Passage through this landscape was a fact of human interaction long before it began to be marked by monuments. One way of looking at the chronological development of the Mycenaean landscape is to examine the increasingly complex inscription of possible patterns of movement in it. It may be suggested that the users of Mycenae were, through time, concerned to add to the complexity of a landscape understood through routines of engagement and tradition. The role of the acropolis itself at any time before the later second millennium is not clear, such that (for example) in the third millennium we have no way of suggesting whether it was in any way marked or unusual (at nearby Tiryns, itself a later site of a Mycenaean 'palace', an unusual, monumental building was constructed at its highest point in the mid-third millennium, and marked after its destruction by a tumulus maintained well into the second millennium: Maran 2016). Third millennium traces of occupation are found in the landscape around Mycenae, for example at the Kalkani hill (Wace 1932, 19). Occupation continued there in the early second millennium, and the acropolis of Mycenae as well as much of the surrounding area has traces of use in this period, although (with the exception of the shaft graves, discussed in Chapter 6) these traces are usually not coherent enough to indicate the structure of the site or the nature of individual buildings.

The shaft graves are discussed in the next chapter. However, they tell us much about Mycenae's development as a place that mattered: here we can examine their role in shaping the way in which Mycenae began to gather people and resources from about 1750 BCE. The earliest shaft graves are located on a ridge running west from the acropolis, where it joins the Panayia ridge. Topographically this forms a crossroads, the point at which all the different possible routes of approach from north, west or south unite into a single route to the acropolis. The shaft graves themselves were placed on the ridge top, not on the slopes, almost at the highest point of that ridge, making their location (marked from the start, or soon after, by a circular enclosure wall) very visible, and causing those moving toward the acropolis to orient themselves in relation to it, and thus acknowledge it, whether their intention was to enter the enclosure or to pass by. Having turned toward the acropolis, walking along the west ridge, the location of the slightly later Grave Circle A (perhaps not at that point a circle) is prominently marked by the jutting bedrock of the acropolis and the pre-existing route of the path. The bedrock behind Grave Circle A forms a natural backdrop, marking its location from afar, and on reaching it, before turning to climb to the summit, stopping, one can survey the near topography of whatever buildings were in existence in the area at that time, and the far vista of the Argive plain.

This was a cultural landscape. Processions of the shaft grave funerals took place here although the routes taken cannot now be reconstructed and the starting points are unknown. If the body were prepared on the acropolis itself (whose configuration at this time is almost entirely unknown: the great walls and buildings all came later), the procession might have been relatively short, although the preparation of the body might have taken place elsewhere, necessitating a longer route. Through time, the use of rare and entrancing materials such as gold and amber had become a key part of the performance. These surely gained the attention of an audience, and the procession extended that audience from the relatively limited number at the graveside to a potentially much larger group lining the route, taking part in the procession, or merely glancing towards the performance (Boyd 2016a).

The centrality of the funerary role of the Mycenae landscape through time was reinforced by the establishment of ever more chamber tomb cemeteries and the construction of the great tholos tombs (Chapter 6). These suggest that until the end of the Bronze Age procession was one of the principal modes through which people came to know the Mycenae landscape and their place in it. Beginning by the middle of the second millennium (Late Helladic I), the chamber tombs, and the tholos tombs to follow, began to spread the cemetery landscape over a far wider area than previously was the case. Areas such as Kalkani began to gain several such tombs, and eventually no less than twenty-seven chamber tomb cemeteries had fanned out around the Mycenae acropolis (Shelton 2003). Individuals and small groups (whether family, kin, village, craft-specialism, or any other reason for banding together), who during shaft grave funerals may have watched or followed the procession, began to inscribe their own identity on the Mycenae landscape in a burgeoning network of movement and funerary deposition thus defining the places that mattered within a wider landscape centred on Mycenae. Their tombs were

Fig. 5.11 Sketch of procession fresco from Pylos. After Lang 1969, pl. 119. Courtesy of The Department of Classics, University of Cincinnati.

conspicuous in a different sort of way from the shaft graves, the passageways to the doors (when not completely filled with earth) inviting the passer-by to wonder at who was buried within. The relationships between the tombs, manifest in the growth of separate cemeteries and the act of placement of each new tomb, mirrored at a larger scale the relationships between the dead, and between the living and the dead, which as we shall see in Chapter 6 underwent a complete change from the principles of the shaft graves.

The idea of procession, with its leaders, participants and observers (Boyd 2016a), became an organizing principle and means of finding one's place within the Mycenaean acropolis itself. By the latter half of the Late Bronze Age (Late Helladic IIIA-B) procession was accommodated in the layout of blocks and design of individual buildings; it was also depicted iconographically, on walls in fresco and in other media (Fig. 5.11). Procession within the more enclosed built spaces of the acropolis would have had to have been more ordered, and potentially more exclusive, as the enclosing architecture demanded. This formalization of procession within the acropolis promoted an exclusivity that reflected on those groups able to act within that sphere, unlike the more open processions practised elsewhere at Mycenae and throughout the southern Greek mainland. Processive activities within Mycenaean 'palatial' complexes, ending in some moment of revelation, not only reinforced the place of those participating within a cosmological order, it also laid claim that the earthly apex of that order was located in that place. At the same time all these practices gained apparent teleology whereby they could all be seen as leading to one particular destiny.

In the latter half of the second millennium the approach to the acropolis at Mycenae began with a passage through the enclosing wall. This wall, subsequently expanded on two further occasions, was a massive undertaking in terms of labour, resources and planning. By the time of its inception Mycenae had already been a place of gathering for centuries. The wall was not initially intended to encircle all of the constructions on the acropolis, hinting at the concerns of different interest groups not all of which may have been fully complicit in a scheme laying such emphasis on an enclosed summit area. The expansion of the enclosure downslope a generation or two later implies the intention to bring those aspects of the acropolis (such as Grave Circle A and the so-called 'Cult Centre') that lay outside the original construction of the wall, within the identity and the authority represented by the buildings, persons and institutions enclosed within the wall (Fig. 5.12). These building episodes inscribed the labour of great numbers of people coming from far and wide upon the very form of the Mycenae acropolis. However, there is no escaping the top-down and directed nature of these gatherings, the accumulation of power now exercised from the acropolis of

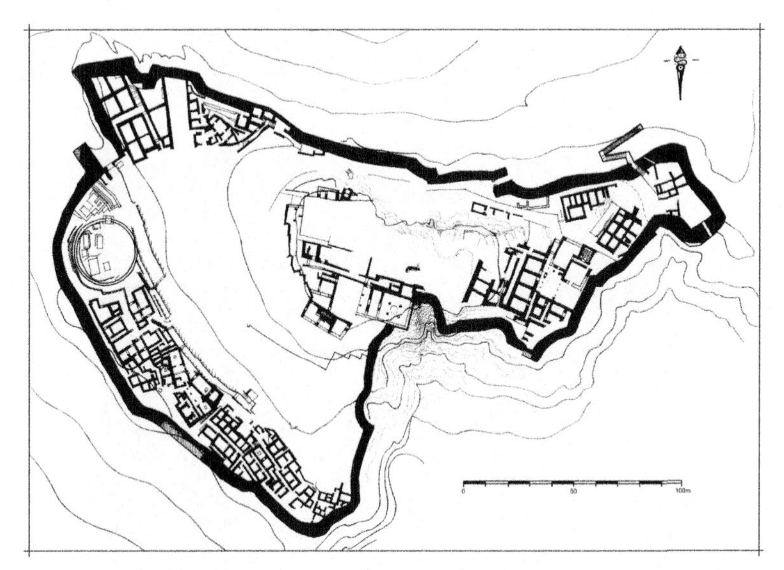

Fig. 5.12 Plan of excavated features at the citadel of Mycenae. After French 2002, Fig. 18. Copyright Mycenae Archive.

Mycenae, and monumentalized in the enclosure wall and the great tholos tombs (Wright 1987; 2006a; 2006b). These construction projects were so immense in scope that one wonders how long they might have lasted; one can imagine decades where the projects were the end in themselves, and actually stopping construction activities may not have been seen as a goal. Vast gangs of people laboured to solidify an exclusivity that was already apparent in the power and class relations between those planning the walls and organizing the labour and those breaking the stones, carting them to the acropolis and building these structures.

The entrance to the acropolis through the enclosure wall is preserved today as the famous Lion Gate, which was constructed as part of the second stage of the enclosure wall. The elongated entrance passage would enforce a certain bodily discipline on those approaching, cutting off their peripheral view of the surrounding landscape, until they were entirely focused on the architectural devices of the entrance gateway itself and the famous emblem above it of two lions, flanking a column, their forepaws resting on a baetyl or altar. The view through the gate frames Mount Zara in the background (Fig. 5.13; we thank Roger Doonan for this observation), and the triangular shape of the lion emblem continues to mirror that of the mountain, juxtaposing secular power, the mythical realm and the Mycenae landscape in

Fig. 5.13 Mount Zara framed by the Lion Gate, Mycenae.

a single vista. The processional route beyond the gate led past the, by now, ancient Grave Circle A by circuitous route to the megaron complex above.

This formalization of movement reached its zenith at the heart of the acropolis, in the so-called megaron. Much recent work has considered the nature of processions at the better-preserved Mycenaean megara of Tiryns and Pylos (Maran 2006; Thaler 2015; 2016; Farmer and Lane 2016) as well as at Mycenae. At both Pylos and Tiryns it is possible to reconstruct specific routes which would have led processions toward the final point at the

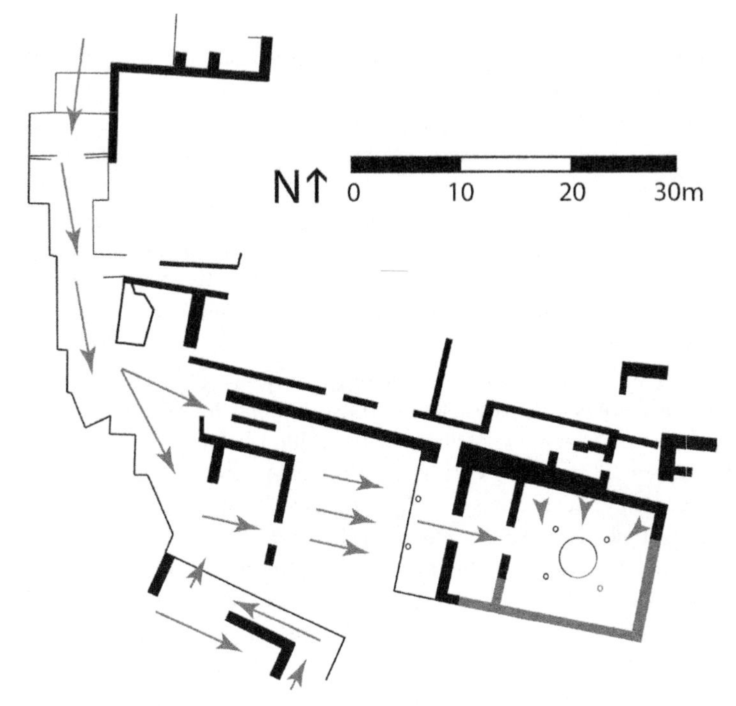

Fig. 5.14 Routes of movement in the megaron complex at Mycenae.

megaron itself. The preservation is less good at Mycenae but after passing through the enclosure wall a procession to the megaron would have turned uphill, through one of two circuitous routes (the Mycenaean architecture is today obscured below later remains) to reach either the propylon or the staircase (Fig. 5.14). Both architectural features brought those participating to a point through which they could not see the subsequent route ahead. At the propylon this was achieved by the use of columns restricting the line of sight through the narrowed entrance which necessitated single file passage, leading onto a corridor that curved, again restricting the line of sight ahead. At the staircase those approaching would have seen a tall construction supporting the megaron complex, which would loom above them as they approached; their route up involved entering a darkened staircase, again single file, with several turns and restricted vision at all times. In both cases, whether approaching by propylon and corridor or by staircase, the darkened route with restricted vision ended at an open court and those arriving would have been confronted by the façade of the megaron itself.

The megaron (Fig. 5.14) has previously been regarded as the primarily secular centre of a Mycenaean state (the throne room of a king); however, the complex is clearly ritual in nature, and many now regard the religious aspect as of equal or greater importance to the secular aspect. The building is elongated, about twice as long as broad (proportionally 9:5 at Mycenae and Pylos, and 11:5 at Tiryns) containing three spaces: a main room, taking up most of the back space (55 per cent of the length of the building in each case), with two smaller rooms of approximately equal size at the front. These front rooms with their central passageways narrow the focus from the large, open façade into the back space of the building. For those approaching, the front space of the building, whose façade consists simply of columns and antae, forms a stage area, where public activities could take place with reference to the interior. Those taking part in the procession and reaching the megaron were probably already a subset of the larger procession, as the size of the court limited numbers, and most interaction between the processants and those occupying the megaron would have taken place between those at the façade and those facing it. It is also possible that a system of circulation would have allowed processants to enter the court via the propylon and leave via the staircase, or vice-versa – thus allowing a potentially much larger number of processants to make their way at least as far as the façade of the megaron, and to take part in the interaction at that point. Similarly, it is clear that at least some persons would make their way into the heart of the megaron itself, and perhaps in a similar way a system of circulation would have facilitated ingress and egress (as perhaps evidenced by additional doorways at Tiryns and Pylos).

For those with rights to enter the megaron, the architectural effect was once again to move from open space through a very focused route into an enclosed and rather dark area. The main room at the back of the megaron has only a single entrance, so this area was never passed through, it was always the point of destination. The interior space was largely open, with a central circular structure forming an oversized hearth which may have imposed a circular, peripheral route of movement on those entering. On the right side of the Tiryns and Pylos megaron rooms an installation was set against the wall (and this may also have been the case at Mycenae, although the evidence was lost in the collapse of the palace terrace). This was evidently a focusing device, perhaps in the form of a seat privileging the position of a single person in relation to all others in the room. The revelation for those entering the room was to see the figure on the seat framed by depictions on the wall (at Pylos, these were mythical animals) and situated in relation to the fire burning in the centre of the room. Those present were presumably attended upon by those carrying out particular roles, the entire performance placed all the participants in relation to each other. Subsequent emergence back into the light of the court, through the framing device of the façade of the megaron made the participants, in the eyes of those observing, the recipients of highly restricted knowledge. Their subsequent movement led them out to the wider world changed and transformed by their experience at the heart of the Mycenaean world.

This description of an evolving architecture and performance of procession at Mycenae from around the middle of the second millennium allows us to see a landscape and a built topography in which people found their place by joining, forming or leading processions. These acts stayed with them once they left Mycenae and went back to their more local communities of more immediate kinship, where they found ways to understand their own, and their community's, relationship to Mycenae through the somatic experiences and the encounters they had while at the great centre of their world.

What we have discovered in the archaeologies of Orkney, Wessex, the Cyclades, Knossos and Mycenae is the development from the third into the second millennia of places and architectures to which travels were undertaken, at some risk, to witness the means by which the order of things, implicit in the routines of daily life, were made explicit when experienced through the lens of formal practice and ceremony. Each of these great centres drew in participants from afar via significant travel to participate in rituals of procession, of commensality, of revelation, wherein communal ties were reforged and networks of people and things were remade. This was what made the third and second millennia different from what had gone before, or what would come after. People found ways to perform themselves and their understanding of the world on a grander scale than had previously been imagined, in so doing anchoring a perception of the world at those places whose ritual and architectural embellishment proceeded from their endless rediscovery by generation after generation. When these shared understandings of the world eventually fell away, such grand projects were not to be enacted again for many centuries.

6

Bodies that Mattered: The Role of the Dead

In August 1952 the object shown in Fig. 6.1 (left) was unearthed in a grave at Mycenae. Some 22cm high, it is, among other things, a depiction of a human face. Whose face is it? What did its maker, and whoever controlled its use, want anyone to think when we looked at it? And what sequence of events led to its deposition in a grave at Mycenae? This is but one of the grave goods recovered at Mycenae that appear to evoke the level of wealth and display that is also associated with burials elsewhere in Europe, including those excavated over a hundred years ago on the Wessex chalkland of southern Britain. At Bush Barrow, 1 kilometre south of Stonehenge, some 4,000 years ago the object shown in Fig. 6.1 (right) was placed on the body as part of an inhumation ceremony. The lozenge was a unique object which not only carried its own history but whose role could be understood by an audience when bestowed upon a corpse.

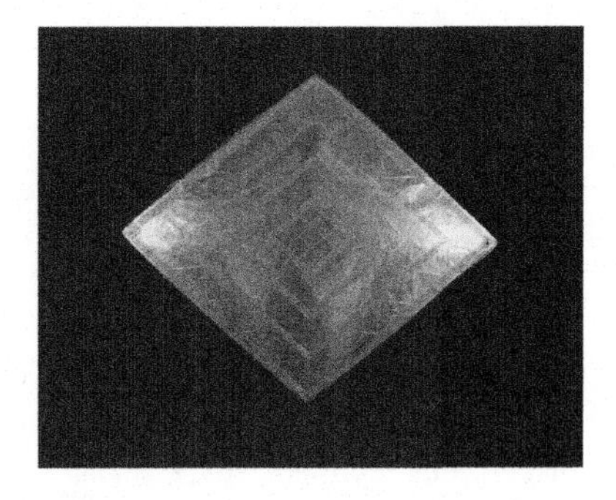

Fig. 6.1 Left: 'Mask' of thin metal alloy found in grave Gamma, Grave Circle B, Mycenae. National Archaeological Museum, Athens/Department of Collection of Prehistoric, Egyptian, Cypriot and Near Eastern Antiquities. Copyright © Hellenic Ministry of Culture and Sports/Archaeological Receipts Fund. Right: Large gold lozenge from Bush Barrow. Copyright Wiltshire Museum, Devizes.

Across Europe new media were in vogue for the construction and manipulation of identity, and increasingly these media were deployed in funerary contexts. If these materials can be regarded as the media by which different kinds of relation between people, and thus the relative status of individuals and groups, could be negotiated and signalled, then funerary rites can be treated as if they were a negotiation between the place, status and identity of the dead and that of the living. The dead might not have buried themselves, but they were certainly active in the ways that their presence, and possible threat, was perceived.

The technologies of metallurgy provided many of the objects that have long been associated by archaeologists with the construction of both individual and group status and identity. It was the deployment of these things in funerary contexts that has so strongly evoked the idea that these deposits included the dead of an elite, as was proposed by Piggott (1938) in discussing the significance of his 'Wessex Culture' burials. In this chapter, we ask how identities were created in funerary rites and how these might relate to analyses offered by funerary archaeology.

The questions posed by the analysis of aDNA

Martin Furholt begins his discussion of what archaeology has identified as a third-millennium pattern of material uniformity in northern and central Europe, the so-called 'Corded Ware Culture', by expressing the concern that:

> All too often, artefacts and practices from different areas that are classified as being similar . . . are uncritically interpreted as the signs of a social phenomenon (such as group identity, ethnicity, etc.) that is likewise shared between these areas.
>
> Furholt 2014, 67

He goes on to warn of the pitfall resulting from the assumption that archaeological categories of material similarity are necessarily the products of, and thus represent, single socially defined populations or ethnic entities (cf. Furholt 2018). A concern similar to that expressed by Furholt might now accompany our understanding of the 'Beaker Culture' in northern Europe and Britain. Named after a distinctive ceramic vessel that also occurs in settlement contexts, this cultural assemblage has dominated the archaeological mind by virtue of the distribution of funerary deposits in which a beaker vessel has been included. The apparent uniformity of the European Beaker Culture has been emphasized by the archaeological practice of identifying a common package of artefacts that are found in only some of the graves of the period (Burgess and Shennan 1976; Shennan 1986), thus downplaying in effect the diversity of funerary rites that had occurred more generally. It appears that a shared resource of material was being worked into a series of common forms, some of which could be employed in funerary rituals. Our argument however is that archaeology needs to understand the strategies by which shared identities were constructed by people, rather than imposing identities upon past populations by means of such classes of archaeological materials as 'cultures'.

The radiocarbon chronology has long since separated the date of the building of the sarsen structure of Stonehenge, around the middle of the third millennium, from that of the grave assemblages of the so-called 'Wessex Culture', the deposition of which occurred in the opening centuries of the second millennium (Needham et al. 2010). The accepted chronology now separates the earlier building of the main stone structure of Stonehenge from the later burial of those whom Atkinson believed had overseen that construction, and it places the origins of the 'Wessex Culture' graves before the citadel of Mycenae, although these burial traditions, along with those with which they had been compared in Amorica and central Europe by Piggott, continued to develop into the second half of the second millennium. These chronological realignments have therefore introduced half a millennium into the southern British sequence between the building of the sarsen structure of Stonehenge and the 'Wessex Culture' burials, during which time metallurgy was fully adopted in Britain and a developing set of grave rituals had become established. In his 1973 model of the social development of the fourth through to the second millennium in Wessex, Renfrew presented the entire sequence as one that was marked by the steady development of an indigenous social complexity, characterized as a process of political ranking and centralization. Much has now changed, and indeed continues to change, and we need to assess possible archaeological interpretations of those changes alongside the new kinds of data that have become available.

In Britain, and indeed across central and northern continental Europe, the third millennium is a period in which the analysis of ancient DNA (aDNA) from human skeletal material has now produced results that have been greeted by both the enthusiasm of welcoming a 'third scientific revolution' in archaeology (Kristiansen 2014, cf. Reich 2018) and by various levels of archaeological reservation (Hofmann 2015; Heyd 2017; Ion 2017; Furholt 2018). In Britain the implication of the aDNA analysis is that those bodies deposited after 2500 BCE and that are associated with beaker vessels, a form and style of ceramic production that appears to have originated in continental Europe, also carried a substantial component of a genetic ancestry that was derived ultimately from populations on the Eurasian Steppe. If we were to take these results at face value, then it appears that the associations that defined 'Beaker Culture' cadavers carried the strong indication of a biological inheritance from one or more migratory populations. The closest genetic comparisons carried by those bodies that have been analysed in Britain is found amongst the occupants of the Beaker graves in Noord-Holland, Netherlands. It is thus implied that the Beaker-associated dead were buried sometime after an earlier third millennium population movement from the Eurasian Steppe had occurred and that this earlier migration is represented by burials assigned to the Corded Ware Culture of northern and central Europe (Olalde and Reich et al. 2018; cf. Haak et al. 2017; Heyd 2017). The complexity of population dynamics occurring in the latter half of the third millennium is further indicated by the isotopic analysis of skeletal material of this date from across Britain (Parker Pearson et al. forthcoming). This analysis provides evidence of both diet and lifetime migrations across different geological zones that had been achieved by individuals, and it indicates a considerable degree of migratory movement, although most of those lifetime migrations appear to have occurred within Britain itself (Parker Pearson et al. 2016).

What are we to make of the fact that the evidence for the third millennium in Britain was read in the 1970s and 1980s to imply both long-term indigenous continuity in social development and is now read, in today's more dramatic terms, as if it marked a discontinuity with a population migration across the North Sea and English Channel? Our own view is simple: we should not conflate two entirely different processes. Lines of biological inheritance do not carry with them cultural badges of identity. This point can easily be missed in an archaeology that treats different material patterns as if they recorded different components or 'levels' of a common historical process. This muddled thinking is then sustained by the assumption that some base level process, such as the biological inheritance of a population, 'explains' (as in 'causes') a cultural pattern of uniformity that is identified archaeologically: it does not. We argue instead that, whilst the evidence for human migrations is clearly important and contributes to our understanding of the ways that networks of communication might have been generated, the creation of cultural identities by those populations may well cut across, and cannot be reduced to, lines of biological inheritance. It is therefore the task of archaeology to understand how people made their identities, and those of their dead, by cultural means as distinguished from the networks that resulted from the biological reproduction of various populations (Barrett 2018).

If we are considering different flows of cultural and biological resources in the making of different forms of human life, then we should perhaps comment upon the idea of a single cultural origin for beaker ceramics. Radiocarbon dates indicate that this style of ceramic was present in the Iberian Peninsula by the second quarter of the third millennium (Cardoso 2014), and whilst such a chronology might suggest an Iberian origin for the European phenomenon (but see Jeunesse 2015), a second origin, based upon a typological development of styles from Corded Ware, has been claimed for the Dutch sequence (Lanting and van der Waals 1976). Attempts to locate a single origin for the Beaker phenomenon and to trace, from that origin, a diffusion of this ceramic style across the rest of Europe have thus continued to pose a considerable archaeological challenge (Needham 2005). Perhaps there was no single origin for Beaker ceramics (Clarke 1976)?

Equating cultural inheritance with that of genetic inheritance involves, as we have argued, the naïve reasoning that the social group is defined both culturally and by a common origin in a shared genetic inheritance. As we have seen, Processual ('New') Archaeology dismissed the archaeological use of 'culture' as an analytical unit, and sought instead to prioritize geographically identifiable systems of human organization as the unit of analysis. In these systems different kinds of behaviour produced an interacting and balanced set of outcomes in relationship with an environmental context. By making the system of behavioural outcomes the unit of analysis, a distinction was drawn between the style of doing something (equated with cultural rules) and the material consequences of that action (equated with functional outcome). The distinction between style and function was one that Robert Dunnell suggested marked a 'fundamental dichotomy' in archaeological reasoning (Dunnell 1978). Analytically this might make some sense if we were to view human practice from the detached view of an external observer, the so-called *etic* perspective. However, if we are concerned, as we are in this book, with the ways that human practices were mobilized to achieve certain ends by developing a particular engagement with an understood order of things, an *emic* perspective, then the distinction between style and function makes no sense at all. As Robin Boast noted some time ago, it is impossible to do anything and thus to have any effect, without having a way of doing it. In other words, given that all actions involve a way of acting then style and function are the two sides of the same coin (Boast 1997).

We have already argued that a form of human life establishes its identity practically and thus relative to the orders that it recognizes in things and in places. Identity is therefore made out of the ability to inhabit a certain order of things in ways that are understandable to others. Movement and migration from one place to another is one such form of life, and it is a practice that must not only display the ability to find a place for itself amongst things afresh, but it must also find the means to make explicit the forces that generated that order. This might place a particular onus upon a mobile material culture: people carried part of these orders, of which their identities were a part, with them in the ways that they moved, spoke and dressed. In addition, the rituals associated with funerary rites might have been one theatre in which the explicit logic of the world was recreated. Taken together this might imply that familiar materials related to appearance, that is dress, technologies of trust, in which we might include the sharing of food and drink, all facilitated the possibilities of the understanding established between participants. We might suspect that these materials could have been drawn into funerary rites.

In the early third millennium of northern and central Europe numerous funerary rituals had ended with the deposition of either an inhumation in a grave or the deposition of cremated remains. In some cases, these deposits were marked with a surrounding ditch or a slight covering mound. The deposition of human material might have been accompanied, among other things, by worked stone in the form of axes and arrow heads, ceramic vessels and beads that included the use of amber. These single deposits, and in particular the inhumations buried in a single grave, are drawn together archaeologically as representing the 'Corded Ware Culture', as if this culture was the normative activity of a single social collective, rather than having encompassed a range of variation in the ways that the practices were executed (Furholt 2014). This perception of uniformity is now overwritten by the aDNA evidence recovered from skeletal material, equating cultural origin with biological migrations from the Yamnaya cultures of the Eurasian Steppe (Haak et al. 2015; Olalde et al. 2017). The migration of these aDNA haplogroups certainly indicates human movement and migration westwards from the Steppe; but the grave assemblages were the products of strategies that were designed to establish various human identities of the living relative to their dead, and not relative to their genetics.

The early funerary sequence in southern Britain

In the early half of the third millennium in Britain archaeology has identified the ways that some human cremated bone was deposited in ditched or palisaded enclosures that might have been places of congregation and of ritual or ceremonial practices (e.g. Atkinson et al. 1951). In some examples these deposits of material, selected at the end of the funerary ritual, might have been employed as foundation deposits associated with particular building events (cf. Speak and Burgess 1999, 26–38), and such foundation deposits could include the cremations from the 'Aubrey Holes' that had been

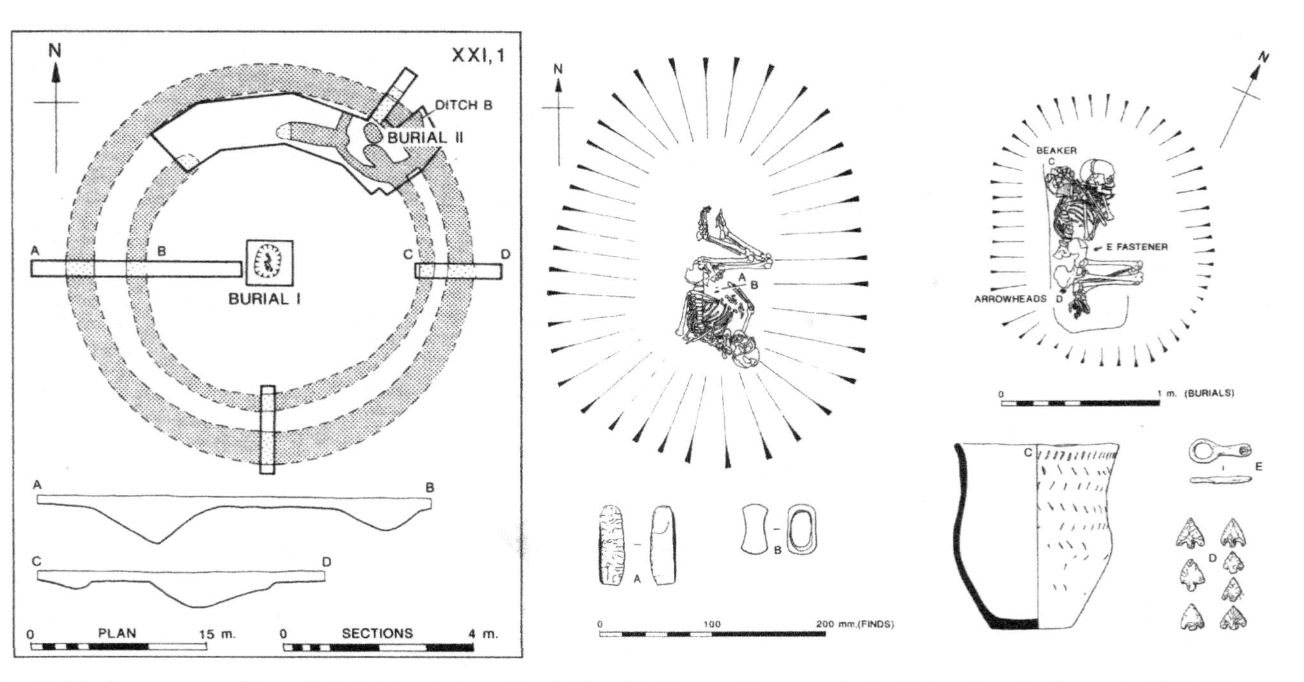

Fig. 6.2 Burial sequence of ring-ditch XXI, and plan of burial 1 and 2, Stanton Harcourt, Oxfordshire. After Barclay et al. 1995, 100. Courtesy of Oxford Archaeology.

dug around the inside of the bank of the early Stonehenge earthwork enclosure (Parker Pearson et al. 2009; Fig. 5.3). In other words, none of these locations need necessarily represent 'cemeteries', if by that we mean the focal places for the funerary ritual itself. None of this human material has been included in the recent aDNA analysis of the human remains of the third and second millennium BCE.

From the middle of the third millennium and over much of Britain and north-western Europe a dug grave tradition had emerged in which the graves were often covered by small mounds and might be surrounded by a circular ditch. The notable associations that are widely taken to begin the barrow burial tradition in Britain in the centuries after 2500 BCE are early metallurgy in the form of copper and bronze artefacts and some small pieces of gold, and Beaker ceramics. When the interpretive emphasis was placed upon the indigenous development of cultural sequences, beakers and early metallurgy were treated as having been drawn into the evolution of systems of social ranking that originated in the British Late Neolithic and were indicated by the specific treatment of a few individuals by single grave internment predating the development of Beaker graves (Thomas 1999, 151–153). One example of such a sequence might be given by excavations of plough-eroded mounds at Stanton Harcourt, Oxfordshire (Fig. 6.2). Among these was the burial of a young female whose flexed corpse was accompanied by a flint knife and jet belt fitting. The grave was surrounded by a double ditch, which was in turn cut by a smaller ditched enclosed grave that held a wooden coffin. This coffin contained the flexed corpse of a young male accompanied by a beaker placed behind the head. A bone belt fitting may have been attached to the corpse and a quiver of seven arrows was probably placed behind the corpse, represented by the surviving flint arrow heads (Grimes 1960, 154–164; cf. Barclay et al. 1995). Few as these earlier deposits are, a round mound, single grave tradition might predate Beaker graves in Britain (Kinnes 1979), and some Beaker burials may then have been made with reference to the objects of that tradition.

There was indeed a continuity of sorts in Britain during the millennium that ran from soon after 2500 until about 1500 BCE. Once a cultural archaeology of Britain and Europe would have depicted this period as marking a sequence of cultural replacements, only for that model to be overturned by Renfrew's narratives of indigenous social evolution. The recent work on aDNA, as we have seen, need not herald a return to a cultural archaeology. Indeed, Renfrew's emphasis upon the processes by which organizational change might have been generated from within a social and economic system, rather than being imposed from outside such a system by cultural diffusion, might continue to guide our thinking. This is because whatever the genomic mix of the populations of Britain and Europe, they generated the cumulative redesign of the material conditions within which they could secure their own identities. Over many areas of northern and western Europe this process involved the steady redesign of the landscape through the execution of funerary rites. Once again, our point is not to treat the patterns represented by the differential treatment of the dead as if it merely represented a structure of social differentiation (Binford 1971), but rather to recognize that social position and identity was being renewed and possibly renegotiated through such practices as the funerary ritual. This shifts our focus away from the corpse as the relic of an individual's proclaimed status to the practices of the mourners who, through their actions in relation to the dead, were actively engaged in renewing the fabric of a social existence.

Burial beneath and within earthen round barrows has often been treated as if it were the normal procedure for Early Bronze Age funerary rites in Europe. However, Atkinson (1972) demonstrated that any population estimate based upon projected numbers of burials in a possible barrow density for England and Wales proved to be remarkably low. The destruction of mounds that may leave no other subsoil trace (cf. Evans 2016) renders any such estimates suspect. Burial without the erection of a covering mound was also a significant component in third and early second millennium funerary rites (Bradley et al. 2016, 126–131) and other rites may have left no archaeological trace. Funerary rites therefore had varying impacts upon landscape architecture, the results of which could then be drawn upon as reference points in future rituals (Evans 2016, 483). In this way the funerary rites of the late third and early second millennia began to bring a new landscape architecture into existence (Garwood 2005). The practices that were structured by the increasingly formalized, entangled relationship between funerary monuments and other elements of the settled landscape is seen clearly around Stonehenge. Here early Beaker burials, often beneath slight mounds, were sited away from the monument, and it was not until the early second millennium that the location of more substantial burial mounds produced a landscape in which these mounds now enhanced the visible horizons to the south, east and north (but significantly not to the west) when viewed from the monument itself (see Fig. 5.5).

Placing the dead in a ritual landscape

Mortuary rites are forms of ritual performance, the formal procedure that effects a transition between different conditions of existence. It might appear that such conditions could only co-exist under the most dangerous of circumstances (such as in 'the living dead'). Such conditions are seen to define a given state of order where a transition from one condition to another involves a momentary break with, or dissolution of, that order. Maurice Bloch has argued that rituals therefore provide a mechanism by which a discursive understanding of those orders and the forces that sustain them can be made available, and thus their legitimacy recognized and extended (Bloch 1985). The simple assumption is that ritual transitions will follow a three-stage sequence, as was originally characterized at the beginning of the last century (Hertz 1907; Van Gennep 1960). In such a *rite de passage* the two states of existence and order are separated by a transitional stage of liminality, and rituals thus facilitate a transformation between the 'relatively fixed or stable states' via a transformative state of 'anti-structure' (Turner 1967, 93).

The Late Neolithic landscape is redolent with ritual and ceremonial activity, and the problem confronting communities at the end of the third millennium was the ways in which the dead might be inserted into those ritual landscapes. The problem was solved in the case of the Stonehenge landscape by utilizing the burial mound as a form of landscape architecture that reworked the visible horizon around that monument. The resulting complexity of this process is illustrated by the ways in which the ceremonies and rituals of burial at that site were integrated into the celestial order which Stonehenge had long addressed.

The image of funerary rites operating as a movement and as a transition is important given the static nature of archaeological deposits. We need to understand this transition in terms of the formation of archaeological residues (Barrett 1988b). For those involved in the process it will have mapped that reality at different moments by means of a spectrum of events such as washing and dressing the corpse, its transportation, the use of cremation, the deposition of the corpse into the grave and the decay of the corpse (for inhumation see Fig. 6.8). This would mean that those attending upon, officiating or otherwise engaged in the process of mourning the dead must have accompanied the corpse and were thus instrumental in performing the rites of transition. They did this through a network of persons, places and materials in which a range of practices resulted, in the case of an inhumation, with the possible deposition of both the corpse and its dress, as well as materials associated with the transitional processes and those of mourning. This process might therefore result in enhancing the quantity and range of artefacts that have been recognized archaeologically as 'grave goods' (Barrett 1994, 64–65; Boyd 2014). It is unfortunate, given the complexity of the processes involved, that the nineteenth-century assumption that mortuary deposits merely provided quarries for the recovery of antiquities continues to inform a great deal of archaeological practice worldwide, although admittedly archaeology now exhibits an increasing refinement in the analysis of the artefacts that have been recovered (cf. Woodward and Hunter 2015). What is needed, however, is for the excavation of mortuary deposits to be treated as an examination of the very rich ritual and material media that enabled a relationship between the states of the living and those of the dead.

This leads to a further observation, that the archaeological residues that result from inhumation grave deposition and those resulting from the deposition of cremated remains result from different stages in the ritual process. Inhumation rites are likely to have closed the initial rites of transition around the infilling of the grave whilst, in the case of cremation, this stage of the ritual process focused upon the pyre (Barrett 1988b). Comparisons of inhumation with cremation deposits, both generally referred to as 'burials', do not compare like with like.

Ritual practices are widely regarded as being highly formulaic and tradition bound, with the implication that long-term regularities should be witnessed in the archaeological deposits resulting from these rites. However, the range of options concerning the processes of transition (such as inhumation or cremation) and of the places and of materials used to mark out the various stages and participants involved are considerable. Thus, whilst ritual practices are processes of rule following, the means by which those rules were rediscovered and elaborated upon allowed perhaps considerable latitude, at least around the symbolic margins of the process, meaning that it is unlikely for there ever to have been a typical example of a particular cultural tradition in burial.

The evolution of Early Bronze Age burial traditions in southern Britain

The mounds of the late third and early second millennium linear barrow cemetery at Barrow Hills, Radley, Oxfordshire, had been largely levelled in the past and were mostly represented by their surrounding ring-ditches which were discovered by aerial photography. The cemetery itself was excavated over several different field campaigns between the 1930s and 1980s (Barclay and Halpin 1999). The mound of Barrow 4A was paired with a second mound by enclosing both within a single ditch (Williams 1948, 1–9; Barclay and Halpin 1999, 153–157). The central grave-pit beneath Barrow 4A contained the corpse of an adult male, lying on its left side, facing north-east and with its legs tightly flexed. The corpse wore two gold hair ornaments (cf. Sherratt 1986) whilst a beaker lay near the feet. Three arrow heads came from the grave fill above the level of the skeleton. This simple assemblage, with the

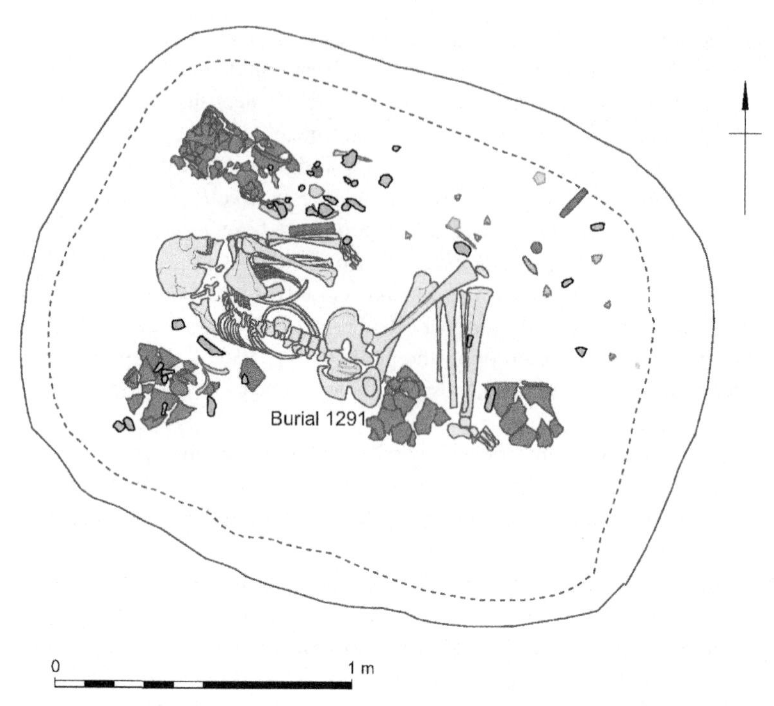

Fig. 6.3 Burial of the Amesbury Archer. Courtesy of Wessex Archaeology.

vessel placed by the mourners against the flexed and prepared corpse with its attached hair ornaments and with the arrow heads belonging with the grave filling, might be compared to the recently excavated and very much more elaborate grave assemblage of the 'Amesbury Archer' (Fig. 6.3). This grave contained one of three Beaker-associated funerary deposits excavated on Boscombe Down, Amesbury, Wiltshire (Fitzpatrick 2011). This particular grave was not surrounded by an enclosing ditch but appears to have been demarcated by wooden shuttering around the edges of the grave-pit. The flexed corpse of an adult male lay on its left side, facing north-east. The additional material from the grave can now be divided into four types of deposit: those things seemingly attached to the corpse, those things placed in direct spatial relation to the corpse, those things from the floor of the grave that did not appear to be spatially ordered in relation to the corpse, and those things included in the grave fill itself. The first of these deposits is represented by a stone 'bracer' found against the left forearm. This is taken to be an outer decorative plate mounted on a leather wrist-guard (Fokkens et al. 2008; Woodward and Hunter 2011). The case for this plate being attached to the corpse is admittedly ambiguous in this case, but other examples listed by Fokkens and his colleagues seem to confirm that such an arrangement was maintained elsewhere. The second kind of deposit includes five beakers which were arranged around the body, two in front of the face and the others at the back of the head, at the buttocks and at the feet. A copper dagger lay under the right shoulder of the corpse and a copper knife in front of the chest. Assuming that the dagger is amongst this second deposit, then neither appear, from their position, to have been attached to the corpse. The third group of material includes a scatter of objects in the north-eastern corner of the grave, beyond the knees of the corpse. This scatter includes another copper knife, two gold hair ornaments, another stone bracer and a bone ring. A cache of flint projectile points lay near this scatter and other caches of flint flakes and projectile points lay in groups around the body whilst a small group of flakes and two projectile points were recovered from the grave fill. Other materials were recovered from the grave along with those mentioned here, and we can now make some general comments based upon what has been described.

Both the Radley and the Amesbury inhumations conformed with a regional regularity by which a flexed male corpse was placed on its left side facing east or north-east. On the basis of comparisons elsewhere it is possible to suggest a limited set of items that could be attached to the corpse itself and were therefore part of its dressing. These were arm bracers, hair ornaments and belt ring fittings. This raises an immediate question as to why it was this set of things that was scattered along one side of the Amesbury grave-pit: it suggests the distinct possibility that the grave had been reopened and an early inhumation removed, leaving this assemblage of things behind. If this had occurred, then the corpse that was excavated archaeologically was the second inhumation placed in this grave, and further post-depositional intervention in the case of this corpse is indicated by the removal of the entire left first rib (McKinley 2011, 86). Removal of corpses or of bones from corpses as part of a continuing concern with the body of the dead might help explain the reasons behind the charnel burial of bodies associated with beakers that was also recovered during the Amesbury excavations (Fitzpatrick 2011, 9–61). Practices involving the mixing of bones and artefacts create a second stage in the transformation of the dead and the living, as the dead move from identifiable individuals to members of the ancestral group.

Obviously, beakers were amongst all the items placed in inhumation graves as part of the mourners' involvement with the ritual, and their placing was always relative to the position of the corpse. What is perhaps more surprising is that knives and daggers, where they occur, also seem to have been placed alongside the corpse rather than attached to it. This might imply that the dagger was one mark of an identity conferred upon the dead by others, and this also alerts us to the wider issue of the ways that codes of appearance and dress were important across Europe as ways of making or conferring an identity upon individuals (see Chapter 4). The importance of this process is not only indicated by the burial assemblages in the case of the dead but also by the anthropomorphic representations that occur on certain continental stelae and plaques (Harrison and Heyd 2007).

Beaker-associated inhumations have, by virtue of the materials deposited with them, tended to dominate our perception of the mortuary deposits of the late third millennium in Britain. It is therefore important that we recognize that a cremation tradition continued throughout this period in both Britain and Ireland (Needham 1996, Fig. 2), but one that by now involved the deposition of cremated remains in pits and sometimes in cists, and only occasionally at the locations of earlier sites of congregation. These deposits were often deposited with accompanying ceramic vessels that appear to have derived from the development of earlier third millennium styles (Waddell 1976, 284). The relationship between these practices and those seen with the Beaker burials might indicate a complex but long-term process of population continuity.

The contrasting mortuary rituals of inhumation and cremation, with their differences in the mapping of the ritualized journey taken by those officiating the path into death, clearly require careful reconsideration. What does appear to happen by the end of the third and the opening decades of the second millennium, at least in some regions and for some cases, is that both traditions converged upon building and embellishing the kinds of round barrow cemeteries that enclosed the landscape around Stonehenge (Fig. 5.5) and that are represented elsewhere by the linear arrangement of ring-ditches, such as those excavated at Barrow Hills, Radley. It was from the excavation of these burial mounds, mainly in the eighteenth and nineteenth centuries, that the associated grave assemblages were recovered that include those taken by Piggott (1938) to mark his Bronze Age 'Wessex Culture'.

The diversity of the finds associated with these later acts of deposition is considerable and an attempt to summarize the material is not only daunting but would inevitably result in over-simplification. We therefore need a way to guide us through this material that will make sense in terms of the practices that brought these assemblages together. If we are correct in our assertion that inhumation burial and the depositing of cremated remains represent different stages in the funerary ritual then this should be supported by differences in the ways that the inhumation and cremation assemblages have been structured. We will begin by examining whether such differences existed with reference to four deposits from the barrows on Normanton Down, Wiltshire, where a

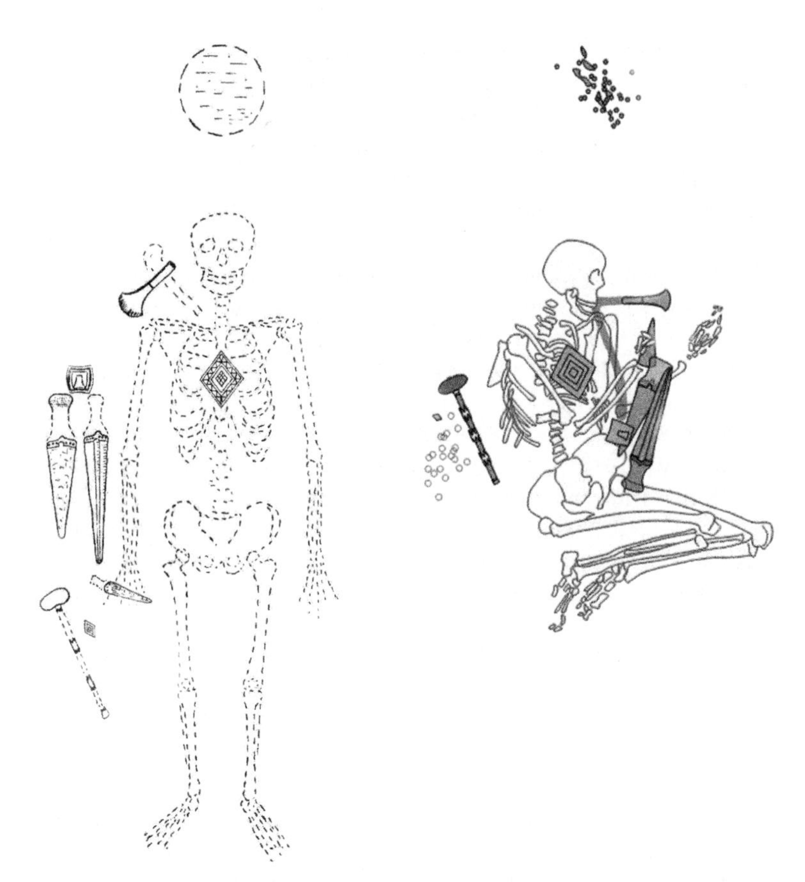

Fig. 6.4 Reconstruction of the Bush Barrow inhumation. After Ashbee 1960, Fig. 24, courtesy of E. Ashbee and K. Massey; and after Needham et al. 2010, Fig. 3, courtesy S. Needham. Copyright S. Needham. Head at the south.

group of mounds include those that sit on the southern horizon when viewed from Stonehenge. We will then examine the development of assemblages associated with cremated deposits with reference to an example from the Radley cemetery.

It is upon Cunnington's early nineteenth-century excavations and Hoare's publication of them that we depend for our understanding of the four deposits from Normanton Down that are discussed here (Hoare 1812). The Bush Barrow (Wilsford G5; Fig. 6.4) produced an inhumation and a mortuary assemblage that remains the best known early 'Wessex' mortuary assemblage from Britain (Piggott 1938, Fig. 3; Needham et al. 2010, 9–24). The account given is of a 'male' inhumation that had been laid with the head to the south and on the ground surface, rather than in a grave-pit (although the cut of a shallow grave might well have been missed), and where a range of objects were then placed around and on the corpse. If the corpse and associated materials were indeed placed upon the old ground surface then we must assume that they had been protected by a mound that was thrown up immediately after deposition rather than being buried by a grave fill. The major ambiguity affecting our understanding of this particular funerary deposit however concerns the arrangement of the corpse for, as we have seen in the case of the Beaker inhumations, the corpse becomes the point of reference around which additional funerary deposits were arranged. The Cunnington/Hoare account is unclear and two reconstructions have been offered; that by Paul Ashbee is of an extended corpse (Ashbee 1960, Fig. 24) and that by Stuart Needham and colleagues offers us the image of a flexed inhumation lying on its left side (Needham et al. 2010, Fig. 3). We would make two observations concerning these suggestions. First, the Ashbee reconstruction offers the image of a more ordered pattern of deposition than that offered by Needham, and in which a clear distinction was made by the deposited material lying on the right and not the left-hand side of the corpse. Both reconstructions do however allow that the large gold lozenge (Fig. 6.1, right) is the only item that might actually have been attached to the clothing of the corpse. Second, Needham's reconstruction not only introduces the image of a more jumbled pattern of deposits, which is not the impression gained from Hoare's description, but the corpse also faces west. Given the emphasis placed upon the east-west (sun-rise and sun-set) axis at Stonehenge and the easterly, sun-rise, facing corpses recorded in earlier graves then, whilst a westerly facing orientation might well have been possible, it is a difficult claim to make, based as it is upon very ambiguous evidence.

Our reading of the mortuary process is therefore as follows. This ritual did not involve the deposition of any ceramic vessels. The corpse was placed on the ground (no trace of bier is recorded) and various objects were placed around it, including two hafted daggers and a smaller knife, some gold work, including an organic plate covered by a decorated gold lozenge which might have been placed upon the corpse's chest (if it was not already attached to the clothing); additional materials included a perforated stone mace head, a 'baton' decorated with bone mounts (Fig. 7.1) and an axe, the latter being placed near the head. An unknown copper and organic object was also placed above the head and which has recently been interpreted as a 'stud hilted dagger' (Needham et al. 2010). This whole deposit was then quickly covered by a mound. Among the many problems of interpretation are the possible indications of organics, including the wooden hafting of the axe, and the

Fig. 6.5 Burial assemblage from Wilsford G8. Courtesy Wiltshire Museum, Devizes.

relation of the hafting of the baton with that of the mace head, where the latter two have recently been reconstructed as a single object (Needham et al. 2010, Fig. 8). The possibility of the bronze axe-head also being hafted when placed in the grave is uncertain; however the axe-head does carry the impression of a textile in the surface corrosion product which might imply that it was un-hafted and wrapped, possibly in linen, when deposited. This alerts us to the evidence for a similar wrapping of an axe-head from another barrow (Weymouth G8: Woodward and Hunter 2015, 131) and the occurrence of axe-heads and daggers contained in three wooden boxes placed in the grave at Kernonen à Plouvorn, Amorica (Briard 1984, Fig. 31). The two surviving daggers from Bush Barrow were also sheathed when deposited (Annable and Simpson 1964, nos. 169 and 170, and pls. 2 and 5). The daggers from the Plouvorn grave are typologically comparable to the two surviving daggers from Bush Barrow and belong with those from the Breton 'dagger-graves' whence Piggott had derived his supposed incoming 'Bronze Age aristocracy'. Some of the material deposited by those officiating at the funerary rites may therefore have been wrapped or otherwise enclosed in containers, and this might call into question the claims that have been made that these were items publicly displayed in acts of conspicuous consumption (although wrapping after display might have been part of the funerary ritual). One final point should be noted concerning the possibility that the axe-head was un-hafted when deposited, as were the French examples: the carvings that are on the sarsens at Stonehenge are of un-hafted axe-heads and not of functioning axes, and it is upon this basis we might accept that the axe-head and the useable axe were regarded with different levels of cultural significance.

Three further mounds (Wilsford G7, G8 and G23) are also among those excavated by Cunnington, reported upon by Hoare and included amongst the Wessex Culture assemblages by Piggott. Whilst two are cremations (Wilsford G8 and G23), the remaining mound covered an inhumation. That inhumation (beneath Wilsford G7) is recorded as lying in a west to east orientation in a shallow grave-pit with an urn at its feet (Longworth 1984, 289 and pl. 10 no. 1716) and with an additional small ceramic vessel in the grave. The corpse was accompanied by three shale beads, one with a gold cover, and four amber pendants, a shale pendant in the shape of the kind of stone battle axe that is mainly known from Ireland and northern Britain (Needham et al. 2010, 27), two fragments of a sheet gold pendant cover and two fragments of fossil encrinite. The cremation deposit from below Wilsford G8 (Fig. 6.5) is also accompanied by what have been described as 'trinkets' which included amber pendants, two gold bound amber discs, a gold covered shale button, a small ceramic vessel and two possible miniature icons: one an amber 'halberd pendant' bound in gold and with a copper blade, the other a gold-covered copper alloy pendant that has sometimes been compared in form with a central European ingot torc (but see Needham et al. 2010, 28).

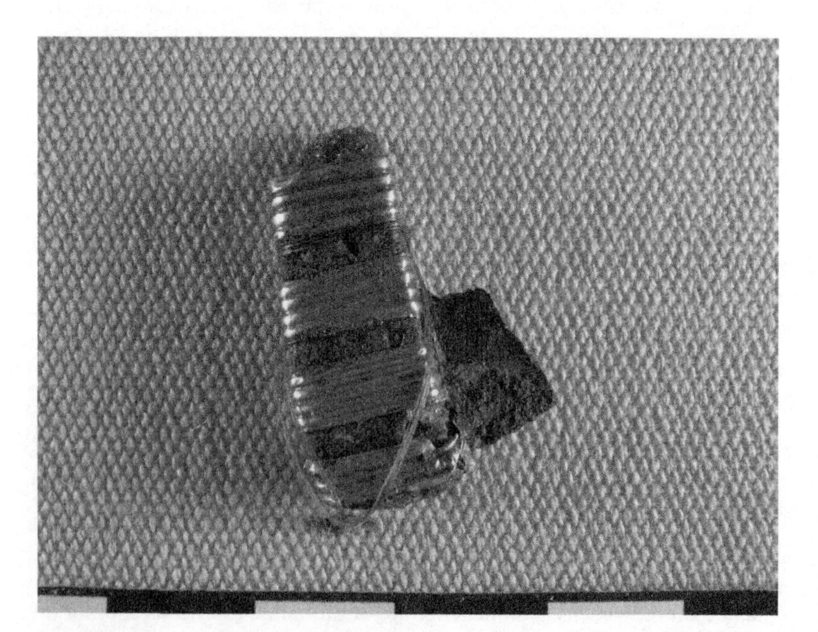

Fig. 6.6 Halberd pendant from Wilsford G8. Courtesy Wiltshire Museum, Devizes.

Two observations may be made concerning these deposits of an inhumation and a cremation. First that the decorative items in the cremation deposit could not have gone through a cremation pyre and survived; they were therefore not attached to the corpse during the funeral process. By extension, this would indicate that neither set formed part of the dress of the corpse but was placed in the grave by those officiating. The impression is of officiates selecting material for deposition from an assemblage of items that might indicate distant cultural contexts and might have conferred identity or status when worn. Whilst the process of selection is therefore likely to have been restricted by the values of convention, such that axe-heads never occur in the earlier Beaker-associated mortuary assemblages and are very rare in these later deposits, a range of options and possibilities could be expressed. For example, the deposit of cremated remains that lay in a chalk-cut pit beneath the turf mound of Wilsford G23 was accompanied by two daggers, a whetstone, a bone pin and a possible flute, or whistle, cut from the long-bone of a swan, implying perhaps a more idiosyncratic way of identifying those involved in the ritual (Grinsell n.d., 36). Our second observation, assuming that our reading of these assemblages is correct, is that they include icons of items from geographically distant contexts of northern Britain and Ireland, in the case of the battle-axe icon, and central Europe in the case of the metal-

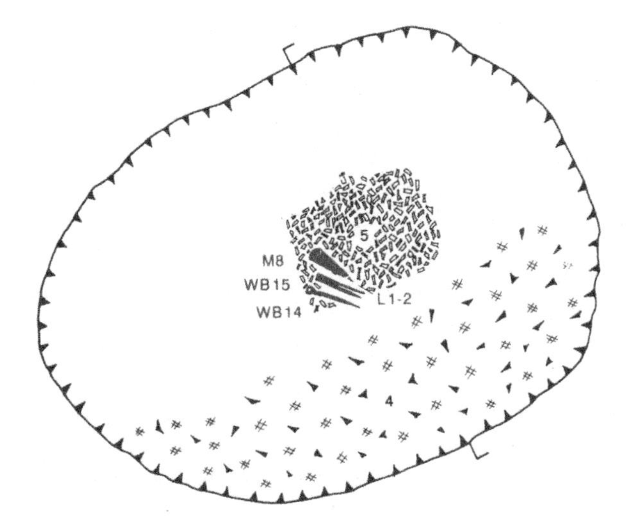

Fig. 6.7 Radley cremation from Barrow 1, showing deposition of pin, tweezers and dagger on top of the cremated remains. After Barclay and Halpin 1999, Fig. 4.82. Courtesy Oxford Archaeology.

bound halberd icon (Fig. 6.6). These icons would have meant nothing if such items could not have been more widely recognized in southern Britain, with the implication that exotic items had become part of a currency of identity and status. This will return us to a further consideration (Chapter 7) of the Bush Barrow mortuary assemblage that includes the bone mounts on the 'baton', and the apparently comparable ivory mounts from Shaft Grave Iota at Mycenae (Harding 1984, Fig. 31).

Given our emphasis upon the actions of the officiants in these rituals let us now consider the assemblage of material that came from the more recently excavated Barrow 1 in the Radley cemetery (Barclay and Halpin 1999, 141–148; Fig. 6.7). Any surviving mound had, in this case, been ploughed away leaving the surrounding ditch and a central oval pit that contained two deposits. A dense concentration of cremated bone which might originally have been held in an organic container lay to the north of the centre of the pit on top of which had been placed a bronze knife or dagger in a leather sheath, a pair of bone tweezers and a bone ring-headed pin. In the southern half of the pit the excavators recovered 'a deposit of deep red-brown sandy loam', which contained charcoal flecks, ash and fragments of cremated bone. The implication is that human cremated bone was collected and bagged for deposition along with some pyre debris that still contained bone fragments. A sheathed knife or dagger was placed on top of the cremation along with a pin and tweezers. The latter remind us of the possibility that the officiants might have modified their own appearance by plucking hair and that the mortuary deposit will have drawn the ritual to a close by containing those items that had been employed in this process (cf. Barrett 1994, 119–121).

All these graves indicate that most of the objects associated with the corpse were not part of its dress, but were placed in the grave by those who were officiating. The implication is that an identity was being conferred upon the dead by means of these objects at a late point of the funerary rite. It may also be significant that the re-entry into the grave that is attested in the case of many Beaker graves (Barrett 1994, 62–69) does not appear to have occurred in the case of the later, non-Beaker deposits which were, instead, buried beneath or within more substantial mounds. This implies a change in how the dead were understood. Previously, stages in the transition from life to death and ancestorhood were marked by interventions in the grave; now, after the closure of the grave, the corpse was no longer a medium in this process, but the newly visible barrow mounds themselves presenced the ancestors in a visible and comprehensible networks of association which created the ancestral landscape of Stonehenge. In light of this understanding as to how material culture might have been employed to construct a relationship between the living and the dead, we will now consider the shaft graves of Mycenae.

The Mycenae shaft graves

In attempting to interpret archaeological data, in many instances worldwide archaeologists have made the mistake of trying to reconstruct a 'snapshot' interpretation of a static archaeological record. We have seen this with the earlier treatment of Piggott's Wessex burials, and similarly the shaft graves of Mycenae have often seemed to offer a snapshot in time. Archaeologists of past generations can perhaps be forgiven for the feeling that such a remarkable, unique archaeological resource should offer a very clear vision of the nature of Mycenaean society, or at least of its golden elite – one which could simply be 'read off' the data. But the synchronic and static pictures offered in such interpretations belie the long continua of human action which resulted in the palimpsest of deposits sometimes referred to as 'the archaeological record'.

The face in Fig. 6.1 (left) was found in a grave located just to the west of the citadel at Mycenae. The shaft graves are so called because of their peculiar construction: deep shafts (from 1.2 to 3.5m deep in Grave Circle B, some perhaps deeper in Grave Circle A) at the bottom of which is a grave, either stone-built or simply made by narrowing the shaft in all directions thus creating a ledge; this ledge was used to support roofing of stone or wood, sealed with clay. Although some of the shaft graves were of modest proportions, the largest were as much as 6.5m × 4m at floor level. Fourteen or sixteen such graves were unearthed in Grave Circle B (the uncertainty in number is due to the exact form of the grave not always being clear) with six in Grave Circle A (and one more nearby; there were also other, non-shaft grave, burials in both areas). The graves of Circle B began earlier than those of A, which finished later, but there was much chronological overlap between the two groups (Schliemann 1878; Mylonas 1973; Dickinson 1977; Graziado 1988; 1991; French 2002; Nafplioti 2009; Prag et al. 2009; Papazoglou-Manioudaki et al. 2010; Dickinson et al. 2012; Boyd 2015b).

Amid the pomp and splendour of the Mycenae shaft graves the faces are almost unique in seemingly offering individual insight into the identity of those buried. Other items, such as swords, exquisite inlaid knives, gold body coverings or amber necklaces, might all have been worn by the dead, and even have been part of their public identity, but the masks promise something more: they let us look upon the faces of the dead. They seem to humanize the dead by giving us an easy insight into aspects of their identities other than their apparent wealth. Like looking at photographs of the long dead, or like the Fayum portraits, which were fixed to the mummified bodies of the dead, these Mycenaean faces seem to offer a direct connection to lives lived millennia ago.

Identity in practice: three shaft grave funerals

In this book we have been concerned to highlight the ways that identity was created, both as lived and as perceived, in how people acted to inhabit the world as they found it and as they shaped it through their actions. We have highlighted the role of material culture and of locale in the creation, projection and transformation of identity, in very different circumstances at different ends of Europe from the mid-third to the late second millennium. The opening of the shaft graves in the late nineteenth century led first and almost exclusively to questions of identity, which are still being asked today. Whose identities were being crafted and displayed in the shaft grave funerals, or protected by the elaborate roofs and deep shafts of the graves?

All funerals consist of a series of events, one often leading to the other, beginning with the initial transformation of a living human, a source of purposeful agency, into an inanimate object, and ending with the deposition of the corpse in the grave and the closure of the latter (Fig. 6.8: Boyd 2016a). Agency is situated within and at the same time transforms the material and immaterial structural conditions of action: a funeral is a time where those conditions have already begun to change through the departure of the lived

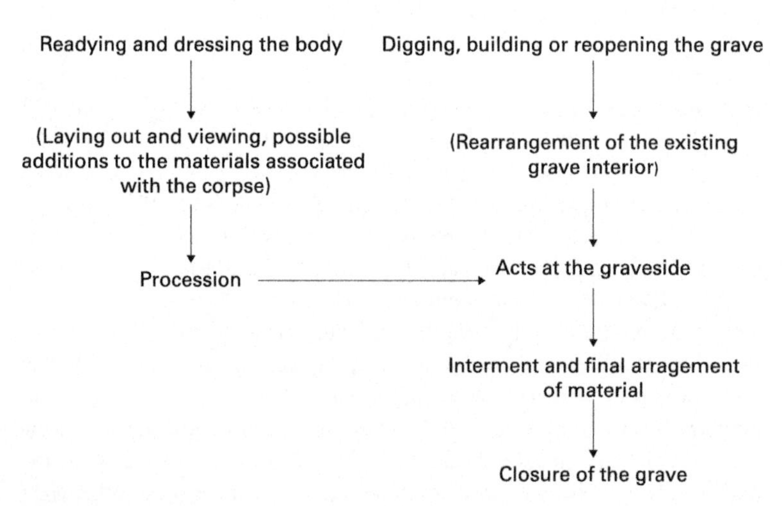

Fig. 6.8 Sequences of action in carrying out an inhumation.

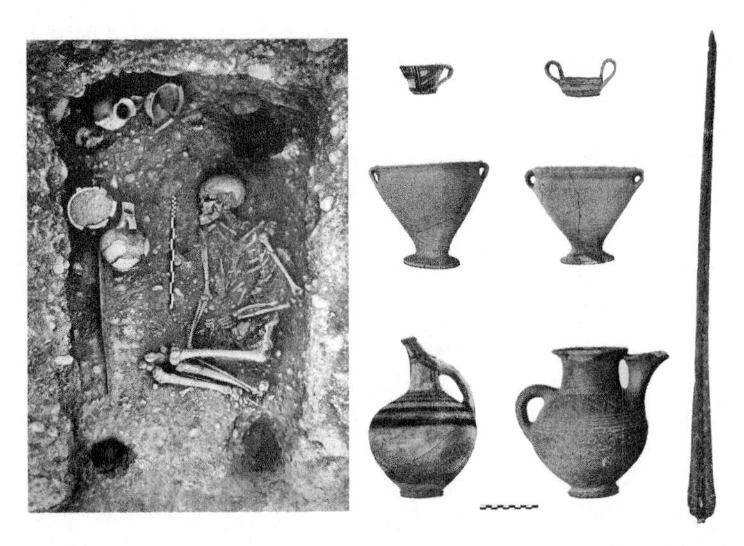

Fig. 6.9 Grave Zeta in Grave Circle B, Mycenae. Objects shown approximately to scale. After Mylonas 1973, pls. 88–90. Courtesy Archaeological Society at Athens.

participation of the deceased, with the decay of the corpse becoming only too evident. So it is clearly wrong to simply 'read off' an identity for the shaft grave dead as if they themselves had chosen the location and form of the grave, their position within it, the material in which they were clothed, or the items placed beside them. All this was done by those who remained; but the agency of those newly dead no doubt played a prior and lingering role in the creation of the material and immaterial structural conditions within which the acts of the funeral were carried out, and which were both reinforced and subtly changed by that funeral. But the funerary tableau – the arrangement of dead and material in the grave just before it was closed – was created by the living in the changed circumstances of life after the death of the subject of the funeral.

In order to pick apart these questions, let us look at three shaft grave funerals. These three funerals took place at around 1750 BCE, 1700 BCE and 1600 BCE, respectively. One of the earliest of the shaft graves is grave Zeta in Grave Circle B, in the north-western group (Fig. 6.9; Mylonas 1973, 102–105). This grave, 1.9m × 1.1m at floor level and about 0.60m deep, was closed by a roof located about 0.25m below the modern surface and (uniquely) supported in the four corners by posts (indicated by the post holes noted during excavation). The grave was oriented east-west, and contained a single inhabitant (a male of about forty-nine years), lying in contracted position along the south side, facing north. Six ceramic items and a sword with ivory pommel were ranged along the north side and in the north-east corner of the grave.

Archaeologists have often fetishized the unspoiled grave. This is because the grave appears perfectly to preserve a moment in time: the moment at the end of the funeral when the covering of wood and clay was placed over the grave and its newly-arranged contents. However, until recently, the interpretations offered of these moments in time have been based on one of two explanations that seemed somehow 'obvious' – that items in the grave were personal possessions that fixed the identity of the dead in death, or that they were items for use in the after-life. In the case of grave Zeta, the ceramic items could be seen as supplies for the journey, and the sword might identify the occupant as part of a warrior class. These interpretations are focused on the reading of an assemblage, but as we said earlier, funerals are arranged and conducted by the living. Before attempting explanations about what objects in a grave *mean*, we should first reconstruct the flow of human action of which they formed both the material conditions and the outcome.

In this example, we see several acts of deposition within the grave. These are anticipated by the size of the grave: although small compared to later shaft graves, the corpse takes up only about 30 per cent of the available floorspace. It was rare for graves of this period to be so much larger than required for a single occupant: those who arranged for the digging of the grave had already anticipated depositional activities beyond the simple contracted burial. How might the objects deposited in the grave have been handled by the mourners? The ceramics are high-quality, rather than quotidian, some in a new, dark-on-light style derived from Minoan Crete (Chapter 4), and all relate to liquids rather than food. There are two small drinking shapes, two large drinking shapes and two large pouring shapes. These suggest the distribution and sharing of liquids as part of the funerary ceremony, perhaps through the act of drinking or the pouring of libations. The larger drinking cups were capable of holding a large volume of liquid, probably close to a standard bottle of wine, whereas the two smaller drinking shapes held between one-seventh and one-eighth that volume. The two pouring vessels could have refilled the two large drinking vessels three or four times each. It is possible, then, to see two types of serving and drinking activity here: one more restricted, where small cups are filled and drunk from, and one more open to wide participation, where the larger cups might be shared among many mourners and refilled several times. Hence despite the restricted number of vessels, it is clear that they would serve adequately the needs both of a small group directing the flow of action at the grave, and a larger group, perhaps gathered around it, or perhaps filing past and partaking of drink while observing the grave. Aside from drinking, each of the vessels could also have been used for libations. Their placement within the grave becomes part of the record of the funeral acts that the grave tableau presents.

The grave's only other object is a sword, with an ivory pommel. A sword was an unusual object in the world of the late Middle Bronze Age Argolid: this sword is one of only two found in the earlier graves (two daggers were also found in other early graves). The decision to deposit such a rare item in this grave must have been extraordinary. The object's history, of which the funeral participants were presumably aware, included highly skilled manufacture (on Crete, or perhaps locally) and the procurement of exotic ivory for the pommel. Such objects would have been carefully curated and passed from hand to hand, won in battle or competition, or bestowed on initiates by leaders (Harrell 2014), each with a growing history of ownership and use through time. Burial with the dead brings that history to an end, associating the sword with the dead in a definitive and unarguable way. As the mourners looked down into the tomb after its arrangement, it is even possible, if the face of the dead were obscured by a shroud, that the sword was the only recognizable and individual element of the grave tableau. Were the grave reopened at some later time when the flesh had decayed (we have no evidence in this particular case that this happened) the sword might be the primary recognizable object, much more so than the bones of the dead, enduring where flesh decayed.

In this early shaft grave funeral we see the active construction of identity at the graveside: both for the living and the dead. The careful positioning of items in the tomb is an act of memory creation, and the role of the shaft grave roof is to preserve the tableau intact, both in memory and in reality: the roof closes that field of discourse and preserves it, to be found again as left (Boyd 2015b). The placement of the dead amid the material employed during the funeral is a reflexive act of identity construction, bearing on the interlinked identities of the dead, of individual living actors, and of that section of the community as a whole taking part in the funeral.

A later shaft grave funeral took place in grave Gamma, where this chapter began. This is a larger grave (3.2m × 1.8m at floor level, which was fully 3.5m below the surface, where the opening of the grave measured 3.8m × 2.8m) with stone and mudbrick walls lining the actual grave at the bottom of the shaft. At floor level in area it is almost three times larger than grave Zeta, and in terms of volume up to ten times larger. In grave Zeta the shaft grave concept was barely developed; in grave Gamma, built in the middle years of use of the Grave Circle, the design had significantly grown in scale. Some fifty or more years may separate the construction of these two graves; many of the

Fig. 6.10 Grave Gamma in Grave Circle B at Mycenae. After Mylonas 1973, pl. 33. Courtesy Archaeological Society at Athens.

same principles of action can clearly be seen in both, with some significant developments.

Grave Gamma (Fig. 6.10) was used up to five times for interment (Voutsaki et al. 2006, 90; Triantaphyllou 2010, 444; pers. comm.). The funeral with which we are concerned is not the earliest. It is the burial taking up most of the space in the north and west part of the grave, a male of about thirty-three years at death. Superficially there are many points of comparison with the burial in grave Zeta. This man has been laid out extended rather than contracted; but, as with grave Zeta, no trace of dressing is preserved: no jewellery or other unperishable components. Like Zeta, on the right (west) side is a sword, this time joined by a shorter sword and a knife. It seems certain that these three objects were deposited at the time of the funeral. What is less certain, however, is which other items within the tomb were either introduced as part of this funeral, or were perhaps moved from one position to another during it. It is important to understand the sequence of actions that might have been possible within the material conditions that would have been revealed to the mourners upon reopening the tomb. So we must step back in time from the completion of the funeral to the prior moment when the grave was reopened.

What the mourners would have seen at this point is two extended inhumations, one close to the east side of the tomb, and one next to it, closer to the centre line of the tomb. The inhumation on the east side was the earlier; the arrangement of material related to the close of the funeral of the more central burial. One of the acts undertaken by the mourners was to move the central skeleton to the east, turning her over so she lay face-down on top of the original eastern skeleton. The high degree of articulation in the body shows this was done fairly soon after her burial (we owe these observations to Ioanna Moutafi: pers. comm. The highly unusual face-down position of this skeleton seems not to have been previously noted).

A group of weapons west of these two earlier corpses consisted of two swords with ivory pommels, three shorter blades and a spearhead; these were found more or less on top of each other, perhaps wrapped up together, or simply placed as a single deposit. Another pair of swords lay in the north-west corner of the grave, against the wall, and close to the face (made of electrum, an alloy of gold and silver) where we began this chapter. The face was found closest to the western inhumation, but not placed over the head of the dead: it was actually located a short distance to the north, and found perpendicular to the ground, next to two cups, a smaller one of gold and a larger one of bronze; inside the latter were two sword pommels of alabaster, six blue paste beads, another of rock crystal and an amethyst bead with a depiction of a bearded face in profile. The excavators thought that all of these objects were contained in a small wooden box, based on a darkened hue to the earth from which they were excavated.

Although it is not possible to be sure when each of these items was introduced into the tomb, or where each was originally positioned, it is possible to discuss the actions of the mourners at the third burial amidst all this material. Perhaps most striking is the number of bladed weapons, consisting of four long swords, three short swords and three or four other bladed weapons – as well as a spearhead. These may have undergone multiple rearrangements by the time of the third funeral, and for this highly potent category normative assumptions about which swords belong to which body are misleading. With grave Zeta, we saw that the identities being created in the funeral, of the dead, those leading the funeral and the burying community, were structured through complex interactions between people and materials. Now, in grave Gamma, we see the same process with the added dimension that all those involved were acting within material and immaterial conditions partly created on previous occasions. How they chose to enact their funeral amidst the detritus of past events was a core element of the identities created, negotiated, bolstered or undermined during the process.

The box containing representations of two faces is a remarkable discovery. We might be inclined to regard such depictions as portraiture. Their location in a closed box, rather than placed on a body, confounds our expectation: whose identity did they express? At least in the grave, these expressions of human individuality were hidden rather than displayed. Did these faces relate at all to the dead of the grave?

The features of the electrum face are simple: approximately triangular in shape, with large, undecorated forehead and chin areas, the features are concentrated in the central third of the face. The closed eyes have always given an impression that the face represents the dead. The act of (re)placement in the box was presumably part of the action of the third funeral, although the box may predate the third funeral. So if the face was either not placed, or did not remain, over the dead, what uses did it have? There are several possible explanations, and indeed more than one of them may be relevant. Dickinson (1977, 45; Dickinson et al. 2012, 177) suggests the mask may have been part of the interment ritual for the female second burial; when she was moved, the mask was moved to the box. There is nothing particularly gendered about the face, so it would be possible to posit that it represents the actual face of the female previously buried here (it now seems that one or two of the Grave Circle A faces may have been associated with female burials: Dickinson et al. 2012, 177). However, the other material perhaps related to the female burial (the ivory comb, and the gold cup, diadem, strip and foil object) were gathered and placed close to the moved skeleton, rather than being placed in the box. Curation in the box suggests a special place and different meaning for the face: not least in that, as with the swords, this rare and idiosyncratic object would have been very recognizable.

But it is important to ask whether the face represents a single individual (perhaps the female dead of grave Gamma). The generic features and closed eyes allow for the possibility that the face was not intended to portray a particular individual. Its role in identity-building might have been more distributed: multiple individuals might have felt themselves in some ways related to the face if, for example, it were taken to represent a specific ancestor, or the mythical progenitor of a group, or the ancestors in general. Its role in multiple funerals could allow the meanings associated with the face to grow each time it was displayed or used. And its production may also have played an important part in how it was understood: which artisan created such an individual piece? Was she or he thought to be channelling the ancestors in creating the representation? More prosaically, where did the metal come from? Electrum is not unknown in the shaft graves, and it does occur naturally in Anatolia. But we can also imagine the act of alloying gold, silver and small amounts of copper as a skilled and knowledgeable act (cf. Demakopoulou et al. 1995) – and it is also possible to imagine the creation of the material for this face through conscious selection of existing objects to be melted and reformed into this object. Thus the retold and embellished history of the face may have included the histories of the objects from which it was made.

The shaft grave acted to preserve the results of the actions of the mourners. The box similarly created a discrete context somehow separate, and requiring its own act of reopening, its contents requiring their separate interpretation. The box, with its own procedure for opening, and its solid borders, attempted to categorize the material within it differently from the other material in the grave. The special treatment suggests the attempt to create a context within which the physical association of these items and the immaterial reasons for this were projected into the future, to a foreseen subsequent reopening of grave and box, creating a special context claiming immunity from the disassociation and reassociation of material as part of further burial activity. The selection and assemblage of the artefacts of the box forms an expression of identity in which the individual – if represented at all by these objects – is subsumed in the creation and projection of a corporate identity, one which the mourners took care to arrange for themselves (or those who came after them) to rediscover in an act of future planning.

The implication of much of this is that there was necessarily a receptive audience. It is clear that the scale of shaft grave funerals was already growing. With grave Zeta we suggested drinking and pouring ceremonies using both larger and smaller vessels, suited both to individual acts of key mourners, and communal acts of consumption. In grave Gamma the ceramic and metal vessels fall into broadly the same categories, including cups of gold and bronze. The grave itself was not filled with ceramics, however: some were found close to the north wall, with another small group near the fourth skeleton. A far greater number was found in the fill of the grave, above the roof, all broken: seventeen large pouring and portage vessels, two large drinking vessels, five small pouring vessels and twelve small drinking vessels. (The vessels on the floor of the grave included six large pouring and portage vessels, two small pouring vessels and four small drinking vessels, supplemented by the two gold and one bronze cups.) In comparison with grave Zeta, it is clear that there is more emphasis on individual drinking shapes than previously, including several fashioned of metal: only two of the communal drinking vessels were found in the fill, and none on the floor. A further change is that many of the vessels were now broken and deposited as part of the refilling of the grave. This implies multiple stages in the funerary feast, some while the tomb remained open, and others after closing the roof and during the refilling of the shaft. Some animal bones, probably sheep or goat, were also found in the shaft, indicating the possibility of eating as part of the refilling ceremony. The wider group of mourners thus participated in creating the meaningful material assemblage of the grave on several levels, through active consumption and through participation in acts of recognition, whereby the funeral leaders in dialogue with the wider mourners created the final funerary tableau.

For our third shaft grave funeral we move to Grave Circle A. Having been excavated so long ago (Schliemann 1878), the details of the exact arrangement of materials within the Circle A graves, or their stratigraphy, are much less reliable than with Grave Circle B (though recent work is extremely informative: Prag et al. 2009; Nafplioti 2009; Papazoglou-Manioudaki et al. 2010; Dickinson et al. 2012). Nonetheless the general picture in each grave is clear enough, and often it is possible to be reasonably sure where items came from.

Grave Circle A properly refers to six shaft graves laid out (with one exception, grave VI) on a north-south (not circular) alignment in an area of about 24m × 12m. Additional probable shaft graves excavated later in the vicinity probably belonged to the same group (Wace 1923, 55–59; Papadimitriou 1955; 1957; Dickinson 1977, 51 disputes whether any of these were in fact true shaft graves). Schliemann and those who came later excavated several non-shaft grave burials within this zone, as well as a pit containing pottery from a preceding phase of the Bronze Age (Alden 2000). The information is too imprecise to reconstruct a reliable history of the use of the area; the earliest of the six numbered shaft graves (II and VI) belong with the latest of Circle B chronologically (Graziado 1991), and the others fall only slightly later.

The funeral in question was of a male, buried in grave V, the second-largest of the shaft graves (6.55m × 3.5m × up to 5.33m deep). Schliemann (1878, 294) and Stamatakis (who was present at the excavation: Papazoglou-Manioudaki et al. 2010, 163–164) both recorded three burials in this large space, with the burial with which we are concerned taking up the whole of the southern half of the tomb, oriented north-south (the others to the north oriented east-west: Fig. 6.11). Recent restudy of the skeletal material suggests the bones of other individuals may have been present in the tomb, although this is not certain (Papazoglou-Manioudaki et al. 2010, 214).

The recent publication of Stamatakis' sketch of the grave gives some idea of its condition when discovered (Fig. 6.11): the body laid out in the centre of the southern part of the grave, with swords at the feet, perpendicular to the axis of the body, and vessels to the west. Schliemann mentions seven copper vessels on the west side of the tomb (Schliemann 1878, 331), while Stamatakis'

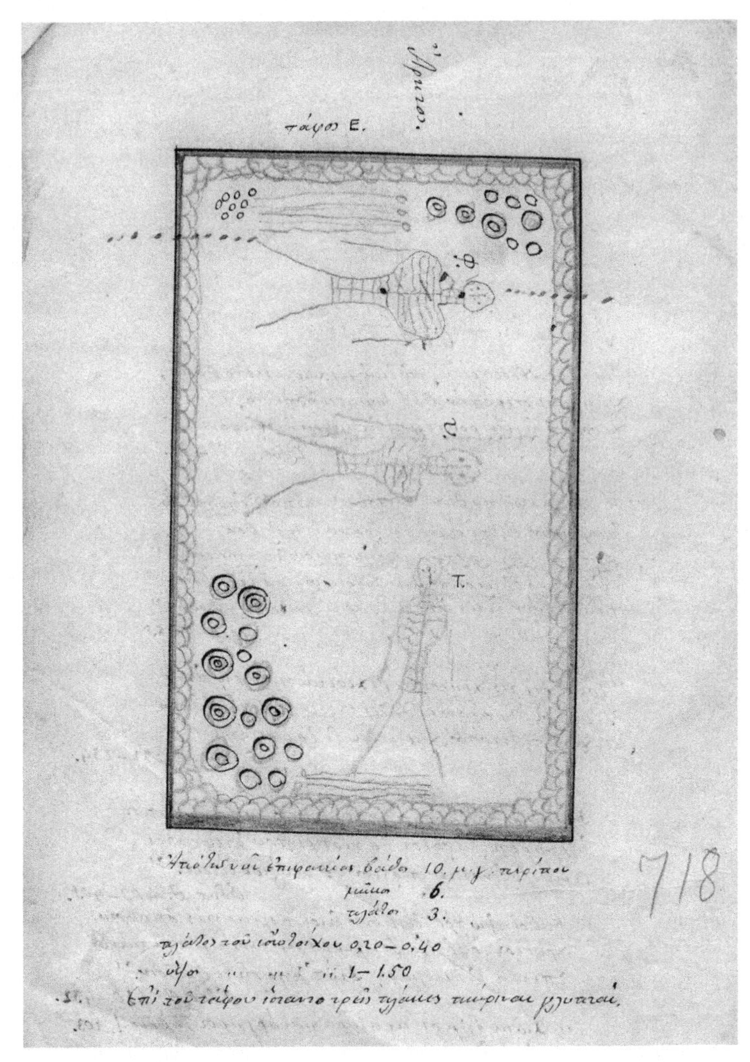

Fig. 6.11 Stamatakis' plan of Grave V in Grave Circle A. After Papazoglou-Manioudaki et al. 2010, Fig. 10. Courtesy L. Papazoglou-Manioudaki.

rough sketch shows fifteen: either some larger ceramic vessels were also placed here, or some of the gold cups described by Schliemann, but not precisely located, should come from this group on the west wall. The body was dressed with a gold face mask (despite popular belief, this was not the face that Schliemann identified with Agamemnon: Dickinson 2005), placed at the head, a large decorated gold breastplate (530mm × 370mm), a gold armband and many other gold discs used on the dress of the corpse. About 100 amber beads come from this tomb, most or almost all probably associated with this burial (Harding and Hughes-Brock 1974). Fifteen shorter and longer swords were associated with this burial, ten at the feet, five elsewhere, with seven alabaster pommels and one of wood. Fragments of silver vases, an alabaster vase, gold tubes, silver tweezers, a gold toggle, and thirty-nine gold button covers (found inside the alabaster vase) are the other objects noted with this burial; it may be the case that other items in grave V should also be associated with this burial.

Although details are lacking we can still marvel at this remarkable funeral and reconstruct some of the actions of this striking event. In arranging the body for the procession and interment, large quantities of gold were employed: with the face, breastplate and other coverings, much of the surface of the body was draped in gold. The body must have been carried on some sort of bier or perhaps on a cart. In sunlight, the gold and the amber adorning the body would have glittered, perhaps reflecting the light blindingly; alternatively, under torchlight, against the darkness as backdrop, these materials would have focused and mesmerized the eyes, the patterns of light reflected in the flickering of the torches and the movement of the bier or cart. The procession was thus a spectacle, and the dead thus transformed was meant to be viewed by a large audience.

Fifteen swords is a large number to imagine as belonging to the deceased. Harrell (2014) has suggested one possible modality for the accumulation of swords toward the end of the shaft grave sequence (she counts forty swords in grave V in total: Harrell 2010, 96). She suggests that swords were presented by faction leaders to initiates and that these were subsequently returned to the dead in the grave. She also suggests many were re-hilted for burial, removing working hilts and replacing them with ornate gold; many were wrapped in a shroud, in a process she sees as analogous to the preparation of the body for burial. If this suggestion is correct, then multiple acts of preparation, and possibly multiple acts of transport, led to these final moments at the graveside. Swords and corpse were worked upon and transformed in order to create and narrate the interconnected identities of the living and the dead, group identities and the individuals who might be part of multiple group identities.

Harrell's is not the only possible hypothesis to explain the presence of large numbers of ornate blades in the later shaft graves. The swords are one of many categories of material to go through hyper consumption in the three graves most replete with material; gold, silver and bronze vessels form another, along with many aspects of ornamentation such as gold body coverings and amber and other beads. The sheer quantities give pause, such as the 1,290 amber beads from grave IV (Harding and Hughes-Brock 1974) or the approximately 900 gold dress items (including 701 gold discs) from grave III (Dickinson 1970, 326). The contribution of such elements of dress at the preparation phase was perhaps one opportunity for different individuals, and representatives of kin or other groups (ritual specialists, social classes or other elements of society, and non-locals), to manifest their presence and their place in the now immensely complex nexus of interaction, negotiation and performance that was the wider funeral. Further such opportunities came during the procession (Boyd 2016a), when the great quantities of vessels and weapons being brought to the graveside could be prominently displayed.

The end of the procession instigated the activities preceding and including the interment. The drinking and toasting ceremonies familiar from the beginning of the shaft grave sequence were writ large, with huge metal containers for liquid, and ever more elaborate gold and silver receptacles from which to drink. There was probably also consumption of meat, perhaps on a very large scale. Swords were dedicated to the grave, having undergone their own transformation in preparation. The most elaborate of the vessels were also now unique items, with histories of their own, each producing a different reaction among the mourners as it was brandished and utilized prior to deposition. Those too far back to observe the events closely would nonetheless have been touched by the procession and would have seen all the gear pass close by at some earlier stage. The stories generated about the incredible acts of consumption and deposition, including the potential divinity of the material employed, bound the actors in with the observers, and manifested the relationships between the living and the dead, and between the living, as articulated through the incredible array of material culture sacrificed in these events.

The simple burial of earlier years with a sword and a few pots in many ways exhibited a much tighter control over meaning and identity: a narrow group selected the items to be deployed, and through their control over the funerary process – including the transport of material and corpse to the grave – would have had more power over asserting the meanings intended to be understood. With the later burials, especially in Grave Circle A, a wider group was involved, not least in simply transporting materials to the grave. This group can be seen to be claiming a direct stake in the conduct of the funeral and in fixing relationships between those taking part; the fabulous level of consumption highlighted the histories of the objects concerned and the networks formed during the processes of procurement and distribution. These later shaft grave burials emphasize ever-widening circles of relationships being remembered, emphasized, negotiated and contested through the deposition of meaningful material with the corpse. These practices can be read as a demonstration of wealth and power, but they can equally be read as suggesting a distribution and dependency of power through wider networks or groups claiming a part in the process—albeit firmly centred on Mycenae and fixated on the by now well-developed shaft grave rituals.

The end of the Mycenae shaft graves

When the earliest shaft graves were being dug, a variety of different practices began to emerge in other locales, driven by one factor that stands in contrast to the practices developing at Mycenae: the predestined reuse of the grave, along with new practices of secondary action on the remains (Boyd 2016b). By the end of the Middle Bronze Age, a tripartite architecture had developed, either dug in soft rock (the 'chamber tomb') or stone-built, partly underground and partly below a mound (the 'tholos tomb'). This form of tomb became common first in the south-west Peloponnese, and then was adopted elsewhere by other groups. The first chamber tombs near Mycenae were built in the earliest years of the Late Bronze Age, while shaft grave burials were still taking place in both grave circles; the first such tomb at Mycenae itself probably dates to the same time period (Boyd 2015b, notes 35, 38).

One candidate for the earliest of these tombs at Mycenae is known as tomb 518 (Fig. 6.12), which was located west of the Panayia ridge, dug into

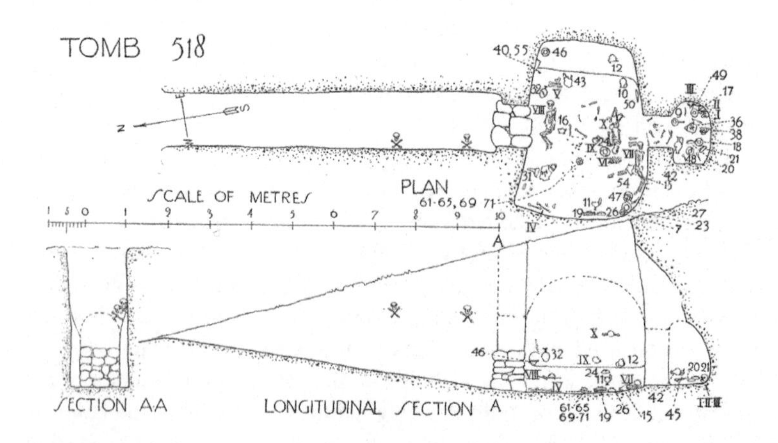

Fig. 6.12 Plan and section of tomb 518 at Mycenae. After Wace 1932, Fig. 29. Courtesy British School at Athens.

the north side of the Kalkani hill, with north-south orientation and, perhaps surprisingly, out of sight of the nearby Mycenae acropolis. The tomb consisted of an 8m-long entrance passage ('dromos') cut into the slope leading to a door situated about 3.3m below the surface. The door ('stomion') was partially blocked by stone walling, and its height is unknown due to the roof's collapse, which occurred after two or more centuries of use. The chamber was rectangular, about 5m × 3.8m, and perhaps originally about 2m tall (Wace 1932, 75).

In the shaft graves, the increase in the quantity, variety and rarity in the deposition of material focused upon the presentation of the dead during the laying out and procession. Once deposited within the grave, however, this strong visual impression was available only to those able to glance down into the shaft before it was closed. The arrangement of the dead and other material in the grave was the last act before closure, and one that was directly observed by only a small group. Alternatively the construction of reusable and inhabitable tombs for the use of a small group of mourners allowed for more emphasis on the deposition of the corpse, the participation of a larger group of people in its presentation in the tomb, and eventually the practice of disarticulation and mingling of pristine burial contexts. The entire funerary process was thus being extended in time and broadened in its scope. Consequently the laying out and procession now led on to a more complex and restricted set of rituals.

Early chamber tombs at Mycenae and elsewhere in the Argolid might seem to have been a considerable challenge to the social order implied and celebrated by the shaft graves. It is of course the case that shaft graves were reused, and especially the larger, later ones were built large enough to accommodate several burials. But there is a crucial difference between the shaft graves and the chamber and tholos tombs that were to supplant them. Shaft graves were initially designed to hold one burial, and when reuse became normal they were enlarged to increase the available floorspace. In most cases (but not all), second and subsequent burials were placed within empty spaces in the tomb, and the tomb was slowly filled over the years with the recognizable detritus of individual funerals. Where previous burials were rearranged, it was often the case that some attempt was made to retain the integrity of the burial context (although other practices, such as removal of bones and pottery, have also been noted). On reopening the tomb, each time the funerary tableau was revealed just as people would have remembered it from the time before – a vista seen from above, appreciated from the outside, experienced by most as a view of things beyond reach, not as a space within which a human might walk, turn and interact with others and with the stuff of the grave.

The first chamber tomb of Mycenae challenged this order. It appeared fully formed, an architectural format imported from elsewhere. Built at some distance and out of sight of the acropolis, it was nonetheless built at Mycenae, on one of the routes toward the acropolis. Its construction took some time – no whim impelled by (say) the death of a visitor from elsewhere. The amount of earth and soft stone removed in its construction was larger than most shaft graves, and the complex format required the participation of an experienced specialist, as the risk of failure was high. Why did those committed to the rituals of the shaft graves tolerate this contrary expression of group identity?

The answer must surely be that the shaft grave group was far less homogenous and established than we might imagine. The group was formed anew at every funeral, ad hoc; its membership on each occasion would reflect social or political opportunities as well as inherited or kin-based obligations. The first chamber tomb, while challenging the shaft grave order, was still built within the emerging parameters of what was acceptable within wider society. Now the chamber tomb form was seized upon as a new way to project distinctiveness. The construction of tomb 518, and the subsequent history of funerary practices at Mycenae, allows us a glimpse of a landscape occupied by newly emergent identities, coming together in different configurations at different times for different purposes: the centrality of Mycenae was not so much that of a single source of authority vested in an individual and kin group, the place an accident of history; instead the place itself was the attraction, and people came there to bring their communities into being in the wider world, and thus inscribe on the landscape a record of different moments in time.

Fig. 6.12 shows the interior of tomb 518 as it was excavated. The remains were found at different levels: the tomb was in use for such a long time that the decay of the sides and roof, and perhaps sometimes minor roof collapses, led to significant deposits of material covering the traces of earlier events. But even on the floor of the chamber, several phases of use can be detected. Remnants of the earliest burials (at least three individuals) seem to have been gathered and placed in the niche at the back of the chamber. On the floor, both articulated burials and disarticulated remains were found, representing at least three further individuals. Four other skeletons were found at different levels higher in the fill.

The practices of disarticulation and rearrangement may be characterized as practices of recontextualization arising from the engagement of the living with the dead via the remains of past funerals, and over time, with the remains of past rearrangements of the interior. Originally conceptualized by archaeologists as a simple process of 'sweeping aside' the remnants of past events to make space for new activities, it has become clear that a number of complex and variable practices are represented, and not merely triggered by the urgency of a new funeral: the return to the tomb for the purpose of reworking the burial context and the creation of a new milieux mixing old and new elements (see Boyd 2016a; 2016b for reviews of the debate and further references). Thus a strong contrast with the shaft grave burials emerged. The remains of the latter represented separate funerary events and were in general maintained as a visible record, while the new chamber tomb burials challenged the entire point of the funerary process: their aim was the curation of communal history, of ancestral remains, where the individual was much less identifiable.

Astonishingly, this alternative world view came to be adopted by the highest echelons of society, thus supplanting the shaft grave rituals. The first of the nine great tholos tombs of Mycenae was built around the time of the last of the shaft grave burials. Even if we imagine the groups using the first chamber tombs as at least partly different from those likely to have been included in shaft grave burials, we must nonetheless accept that those who arranged for the construction of the first Mycenae tholos tombs did so partly to resituate their burial practices within the emerging wider social practices in which the chamber tombs were used. This change in practice can be seen to be derived partly from below rather than being imposed from above, and those burying in the Mycenae tholos tombs sought new legitimacy for their burial practices by wholesale borrowing of architectural form from other places, and practice from differently constituted groups using the chamber tombs.

It remains an unfortunate circumstance of history that no intact contexts have been excavated in Mycenae's nine tholos tombs. Tholos tombs elsewhere that have preserved contexts indicate that the mode of use was the same as the chamber tombs: multiple burials and multiple instances of rearrangement. One clear fact is that the Mycenae tholos tombs were large: whereas elsewhere both large and small tholos tombs are found, at Mycenae only large, difficult to construct tombs were built. When it was decided to build the first such tomb, an experienced architect was imported from elsewhere and given the task and the required resources, including time and labour. The smaller Mycenae tholos tombs have chamber areas about four times that of the average Mycenae chamber tomb; others are up to eight times larger, and the largest of the early Mycenae tholoi (the Lion Tomb) is twelve times larger than the average chamber tomb (Boyd 2015b, Table 2). This is not merely extravagant in terms of construction effort and materials; the scale of these tombs is important in two ways: the number of persons who can take part in activities in the chamber, stomion and dromos, and in the relationship between the scale of the architecture and the affordances of the human body. It is not too much of a stretch of the imagination that the first burials in the new tombs would have tried to replicate many of the practices of the shaft graves, with much of the audience now able to enter the tomb as witness. But it is also certain that the long period of use of the tombs ensured that, unlike the shaft graves, their contents were rearranged, reused, reimagined and remembered over the years. Meanwhile the ability to command resources and to plan construction events extending years into the future was also now being focused on the acropolis of Mycenae itself, and on the creation of ever more focused endpoints for processions where different kinds of revelations might take place (Chapter 5).

The remarkable funerary sequence from Mycenae records endless engagements, both intimate at the scale of the grave and more widely at the scale of the southern Aegean. At the intimate scale of co-presence, mourners and other participants engaged with each other within the circumstances of death and the material resource available to create events in which the identity of the dead, the identities of key participants, and a sense of communal identity were all foregrounded. Such events came at times to draw in participants, material and ideas from great distances. These elements brought a cosmopolitan flavour to the proceedings, generating a view of the world that came to be comprehensible throughout southern Greece by adopting disparate new elements. Thus the identities created at Mycenae were always intended to be understood widely, and the changes noted in the ways funerals were carried out were intended to make the acts at Mycenae more relevant in the wider world. The intention was never to project a Mycenaean identity that would overshadow other ways of understanding the world; the intention was to co-opt those ways of understanding the world in an overarching world view with Mycenae at its very core.

In previous chapters we have indicated that the third and second millennia were different to what came before, and what came after, in terms of material complexity, movement and place. Similarly, the third to second millennia in both Britain and the Aegean witnessed an increased investment in the funerals of at least certain individuals. That investment was marked, amongst other things, by the efforts expended in the construction of the grave and the rituals themselves, the materials that conferred a new status upon the dead by their inclusion in the grave, and by the redesign of the landscape through the location of the grave and the funerary monuments. The dead were not absent in these worlds but continued to play a part in the ways that the land was occupied and used. Thus the roles of the dead, the funeral and the cemetery, were fully implicated in expanded world views of this time, so that much of the material complexity we have described came to be oriented toward the dead, and the place of the dead in the landscape was often oriented to the great communal centres of the time.

7

Living amongst Things: Practice, Place and Identity in Expanding Worlds

The excavations by Cunnington's workmen of the Bush Barrow (Wilsford G5) recovered from amongst the finds associated with the corpse a set of bone mounts that appear to have once been set on a wooden haft. The suggestion made by Ashbee and others (see Figs 6.4 and 7.1; Needham et al. 2010), that the perforated stone mace head from the burial (Annable and Simpson 1964, no. 175) was hafted onto this composite artefact finds little support in Hoare's admittedly ambiguous account of the excavations (Hoare 1812). The cut 'zig-zag' shape of these mounts finds only a general comparison with a set of ivory mounts recovered from grave Iota in Grave Circle B at Mycenae, a comparison that is illustrated by Anthony Harding (Harding

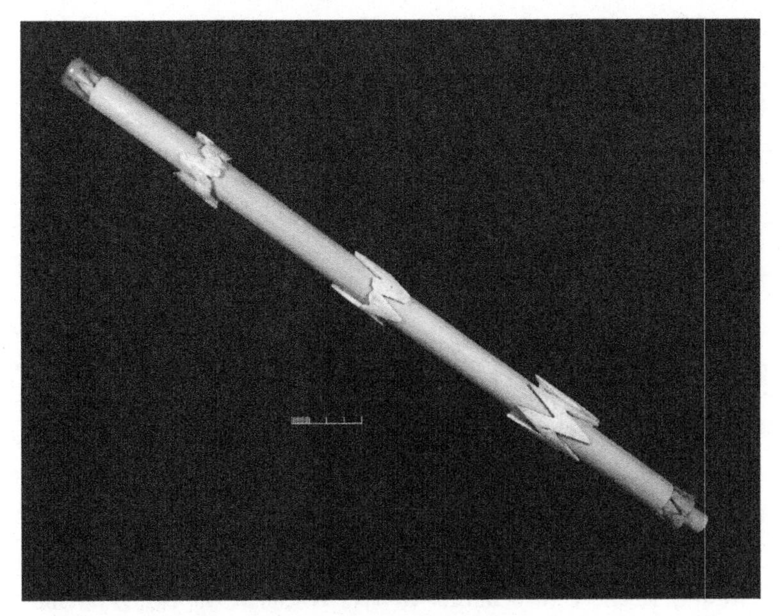

Fig. 7.1 Reconstructed baton from Bush Barrow with bone zig-zag mounts. Courtesy Wiltshire Museum, Devizes.

1984, 114–115). Bush Barrow is dated by Needham and colleagues to the period 1950–1750/1700 BCE (Needham et al. 2010, Table 1), a comparable date with that for grave Iota which probably lies within the years 1750–1700 BCE. In comparing the form of these objects Harding also draws attention to the roughly similar form of four gold 'crowns' from the Kerlagat dolmen, Carnac (Taylor 1980, pl. 25f) and the two mounts from the area of the Mycenae Acropolis, although lacking in a more specific context (Harding 1984, 114 and Fig. 31; 1990, 148 and Fig. 10). Harding comments: 'In the absence of more comparative material it is impossible to form an objective judgement about this analogy' (Harding 1990, 148). The problem would seem to be that: 'Tempting though it may be to imagine a direct correspondence between Mycenae and Wessex to account for these extraordinary objects, other explanations are possible' (Harding 1984, 114–115). It remains unclear as to what those explanations might be.

In this book we have attempted to move away from treating the material as if it could only be interpreted as the representation of those historical processes that resulted in its formation. This representational model of archaeological data limits the understanding of historical conditions to the procedures resulting in archaeological deposits. Given that only these formation processes are visible, it follows that only these processes can be established with a degree of objectivity (Binford 1987). It was upon this basis that theoretical claims for the importance of historical processes that either generated an ambiguous material record (such as the symbolic representations of an agent's motivations), or generated no record at all, could quite logically be dismissed as lying beyond the limits of archaeological visibility. The problem, as Harding appears to have discovered, is that even if we can map the distribution of materials whose geographical origins are securely established, then this mapping can only ever represent the fact that materials have moved, it does not represent the political and economic processes that resulted in that movement.

Renfrew attempted to address the historical interpretation of archaeological distribution patterns by establishing a topography that equated a type of distribution pattern with a type of exchange mechanism (Renfrew 1975). The problem is that to model the different fall-off in material density from source in this way requires consistency in the process of both deposition and recovery, neither of which are likely to have existed or to exist. For example, the differential recovery of the various amber necklace plates dating to the early second millennium BC that has resulted in clusters of finds in southern Britain (Wessex), central Europe and the Aegean (Harding 1990, Fig. 5) certainly indicates the movement of such worked material derived ultimately from raw material sources occurring around the Baltic or the eastern British coastlines.

But a mapping such as this does not reveal the mechanism for that movement, nor does it indicate where such material circulated but was not deposited in archaeologically recognizable contexts.

One possible solution to such questions is to model a world where continent-wide networks are taken as a pre-existing condition which provided a framework within which a shared cosmology and social structure could develop (Kristiansen and Rowlands 1998; Kristiansen 1998; Kristiansen and Larsson 2005). In all this work the European and Eurasian Bronze Ages are treated as geographically extensive systems of human movement, material exchanges, political alliances, ideological commitments and cosmological uniformities. The tension that has been exposed by some of the criticisms directed towards this work (e.g. Nordquist and Whittaker 2007) is that whilst the expectation is that the historical processes operating in the late third and early second millennium BCE were geographically extensive, the material details that might support the existence of those processes cannot be related with any certainty to the patterns recovered in the archaeological data. For example, the comparisons of certain stylistic motifs that play such a central role in Kristiansen's and Larsson's arguments for the existence of a commonality in Eurasian cosmologies might, it is argued, be treated as little more than patterns of coincidence. 'The trouble with this whole discussion' Harding comments when considering the controversial study of 'Mycenaean' motifs elsewhere in Europe, 'is that it is almost totally unsusceptible to objective analysis' (Harding 1984, 189). We might add that fragmented patterns of circulation of materials do not in themselves encode past beliefs, social systems or even networks of interaction.

If the comprehensive systems Kristiansen and Larsson argue for are not self-evidently indicated by the data, it is nonetheless the case that the widespread exchange of materials, human movement and shared cosmological understandings were likely to have been significant factors in the Eurasian Bronze Age. In this book we have set out to show how we can understand the role these factors played in the historical conditions of the past by situating human action within its material and discursive context.

This brings us to the heart of the case that we are making. In reviewing a period in Europe that runs from about 3200 BCE to about 1200 BCE, we are dealing with two millennia over which the material world became increasingly more complex, not simply in terms of the range of things that existed (although that certainly occurs), but in terms of the range of material conditions that people had to engage with and thus had to understand in order to behave effectively. In Hodder's terms, the density of the entangled relations between people and things therefore increased with new technologies that worked directly upon the ways that the body might perform in terms of productive activities, the architectures of movement, and the technologies of trust and engagement, both with others (notably in the service of food and drink) and with the dead. Any engagement with these changing conditions of existence must have involved movement from one place to another. Whilst it is for this reason that we have placed such an emphasis upon voyaging and upon processions, the fundamental point is that to exist and to develop as a person at this time was to move.

The importance of places such as Stonehenge or Knossos is that people came to orient themselves and their world in relation to them. The reason why such places came to exert a hold on the imagination of such far-flung populations was not because of what power they represented, be that sacred or profane; these places provided the backdrop in which people could adopt and express identity, and make their place in the world through the very act of going there. Places like Stonehenge fulfilled a role whereby ever larger and more diverse groups could be brought together in gatherings that reaffirmed expanding views of the world.

In a similar way, portable objects became props through which identity could be expressed and augmented. Material culture carries no meaning of itself; but new and ever-more complex objects served as media through which the self or the community might be expressed, and by adopting new materials and the practices that went with them people could adopt new elements of identity.

In contrast, then, with archaeologies that seek monolithic group identities through distributions of material style, we suggest that in the third and second millennia identity was constantly recreated through acts of movement and communication made possible by the changing technologies and the material conditions which people brought about. This means not that people knew the meaning of the Bush Barrow lozenge because it was one member of a class of material used throughout Europe, or because it carried universally recognizable symbols, but that to the people of Europe at that time the expression of kinds of identity through such material practices was part of a comprehensible order of the world.

The leads to the methodological thrust of our argument, which is that archaeologists record the material conditions through which those movements once occurred, as well as the material consequences of the actions that followed from those movements, whether these be the debris that might have been generated, or the architectural embellishment of the places that were passed through. These material conditions thus describe the 'fields' within which performances occurred. The archaeological task now becomes not simply to reconstruct such fields but to understand how their changing architectures and the available technologies facilitated the emergence of different forms of life. This moves us away from an archaeology that attempts to trace human life in terms of the debris that it generated, but more importantly it implies that the meaning of things was the product of an understanding and use of those things, it was not carried by the things themselves. It is therefore pointless for archaeology to claim that things have carried a consistent meaning across time and space and that this supposed meaning can be recovered archaeologically. People understood things because they knew how to live amongst them and the task of archaeology, as we have attempted to demonstrate, is to understand how that 'living amongst things' was practised in different parts of Europe over the period that saw, amongst other things, the widespread adoption of metallurgy.

Let us now return to those small pieces of bone, ivory and gold that come from the Bush Barrow in Wessex, shaft grave Iota at Mycenae, and the Kerlagat dolmen, Carnac with which we began this discussion. No source material analysis can possibly link these finds and their design is not only simple but the comparisons between them are imprecise. Consequently, few would accept that this material represents an objective record of early second millennium contacts between these regions. This is not, however, the point. If these were mounted on simple batons, then we would argue that they can only be understood relative to the practices of the body itself. They did not signify some form of social status, but to know how to carry and to display such an object, the dignity that was demanded by its presence and the way that such dignity was borne, to have performed in this way and to have been recognized for it, these were the conditions out of which a social identity was practised. This argument does not require a direct link to have existed between Wessex, Amorica and Mycenae, but is does allow that in different parts of Europe in this period the display and performance of bodies that evoked authority would have been recognizable to a significant level of detail.

Our argument throughout this book has been to find an alternative from the conventional treatment of archaeological data as if they represented either cultural, economic or socially determined behaviour. Our point has been that material conditions do not so much represent but rather enable particular kinds of human behaviour to come into being. This has not caused us to revise arguments concerning the relationship between Bronze Age Mycenae and Wessex, but it has explored some of the ways that the movement of things and people through different regions of Eurasia enabled different forms of human life to come into existence.

References

Alden, M. (2000), *Well Built Mycenae 7. The Prehistoric Cemetery: Pre-Mycenaean and Early Mycenaean Graves*. Oxford: Oxbow.

Annable, F.K. and D.D.A. Simpson (1964), *Guide Catalogue of the Neolithic and Bronze Age Collections in Devizes Museum*. Devizes: Wiltshire Archaeological and Natural History Society.

Aruz, J., K. Benzel and J.M. Evans (2008), eds, *Beyond Babylon: Art, Trade, and Diplomacy in the Second Millennium B.C.* New York: Metropolitan Museum of Art.

Ashbee, P. (1960), *The Bronze Age Round Barrow in Britain*. London: Phoenix House.

Atkinson, R.J.C. (1960 [1956]), *Stonehenge*. Harmondsworth: Penguin Books.

Atkinson, R.J.C. (1972), Burial and Population in the British Bronze Age. In F. Lynch and C. Burgess (eds) *Prehistoric Man in Wales and the West*, 107–116, Bath: Adams and Dart.

Atkinson, R.J.C., C.M. Piggott and N.K. Sanders (1951), *Excavations at Dorchester, Oxon*. Oxford: Ashmolean Museum.

Banton, S., M. Bowden, T. Dawe, D. Grady and S. Soutar (2014), Parchmarks at Stonehenge, July 2013. *Antiquity*, 88, 733–739.

Barclay, A., M. Gray and G. Lambrick (1995), *Excavations at the Devil's Quoits Stanton Harcourt, Oxfordshire 1972–3 and 1988*. Oxford: Oxford Archaeological Unit.

Barclay, A. and C. Halpin (1999), *Excavations at Barrow Hills, Radley, Oxfordshire. Volume 1: The Neolithic and Bronze Age Monument Complex*. Oxford: Oxford Archaeological Unit.

Barrett, J.C. (1988a), Fields of Discourse: Reconstituting a Social Archaeology. *Critique of Anthropology*, 7(3), 5–16.

Barrett, J.C. (1988b), The Living, the Dead and the Ancestors: Neolithic and Early Bronze Age Mortuary Practices. In J.C. Barrett and I.A. Kinnes (eds) *The Archaeology of Context in the Neolithic and Bronze Age: Recent Trends*, 30–41, Sheffield: John R. Collis.

Barrett, J.C. (1991), Towards an Archaeology of Ritual. In P. Garwood, D. Jennings, R. Skeates and J. Toms (eds) *Sacred and Profane: Proceedings of a Conference on Archaeology, Ritual and Religion Oxford 1989*, 1–9, Oxford: Oxford Committee for Archaeology.

Barrett, J.C. (1994), *Fragments form Antiquity: An Archaeology of Social Life in Britain, 2900–1200BC*. Oxford: Blackwell.

Barrett, J.C. (2014), The Material Constitution of Humanness. *Archaeological Dialogues*, 21(1), 65–74.

Barrett, J.C. (2018), The Dutch Abroad? Interpreting the Distribution of the 'Beaker Culture'. In C.C. Bakels, Q.P.J. Bourgeois, D.R. Fontijn and R. Jansen (eds) *Local Communities in the Big World of Prehistoric Northwest Europe*, 13–22, Leiden: Sidestone Press.

Barth, F. (1969), ed. *Ethnic Groups and Boundaries: The Social Organization of Culture Difference*. Oslo: Univ-furl.

Bass, G.F., P. Throckmorton, J. DuP. Taylor, J.B. Hennessy, A.R. Shulman and H-G. Bucholz (1967), Cape Gelidonya: A Bronze Age Shipwreck. *Transaction of the American Philosophical Society*, 57(8), 1–177.

Bassiakos, Y. and T. Tselios (2012), On the Cessation of Local Copper Production in the Aegean in the 2nd Millennium BC. In V. Kassianidou and G. Papasavvas (eds) *Eastern Mediterranean Metallurgy and Metalwork in the Second Millennium BC: A Conference in Honour of James D. Muhly, Nicosia, 10th–11th October 2009*, 151–161, Oxford: Oxbow Books.

Beck, C.W., E. Wibur and S. Meret (1964), Infrared Spectra and the Origin of Amber. *Nature*, 201, 256–57.

Beck, C. and S. Shennan (1991), *Amber in Prehistoric Britain*. Oxford: Oxbow Books.

Bell, C. (2012), The Merchants of Ugarit: Oligarchs of the Late Bronze Age Trade in metals? In V. Kassianidou and G. Papasavvas (eds) *Eastern Mediterranean Metallurgy and Metalwork in the Second Millennium BC: A Conference in Honour of James D. Muhly, Nicosia, 10th–11th October 2009*, 180–187, Oxford: Oxbow Books.

Bennett, J. (2010), *Vibrant Matter: A Political Ecology of Things*. Durham, NC: Duke University Press.

Betancourt, P.P. (2006), *The Chrysokamino Metallurgy Workshop and its Territory* (Hesperia Supplement 36). Princeton: American School of Classical Studies at Athens.

Betancourt, P.P. (2012), Cyprus and Crete: The Transformation of the Minoan Metalworking Industry. In V. Kassianidou and G. Papasavvas (eds) *Eastern Mediterranean Metallurgy and Metalwork in the Second Millennium BC: A Conference in Honour of James D. Muhly, Nicosia, 10th–11th October 2009*, 129–134, Oxford: Oxbow Books.

Bickle, P and A. Whittle. (2013), eds, *The First Farmers of Central Europe: Diversity in LBK Lifeways*. Oxford: Oxbow Books.

Binford, L.R. (1962), Archaeology as Anthropology. *American Antiquity*, 28(2), 217–225.

Binford, L.R. (1971), Mortuary Practices: Their Study and Potential. In J.A. Brown (ed.) Approaches to the Social Dimensions of Mortuary Practices. *American Antiquity*, 36(3:2), 6–29.

Binford, L.R. (1983), *In Pursuit of the Past: Decoding the Archaeological Record*. London: Thames and Hudson.

Binford, L.R. (1987), Data, Relativism and Archaeological Science. *Man* (n.s.), 22(3), 391–404.

Binford, L.R. (2001), *Constructing Frames of Reference: An Analytical Method for Archaeological Theory Building Using Ethnographic and Environmental Data Sets*. Berkeley: University of California Press.

Birtacha, K. (2017), Examining the Paint on Cycladic Figurines. In M. Marthari, C. Renfrew and M.J. Boyd (eds) *Early Cycladic Sculpture in Context*, 491–502, Oxford: Oxbow.

Bloch, M. (1985), From Cognition to Ideology. In R. Fardon (ed.) *Power and Knowledge: Anthropological and Sociological Approaches*, 21–48, Edinburgh: Scottish Academic Press.

Bloch, M. (2012), *Anthropology and the Cognitive Challenge*. Cambridge: Cambridge University Press.

Boast, R. (1997), A Small Company of Actors: A Critique of Style. *Journal of Material Culture*, 2(2), 173–198.

Bossert, E-.M. (1967), Kastri auf Syros. Vorbericht ueber eine untersuchung der praehistorischen siedlung. *Archaiologikon Deltion 22A*, 53–76.

Botterill, G. (2010), Two Kinds of Causal Explanation. *Theoria*, 76, 287–313.

Boyd, M.J. (2013), The Structure and Architecture of the Settlement. In C. Renfrew, O. Philaniotou, N. Brodie, G. Gavalas and M.J. Boyd (eds) *The Sanctuary on Keros and the Origins of Aegean Ritual Practice, Volume I: The Settlement at Dhaskalio*, 341–85, Cambridge: McDonald Institute for Archaeological Research.

Boyd, M.L. (2014), The Materiality of Performance in Myceneaean Funerary Practices. *World Archaeology*, 46, 192–205.

Boyd, M.J. (2015a), The Architectural Features of Kavos. In C. Renfrew, O. Philaniotou, N. Brodie, G. Gavalas and M.J. Boyd (eds) *The Sanctuary on Keros and the Origins of Aegean Ritual Practice, Volume II: Kavos and the Special Deposits*, 533–548, Cambridge: McDonald Institute for Archaeological Research.

Boyd, M.J. (2015b), Explaining the Mortuary Sequence at Mycenae. In A.-L. Schallin and I. Tournavitou (eds) *Mycenaeans up to Date: The Archaeology of the Northeastern Peloponnese – Current Concepts and New Directions*, 375–389, Athens: Swedish School.

Boyd, M.J. (2016a), Fields of Action in Mycenaean Funerary Practices. In A. Dakouri-Hild and M.J. Boyd (eds) *Staging Death: Funerary Performance, Architecture and Landscape in the Aegean*, 57–87, Berlin: De Gruyter.

Boyd, M.J. (2016b), Becoming Mycenaean? The Living, the Dead and the Ancestors in the Transformation of Society in the Second Millennium BC in southern Greece. In C. Renfrew, M.J. Boyd and I. Morley (eds) *Death Shall Have No Dominion: The Archaeology of Mortality and Immortality – a Worldwide Perspective*, 200–220, Cambridge: Cambridge University Press.

Boyd, M.J. and J. Dixon (2013), The Stone Discs from Dhaskalio. In C. Renfrew, O. Philaniotou, N. Brodie, G. Gavalas and M.J. Boyd (eds) *The Sanctuary on Keros and the Origins of Aegean Ritual Practice, Volume I: The Settlement at Dhaskalio*, 598–644, Cambridge: McDonald Institute for Archaeological Research.

Boyd, M.J. and C. Renfrew (2018), The Contrasting Material Worlds of Dhaskalio and Kavos. In C. Renfrew, O. Philaniotou, N. Brodie, G. Gavalas and M.J. Boyd (eds) *The Sanctuary on Keros and the Origins of Aegean Ritual Practice,*

Volume III: The Marble Finds from Kavos and the Archaeology of Ritual, 533–545, Cambridge: McDonald Institute for Archaeological Research.
Bradley, R. (1984), *The Social Foundations of Prehistoric Britain: Themes and Variations in the Archaeology of Power*. London: Longman.
Bradley, R., C. Haselgrove, M. Vander Linden and L. Webley (2016), *The Later Prehistory of North-West Europe: The Evidence of Development-led Fieldwork*. Oxford: Oxford University Press.
Branigan, K. (1974), *Aegean Metalwork of the Early and Middle Bronze Ages*. Oxford: Clarendon Press.
Bray, P.J. and A.M. Pollard (2012), A New Interpretive Approach to the Chemistry of Copper-alloy Objects: Source, Recycling and Technology. *Antiquity*, 86, 853–867.
Briard, J. (1984), *Les Tumulus D'Amorique: L'age du bronze en France 3*. Paris: Picard.
Brodie, N. and M. Georgakopoulou (2015), Investigations on Kavos Promontory. In C. Renfrew, O. Philaniotou, N. Brodie, G. Gavalas and M.J. Boyd (eds) *The Sanctuary on Keros and the Origins of Aegean Ritual Practice, Volume II: Kavos and the Special Deposits*, 507–523, Cambridge: McDonald Institute for Archaeological Research.
Bronk Ramsey, C., C. Renfrew and M.J. Boyd (2013), The Radiocarbon Determinations. In C. Renfrew, O. Philaniotou, N. Brodie, G. Gavalas and M.J. Boyd (eds) *The Sanctuary on Keros and the Origins of Aegean Ritual Practice, Volume I: The Settlement at Dhaskalio*, 695–703, Cambridge: McDonald Institute for Archaeological Research.
Broodbank, C. (2000), *An Island Archaeology of the Early Cyclades*. Cambridge: Cambridge University Press.
Broodbank, C. (2004), Minoanisation. *The Cambridge Classical Journal*, 50, 46–91.
Brown, J.A. (1971), *Approaches to the Social Dimensions of Mortuary Practices*. Memoirs of the Society for American Archaeology No. 25.
Burgess, C. and S. Shennan (1976), The Beaker Phenomenon: Some Suggestions. In C. Burgess and R. Miket (eds) *Settlement and Economy in the Third and Second Millennia BC*, 309–331, Oxford: British Archaeological Reports.
Burns, B.E. (2010), *Mycenaean Greece, Mediterranean Commerce, and the Formation of Identity*. Cambridge: Cambridge University Press.
Card, N., I. Mainland, S. Timpany, R. Towers, C. Batt, C.B. Ramsey, E. Dunbar, P. Reimer, A. Bayliss, P. Marshall and A. Whittle (2018), To Cut a Long Story Short: Formal Chronological Modelling for the Late Neolithic site of Ness of Brodgar, Orkney. *European Journal of Archaeology*, 21(2), 217–263.
Cardoso, J.L. (2014), Absolute Chronology of the Beaker Phenomenon North of the Tagus Estuary: Demographic and Social Implications. *Trabajos de Prehistoria*, 71(1), 56–75.
Carter, T. (2007), The Theatrics of Technology: Consuming Obsidian in the Early Cycladic Burial Arena. *Archaeological Papers of the American Anthropological Association*, 17, 88–107.

Carter, T. and M. Milić (2013), The Chipped Stone Industry from Dhaskalio. In C. Renfrew, O. Philaniotou, N. Brodie, G. Gavalas and M.J. Boyd (eds) *The Sanctuary on Keros and the Origins of Aegean Ritual Practice, Volume I: The Settlement at Dhaskalio*, 531–556, Cambridge: McDonald Institute for Archaeological Research.

Carter, T. and M. Milić (2015), The Obsidian Industry. In C. Renfrew, O. Philaniotou, N. Brodie, G. Gavalas and M.J. Boyd (eds) *The Sanctuary on Keros and the Origins of Aegean Ritual Practice, Volume II: Kavos and the Special Deposits*, 269–285, Cambridge: McDonald Institute for Archaeological Research.

Caskey, J.L. (1959), Activities at Lerna, 1958–1959. *Hesperia*, 28, 202–207.

Chapman, J. (2000), *Fragmentation in Archaeology: People, Places and Broken Objects in the Prehistory of South Eastern Europe*. Abingdon: Routledge.

Cherry, J. (1983), Evolution, Revolution and the Origins of the State in Minoan Crete. In O. Krzyszkowska and L. Nixon (eds) *Minoan Society*, 33–45, Bristol: Bristol Classical Press.

Cherry, J. (1984), The Emergence of the State in the Prehistoric Aegean. *Proceedings of the Cambridge Philological Society*, 30, 18–48.

Cherry, J. (1986), Polities and Palaces: Some Problems in Minoan State Formation. In C. Renfrew and J. Cherry (eds) *Peer Polity Interaction and Socio-political Change*, 19–45, Cambridge: Cambridge University Press.

Childe, V.G. (1925), *The Dawn of European Civilization*. London: Kegan Paul (First edition).

Childe, V.G. (1929), *The Danube in Prehistory*. Oxford: Clarendon Press.

Childe, V.G. (1931), *Skara Brae: A Pictish Village in Orkney*. London: Kegan Paul, Trench, Turner & Co. Ltd.

Childe V.G. (1957a), The Bronze Age. *Past and Present*, 12, 2–15.

Childe, V.G. (1957b), *The Dawn of European Civilization*. London: Routledge & Kegan Paul (Sixth edition).

Childe, V.G. (1958), *The Prehistory of European Society*. London: Penguin Books.

Chomsky, N. (1959), Verbal Behaviour. By B.F. Skinner. *Language*, 35, 26–58.

Chomsky, N. (1972), *Language and Mind* (Enlarged edition). New York: Harcourt Brace Javanovich, Inc.

Clarke, D.L. (1968), *Analytical Archaeology*. London: Methuen.

Clarke, D.L. (1976), The Beaker Network – Social and Economic Models. In J.N. Lanting and J.D. van der Waals (eds) *Glockenbechersymposion Oberried*, 459–476. Haarlem: Fibula-van DishoecK.

Cleal, R.M.J., K.E. Walker and R. Montague (1995), *Stonehenge in its Landscape: Twentieth-century Excavations*. London: English Heritage.

Cline, E.H. (2014), *1177 B.C. The Year Civilisation Collapsed*. Princeton: Princeton University Press.

Cline, E.H. and S.M. Stannish (2011), Sailing the Great Green Sea? Amenhotep III's 'Aegean List' from Kom el-Hetan, Once More. *Journal of Ancient Egyptian Interconnections*, 3, 6–16

Coleman, J.E. (1977), *Keos I: Kephala: A Late Neolithic Settlement and Cemetery*. Princeton: Princeton University Press.

Craig, O.E., I.M, Shillito, U. Albarella, S. Viner-Daniels, B. Chan, R. Cleal, R. Ixer, M. Jay, P. Marshall, E. Simmons, E. Wright and M.P. Pearson (2015), Feeding Stonehenge: Cuisine and Consumption at the Late Neolithic Site of Durrington Walls. *Antiquity*, 80, 1096–1109.

Cunnington, M.E. (1929), *Woodhenge: A Description of the Site as Revealed by Excavations Carried out there by Mr. and Mrs. B.H. Cunnington, 1926-7-8. Also of Four Circles and an Earthwork Enclosure south of Woodhenge*. Devizes: George Simpson & Co.

Czebreszuk, J. (2013), Mysterious Raw Material from the Far North: Amber in Mycenaean Culture. In S. Bergerbrant and S. Sabatini (eds) *Counterpoint: Essays in Archaeology and Heritage Studies in Honour of Professor Kristian Kristiansen*, 557–563, Oxford: Archaeopress.

Daniel, G. (1958), *The Megalith Builders of Western Europe*. London: Hutchinson

Darvill, T. (2016), Houses of the Holy: Architecture and Meaning in the Structure of Stonehenge, Wiltshire, UK. *Time and Mind*, 9(2), 89–121.

Darvill, T., M. Parker Pearson, P. Marshall and G. Wainwright (2012), Remodelling Stonehenge. *Antiquity*, 86, 1021–1040.

Day, P.M. and D.E. Wilson (2002), Landscapes of Memory, Craft and Power: Prepalatial and Protopalatial Knossos. In Y. Hamilakis (ed.) *Labyrinth Revisited: Rethinking 'Minoan' Archaeology*, 143–166, Oxford: Oxbow.

Demakopoulou, K., E. Mangou, R.E. Jones and E. Photos-Jones (1995), Mycenaean Black Inlaid Metalware in the National Archaeological Museum, Athens: A Technical Examination. *Annual of the British School at Athens*, 90, 137–153.

Descombes, V. (1986), *Objects of All Sorts: A Philosophical Grammar*. Oxford: Blackwell.

Dickinson, O. (2005), The 'Face of Agamemnon'. *Hesperia*, 74, 299–308.

Dickinson, O.T.P.K. (1970), *The Origins and Development of Early Mycenaean Culture*. PhD thesis, University of Oxford.

Dickinson, O.T.P.K. (1977), *The Origins of Mycenaean Civilisation*. Göteborg: Paul Åströms Förlag.

Dickinson, O.T.P.K., L. Papazoglou-Manioudaki, A. Nafplioti and A.J.N.W. Prag (2012), Mycenae Revisited Part 4: Assessing the New Data. *Annual of the British School at Athens*, 107, 161–188.

Dixon, J., (2013), The Petrology of the Walls. In C. Renfrew, O. Philaniotou, N. Brodie, G. Gavalas and M.J. Boyd (eds) *The Sanctuary on Keros and the Origins of Aegean Ritual Practice, Volume I: The Settlement at Dhaskalio*, 309–323, Cambridge: McDonald Institute for Archaeological Research.

Doonan, R.C.P., P.M. Day and N. Dimopoulou-Rethemiotaki (2007), Lame Excuses for Emerging Complexity in Early Bronze Age Crete: The Metallurgical Finds from Poros Katsambas and their Context. In P.M. Day and R.C.P. Doonan (eds) *Metallurgy in the Early Bonze Age Aegean*, 98–122, Oxford: Oxbow Books.

Douglas, M. (1966), *Purity and Danger: An Analysis of the Concepts of Pollution and Taboo*. London: Routledge & Kegan Paul.
Dunnell, R.C. (1978), Style and Function: A Fundamental Dichotomy. *American Antiquity*, 43(2), 192–202.
Earle, T. (1977), A Reappraisal of Redistribution: Complex Hawaiian Chiefdoms. In T.K. Earle and J. Ericson (eds) *Exchange Systems in Prehistory*, 213–229, London: Academic Press.
Earle, T. (1997), *How Chiefs Come to Power: The Political Economy in Prehistory*. Stanford: Stanford University Press.
Earle, T. (2002), *Bronze Age Economics*. Oxford: West View Press.
Efstratiou, N., A. Karetsou, E.S. Banou and D. Margomenou (2004), The Neolithic settlement of Knossos: New Light on an Old Picture. In G. Cadogan, E. Hatzaki and A. Vasilakis (eds) *Knossos: Palace, City, State*, 39–45, London: British School at Athens.
Evans, A.J. (1921), *The Palace of Minos*, Vol. 1. London: Macmillan.
Evans, A.J. (1928), *The Palace of Minos*, Vol. 2. London: Macmillan.
Evans, A.J. (1930), *The Palace of Minos*, Vol. 3. London: Macmillan.
Evans, A.J. (1935), *The Palace of Minos*, Vol. 4. London: Macmillan.
Evans, C. (2016), *Twice Crossed River: Prehistoric and Palaeoenvironmental Investigations at Barleycroft Farm/Over, Cambridgeshire*. Cambridge: McDonald Institute.
Evans, J.G. (1984), Stonehenge – the Environment in the Late Neolithic and Early Bronze Age and a Beaker-age Burial. *Wiltshire Archaeological and Natural History Magazine*, 78, 7–30.
Farmer, J.L. and M.F. Lane (2016), The Ins and Outs of the Great Megaron: Symbol, Performance, and Elite Identities around and between Mycenaean Palaces. *Studi Micenei ed Egeo-Anatolici*, Nuova Serie 2, 41–79.
Fitzpatrick, A.P. (2011), *The Amesbury Archer and the Boscombe Bowmen: Bell Beaker Burials at Boscombe Down, Amesbury, Wiltshire*. Salisbury: Wessex Archaeology Ltd.
Fleming, A. (2004), Hail to the Chiefdom? The Quest for Social Archaeology. In J. Cherry, C. Scarre and S. Shennan (eds) *Explaining Social Change: Studies in Honour of Colin Renfrew*, 141–147, Cambridge: McDonald Institute for Archaeological Research.
Fokkens, H., Y. Achterkamp and M. Kuipers (2008), Bracers or Bracelets? About the Functionality and Meaning of Bell Beaker Wrist-guards. *Proceedings of the Prehistoric Society*, 74, 109–140.
Fowler, C. (2013), *The Emergent Past: A Relational Realist Archaeology of Early Bronze Age Mortuary Practices*. Oxford: Oxford University Press.
Frankenstein, S. and M.J. Rowlands (1978), The Internal Structure and Regional Context of Early Iron Age Society in South-western Germany. *Institute of Archaeology Bulletin*, 15, 73–112.
French, E. (2002), *Mycenae Agamemnon's Capital*. Stroud: Tempus.
Friedman, J. and M.J. Rowlands (1977), eds, *The Evolution of Social Systems*. London: Duckworth.

Furholt, M. (2014), Upending a 'Totality': Re-evaluating Corded Ware Variability in Late Neolithic Europe. *Proceedings of the Prehistoric Society*, 80, 67–86.

Furholt, M. (2018), Massive Migrations? The Impact of Recent aDNA Studies on our View of Third Millennium Europe. *European Journal of Archaeology*, 21(2), 159–191.

Garwood, P. (2005), Before the Hills in Order Stood: Chronology, Time and History in the Interpretation of Early Bronze Age Round Barrows. In J. Last (ed.) *Beyond the Grave: New Perspectives on Barrows*, 30–52, Oxford: Oxbow Books.

Gavalas, G. (2013), The Marble Vessels from Dhaskalio. In C. Renfrew, O. Philaniotou, N. Brodie, G. Gavalas and M.J. Boyd (eds) *The Sanctuary on Keros and the Origins of Aegean Ritual Practice, Volume I: The Settlement at Dhaskalio*, 505–516, Cambridge: McDonald Institute for Archaeological Research.

Georgakopoulou, M. (2007), Metallurgical Activities within Early Cycladic Settlements: The Case of Daskalio-Kavos. In P.M. Day and R.C.P. Doonan (eds) *Metallurgy in the Early Bronze Age Aegean*, 123–134, Oxford: Oxbow.

Georgakopoulou, M. (2013), Metal Artefacts and Metallurgy. In C. Renfrew, O. Philaniotou, N. Brodie, G. Gavalas and M.J. Boyd (eds) *The Sanctuary on Keros and the Origins of Aegean Ritual Practice, Volume I: The Settlement at Dhaskalio*, 667–692, Cambridge: McDonald Institute for Archaeological Research.

Georgakopoulou, M. (2016), Mobility and Early Bronze Age Southern Aegean Metal Production. In E. Kiriatzi and C. Knappett (eds) *Human Mobility and Technological Transfer in the Prehistoric Mediterranean*, 46–67, Cambridge: Cambridge University Press.

Gerloff, S. (1975), *The Early Bronze Age Daggers in Great Britain and a Reconsideration of the Wessex Culture*. Munich: Prähistorische Bronzefunde Ab.VI, Band 2.

Getz-Gentle, P. (2008), The Keros Hoard Revisited. *American Journal of Archaeology*, 112, 299–305.

Gill, D.W.J. and C. Chippindale (1993), Material and Intellectual Consequences of Esteem for Cycladic Figures. *American Journal of Archaeology*, 97, 601–59.

Gilman, A. (1981), The Development of Stratification in Bronze Age Europe. *Current Anthropology*, 22(1), 1–24.

Gilman, A. (1991), Trajectories toward Social Complexity in the Later Prehistory of the Mediterranean. In T. Earle (ed.) *Chiefdoms: Power, Economy, and Ideology*, 146–168, Cambridge: Cambridge University Press.

Goldhan, J. (2013), Rethinking Bronze Age Cosmology: A North European Perspective. In H. Fokkens and A. Harding (eds) *The Oxford Handbook of the European Bronze Age*, 248–269, Oxford: Oxford University Press.

Graziado, G. (1988), The Chronology of the Graves of Circle B at Mycenae: A New Hypothesis. *American Journal of Archaeology*, 92, 343–372.

Graziado, G. (1991), The Process of Social Stratification at Mycenae in the Shaft Grave Period: A Comparative Examination of the Evidence. *American Journal of Archaeology*, 95, 403–440.

Green, C. and S. Rollo-Smith, (1984) The Excavation of Eighteen Round Barrows near Shrewton Wiltshire. *Proceedings of the Prehistoric Society*, 50, 255–318.

Grimes, W.F. (1960), *Excavations on Defence Sites 1939–1945 1. Mainly Neolithic-Bronze Age*. London: Her Majesty's Stationary Office.

Grinsell, L.V. (n.d.), *The Stonehenge Barrow Groups*. Salisbury: Salisbury and South Wiltshire Museum.

Haak, W., I. Lazaridis, N. Patterson, N. Rohland, S. Mallick, B. Llamas, G. Brandt, S. Nordenfelt, E. Harney, K. Stewardson, Q. Fu, A. Mittnik, E. Bánffy, C. Economou, M. Francken, S. Friederich, R. Garrido Pena, F. Hallgren, V. Khartanovich, A. Khokhlov, M. Kunst, P. Kuznetsov, H. Meller, O. Mochalov, V. Moiseyev, N. Nicklisch, S.L. Pichler, R. Risch, M.A. Rojo Guerra, C. Roth, A. Szécsényi-Nagy, J. Wahl, M. Meyer, J. Krause, D. Brown, D. Anthony, A. Cooper, K.W. Alt and D. Reich (2015), Massive Migration from the Steppe was a Source for Indo-European Languages in Europe, *Nature* 522, 207–11. https://doi.org/10.1038/nature14317

Hachmann, R. (1957), Bronzezeitliche Bernsteinschieber, *Beyerische Vorgechichtsblätter*, 22, 1–36.

Harbison, P. (1969), *The Axes of the Early Bronze Age in Ireland*. Munich: Pràhistorische Bronzefunde, Ab IX, Band 1.

Harding, A.F. (1984), *The Mycenaeans and Europe*. London: Academic Press.

Harding, A. (1990), The Wessex Connection: Developments and Perspectives. In T. Bader (ed.) *Orientalisch-Ägäische einflüsse in der Europä. ischen bronzezeit*, 139–154, Bonn: R. Habelt.

Harding A. (2013a), World Systems, Cores, and Peripheries in Prehistoric Europe. *European Journal of Archaeology*, 16(3), 378–400.

Harding, A. (2013b), Trade and Exchange. In H. Fokkens and A. Harding (eds) *The Oxford Handbook of the European Bronze Age*, 370–381, Oxford: Oxford University Press.

Harding, A. and H. Hughes Brock (1974), Amber in the Mycenaean World. *Annual of the British School at Athens*, 69, 145–172.

Harrell, K. (2010), Mycenaean Ways of War: The Past, Politics, and Personhood. University of Sheffield: unpublished doctoral dissertation.

Harrell, K. (2014), The Fallen and their Swords: A New Explanation for the Rise of the Shaft Graves. *American Journal of Archaeology*, 118, 3–17.

Harrison, R.J. and V. Heyd (2007), The Transformation of Europe in the Third Millennium BC: The Example of 'Le Petit-Chasseur I + III' (Sion, Valais, Switzerland). *Praehistorische Zeitschrift*, 82, 129–214.

Hawkes, C.F.C. (1959) The ABC of the British Iron Age. *Antiquity*, 33, 170–182.

Hein, A. and V. Kilikoglou (2018), Appendix: Neutron Activation Analysis of Early Cycladic Ceramics from Kavos and Dhaskalio (Keros). In C. Renfrew, O. Philaniotou, N. Brodie, G. Gavalas and M.J. Boyd (eds) *The Sanctuary on*

Keros and the Origins of Aegean Ritual Practice: The Excavations of 2006–2008, Volume III: The Marble Finds from Kavos and the Archaeology of Ritual, 494–500, Cambridge: McDonald Institute for Archaeological Research.

Hendrix, E. (2003), Painted Early Cycladic Figurines: An Exploration of Context and Meaning. *Hesperia*, 72, 405–446.

Hertz, R. (1907), Contribution à une étude sur la représentation collective de la mort. *Année Sciologique*, 10, 48–137.

Heyd, V. (2017), Kossina's Smile. *Antiquity*, 91, 348–359.

Higgs, E.S. and M.R. Jarman (1975), Palaeoeconomy. In E.S. Higgs (ed.) *Palaeoeconomy: Being the Second Volume of Papers in Economic Prehistory by Members and Associates of the British Academy Major Research Project in the Early History of Agriculture*, 1–7, Cambridge: Cambridge University Press.

Higham, T., J. Chapman, V. Slavchev, B. Gaydarska, N. Honch, Y. Yordanov and B. Dimitrova (2007), New Perspectives on the Varna Cemetery (Bulgaria) – AMS Dates and Social Implications. *Antiquity*, 8, 640–654.

Hilditch, J. (2013), The Fabrics of the Ceramics at Dhaskalio. In C. Renfrew, O. Philaniotou, N. Brodie, G. Gavalas and M.J. Boyd (eds) *The Sanctuary on Keros and the Origins of Aegean Ritual Practice, Volume I: The Settlement at Dhaskalio*, 465–482, Cambridge: McDonald Institute for Archaeological Research.

Hilditch, J. (2015), The Ceramic Fabrics of the Special Deposit South. In C. Renfrew, O. Philaniotou, N. Brodie, G. Gavalas and M.J. Boyd (eds) *The Sanctuary on Keros and the Origins of Aegean Ritual Practice, Volume II: Kavos and the Special Deposits*, 229–247, Cambridge: McDonald Institute for Archaeological Research.

Hilditch, J. (2018), The Fabric Study of the Pottery of Dhaskalio and Kavos. In C. Renfrew, O. Philaniotou, N. Brodie, G. Gavalas and M.J. Boyd (eds) *The Sanctuary on Keros and the Origins of Aegean Ritual Practice: The Excavations of 2006–2008, Volume III: The Marble Finds from Kavos and the Archaeology of Ritual*, 445–493, Cambridge: McDonald Institute for Archaeological Research.

Hoare, R.C. (1807), *Journal of a Tour in Ireland A.D. 1806*. London: William Miller.

Hoare, R.C. (1812), *The Ancient History of South Wiltshire*. London: William Miller.

Hodder, I. (1984), Archaeology in 1984. *Antiquity*, 58, 25–32.

Hodder, I. (2012), *Entangled: An Archaeology of the Relationship between Humans and Things*. Chichester: Wiley-Blackwell.

Hoffman, G.L. (2002), Painted Ladies: Early Cycladic II Mourning Figures? *American Journal of Archaeology*, 106, 5525–550.

Hofmann, D. (2015), What Have Genetics Ever Done for Us? The Implications of aDNA Data for Interpreting Identity in Early Neolithic Central Europe. *European Journal of Archaeology*, 18, 454–476.

Horejs, B. (2017), *Çukuriçi Höyük 1: Anatolia and the Aegean from the 7th to the 3rd Millennium* BC. Vienna: Austrian Academy of Sciences.

Horejs, B., S. Grasböck and M. Röcklinger (2017), Continuity and Change in an Early Bronze Age 1 Metal Workshop. In B. Horejs *Çukuriçi Höyük 1: Anatolia and the Aegean from the 7th to the 3rd Millennium BC*, Vienna: Austrian Academy of Sciences.

Ingold, T. (2001), From Complementarity to Obviation: On Dissolving the Boundaries between Social and Biological Anthropology, Archaeology and Psychology. In S. Oyama, P.E. Griffiths and R.D. Gray (eds) *Cycles of Contingency: Developmental Systems and Evolution*, 255–279, Cambridge, MA: The MIT Press.

Ingold, T. and G. Palsson. (2013), eds, *Biosocial Becomings: Integrating Social and Biological Anthropology*. Cambridge: Cambridge University Press.

Ion, A. (2017), How Interdisciplinary is Interdisciplinarity? Revisiting the Impact of aDNA Research for the Archaeology of Human Remains. *Current Swedish Archaeology*, 25, 87–108.

Ivanov, I. (1975), Razkopki na Varnenskiva eneoliten nekropol prez 1972g. *Izvestia na Narodniya Muzej Varna*, 11, 1–16.

Ivanov, I. (1991), Der Bestattungsritus in der chalkolitischen Nekropole von Varna (mit einem Katalog der wichstigsten Gräber). In J. Lichardus (ed.) *Die Kupferzeit als historische Epoche* (Saabrücker Beiträge zum Altertumskunde 55), 125–150, Saarbrücken: Saarland Museum.

Jeunesse, C. (2015), The Dogma of the Iberian Origin of the Bell Beaker: Attempting Its Deconstruction. *Journal of Neolithic Archaeology*. doi 10.12766/jna.2014.5

Johnson, A.W. and T. Earle (1987), *The Evolution of Human Societies: From Foraging Group to Agrarian State*. Stanford: Stanford University Press.

Jones, A. (2002), *Archaeological Theory and Scientific Practice*. Cambridge: Cambridge University Press.

Junk, K., R. Krause and E. Pernicka (2001), Össenringbarren and the Classic Össenring Copper. In W.H. Metz, B.L. van Beck and H. Steegstra (eds) *PATINA: Essays presented to Jay Jordan Butler on the occasion of his 80th birthday*, 353–366, Amsterdam: Metz, Van Beek & Steegstra.

Keskin, H.L. (2016), A Survey of West Anatolian Metallurgy Prior to Middle Bronze Age (2000 BC). *International Journal of Humanities & Social Studies*, 4, 187–195.

Killen, J.T. (2006), Conscription and Corvée at Mycenaean Pylos. In M. Perna (ed.) *Fiscality in Mycenaean and Near Eastern Archives: Proceedings of the Conference Held in Soprintendeza Archivistica per la Campania, Naples, 21–23 October 2004*, 78–87, Paris: De Boccard.

Kinnes, I. (1979), *Round Barrows and Ring-ditches in the British Neolithic*. London: Trustees of the British Museum.

Knapp, A.B and P. van Dommelen (2010), Material Connections: Mobility, Materiality and Mediterranean Identities. In P. van Dommelem and A.B. Knapp (eds) *Material Connections in the Ancient Mediterranean: Mobility, Materiality and Mediterranean Identities*, 1–18, London: Routledge.

Kristiansen, K. (1978), The Consumption of Wealth in Bronze Age Denmark: A Study in the Dynamics of Economic Processes in Tribal Societies. In

K. Kristiansen and C. Paludan-Müller (eds) *New Directions in Scandinavian Archaeology*, 158–190, Copenhagen: National Museum Press.

Kristiansen, K. (1998), *Europe Before History*. Cambridge: Cambridge University Press.

Kristiansen, K. (2014), Towards a New Paradigm? The Third Science Revolution and Its Possible Consequences in Archaeology. *Current Swedish Archaeology*, 22, 11–34.

Kristiansen, K. and T. Larsson (2005), *The Rise of Bronze Age Society: Travels, Transmissions and Transformations*. Cambridge: Cambridge University Press.

Kristiansen, K. and M. Rowlands (1998), *Social Transformations in Archaeology: Global and Local Perspectives*. London: Routledge.

Lang, M.L. (1969), *The Palace of Nestor at Pylos in Western Messenia, Volume II: The Frescoes*. Princeton: Princeton University Press.

Lanting, J.N. and J.D. Van der Waals (1976), Beaker Culture Relations in the Lower Rhine Basin. In J.N. Lanting and J.D. Van der Waals (eds) *Glockenbecher Symposion, Oberreid 1974*, 1–80, Haarlem: Fibula-Van Dishoeck.

Laporte, L. and C. Scarre (2015), eds, *The Megalithic Architectures of Europe*. Oxford: Oxbow Books.

Larsen, M.T. (1989), Orientalism and Near Eastern Archaeology. In D. Miller, M. Rowlands and C. Tilley (eds) *Domination and Resistance*, 229–239, London: Unwin Hyman.

Leach, E. (1964), *Political Systems of Highland Burma: A Study of Kachin Social Structure*. London: Athlone.

Leach, E. (1973), Concluding Address. In C. Renfrew (ed.) *The Explanation of Culture Change: Models in Prehistory*, 761–771, London: Methuen.

Leach. E. (1976), *Culture and Communication: The Logic by which Symbols are Connected*. Cambridge: Cambridge University Press.

Leary, J., D. Field and G. Campdell (2013), *Silbury Hill, the Largest Prehistoric n=mound in Europe*. London: English Heritage.

Levi-Strauss, C. (1982), *The Way of the Masks*. Seattle: University of Washington Press (Translated by S. Modelski).

Ling, J., E. Hjärthner-Holdar, L. Grandin, K. Billström and P-O. Petersen (2013), Moving Metals or Indigenous Mining? Provenancing Scandinavian Bronze Age Artefacts by Lead Isotopes and Trace Elements. *Journal of Archaeological Science*, 40, 291–304.

Ling, J., Z. Stos-Gale, L. Grandin, K. Billström, E. Hjärthner-Holdar (2014), Moving Metals II: Provenancing Scandinavian Bronze Age Artefacts by Lead Isotope and Elemental Analysis. *Journal of Archaeological Science*, 41, 106–132.

Longworth, I.H. (1984), *Collard Urns of the Bronze Age in Great Britain and Ireland*. Cambridge: Cambridge University Press.

Lucas, A. and J.R. Harris (1962), *Ancient Egyptian Materials and Industries*. London: Edward Arnold.

Lucas, G. (2012), *Understanding the Archaeological Record*. Cambridge: Cambridge University Press.

Lupack, S. (2011), A View from Outside the Palace: The Sanctuary and the *Damos* in Mycenaean Economy and Society. *American Journal of Archaeology*, 115, 207–217.
Manning, S. (2015), Radiocarbon Dating and Archaeology: History, Progress and Present Status. In R. Chapman and A. Wylie (eds) *Material Evidence: Learning from Archaeological Practice*, 128–158, Abingdon: Routledge.
Maran, J. (2006), Mycenaean Citadels as Performative Space. In J. Maran, C. Juwig, H. Schwengel and U. Thaler. *Constructing Power – Architecture, ideology and Social Practice*, 75–91, Hamburg: LIT.
Maran, J. (2013), Bright as the Sun: The Appropriation of Amber Objects in Mycenaean Greece. In H.P. Han and H. Weiss (eds) *Mobility, Meaning and the Transformations of Things: Shifting Contexts of Material Culture through Time and Space*, 147–169, Oxford: Oxbow Books.
Maran, J. (2016), The Persistence of Place and Memory: The Case of the Early Helladic *Rundbau* and the Mycenaean Palatial *Megara* of Tiryns. In M. Bartelheim, B. Horejs and R. Krauss (eds) *Von Baden bis Troia: Ressourcennutzung, Metallurgie und Wissenstransfer*, 153–173, Vienna: Austrian Academy of Sciences.
Margaritis, E. (2013a), Distinguishing Exploitation, Domestication, Cultivation and Production: The Olive in the Third Millennium Aegean. *Antiquity*, 87, 746–757.
Margaritis, E. (2013b),Foodstuffs, Fruit Tree Cultivation and Occupation Patterns at Dhaskalio. In C. Renfrew, O. Philaniotou, N. Brodie, G. Gavalas and M.J. Boyd (eds) *The Sanctuary on Keros and the Origins of Aegean Ritual Practice, Volume I: The Settlement at Dhaskalio*, 389–404, Cambridge: McDonald Institute for Archaeological Research.
Marx, K. (1930 [1867]), *Capital*. London: Dent
McKinley, J.I. (2011), Human Remains (Graves 1236 and 1289). In A.P. Fitzpatrick *The Amesbury Archer and the Boscombe Bowmen: Bell Beaker Burials at Boscombe Down, Amesbury, Wiltshire*, 77–87, Salisbury: Wessex Archaeology Ltd.
Mee, C. (2008), Mycenaean Greece, the Aegean and Beyond. In C.W. Shelmerdine (ed.) *The Cambridge Companion to the Aegean Bronze Age*, 362–386, Cambridge: Cambridge University Press.
Mehofer, M. (2014), Metallurgy during the Chalcolithic and the Beginning of the Early Bronze Age in Western Anatolia. In B. Horejs and M. Mehofer (eds) *Western Anatolia before Troy Proto-Urbanisation in the 4th Millennium BC?*, 463–487, Vienna: Austrian Academy of Sciences.
Miller, D. and C. Tilley (1984), eds, *Ideology, Power and Prehistory*. Cambridge: Cambridge University Press.
Monroe, C.M. (2009), *Scales of Fate: Trade, Tradition, and Transformation in the Eastern Mediterranean, ca. 1350-1175 BCE*. Alter Orient und Altes Testament 357. Munster: Ugarit-Verlag.
Monroe, C.M. (2010), Sunk Costs at Late Bronze Age Uluburun. *Bulletin of the American School of Oriental Research*, 357, 19–33.

Montelius, O. (1903), *Die ältern Kulturperioden im Orient und Europa*. Stockholm: Selbstverlag des Verfassers.

Musgrave, J.H., R.A.H. Neave, A.J.N.W. Prag, R.A. Musgrave and D.I. Thimme (1995), Seven faces from Grave Circle B at Mycenae. *Annual of the British School at Athens*, 90, 107–136.

Mylonas, G.E. (1973), *Ὁ ταφικὸς κύκλος Β τῶν Μυκηνῶν*. Athens: Archaeological Society.

Nafplioti, A. (2009), Mycenae Revisited Part 2. Exploring the Local versus Non-local Geographical Origin of the Individuals from Grave Circle A: Evidence from Strontium Isotope Ratio ($^{87}Sr/^{86}Sr$) Analysis. *Annual of the British School at Athens*, 104, 279–291.

Nakassis, D., W.A. Parkinson and M.L. Galaty (2011), Redistributive Economies from a Theoretical and Cross-Cultural Perspective. *American Journal of Archaeology*, 115, 177–84.

Nakassis, D., M.L. Galaty and W.A. Parkinson (2016), Introduction. *Journal of Mediterranean Archaeology*, 29, 61–70.

Nakou, G. (1995), The Cutting Edge: A New Look at Early Aegean Metallurgy. *Journal of Mediterranean Archaeology*, 8, 1–32.

Needham, S. (1996), Chronology and Periodisation in the British Bronze Age. *Acta Archaeologica*, 67, 121–140.

Needham, S. (2005), Transforming Beaker Culture in North-West Europe; Processes of Fusion and Fission. *Proceedings of the Prehistoric Society*, 71, 171–217.

Needham, S., K. Parfitt and G. Varndell (2006), eds, *The Ringlemere Cup: Precious Cups and the Beginning of the Channel Bronze Age*. London: British Museum Press.

Needham, S., A.J. Lawson and A. Woodward (2010a), 'A Noble Group of Barrows': Bush Barrow and the Normanton Down early Bronze Age Cemetery Two Centuries on. *The Antiquaries Journal*, 90, 1–39.

Needham S., M. Parker Pearson, A. Tyler, M. Richards and M. Jay (2010b), A First 'Wessex 1' Date from Wessex. *Antiquity*, 84, 363–373.

Nicholson, P.T., C.M. Jackson and K.M. Trott (1997), The Uluburun Glass Ingots, Cylindrical Vessels and Egyptian Glass. *The Journal of Egyptian Glass Archaeology*, 83, 143–153.

Nordquist, G. and H. Whittaker (2007), Comments on Kristian Kristiansen and Thomas B. Larsson () [sic]: The Rise of Bronze Age Society. Travels, Transmissions and Transformations. Cambridge University Press, Cambridge. *Norwegian Archaeological Review*, 40(1), 75–84.

Nosch, M-L. B. (2006), More Thoughts on the Mycenaean *Ta-ra-si-ja* System. In M. Perna (ed.) *Fiscality in Mycenaean and Near Eastern Archives: Proceedings of the Conference Held in Soprintendeza Archivistica per la Campania, Naples, 21-23 October 2004*, 161–187, Paris: De Boccard.

O'Brien, W. (2004), *Ross Island: Mining, Metal and Society in Early Ireland*. Galway: Galway University Press.

Oka, R. and C.M. Kusimba (2008), The Archaeology of Trading Systems, Part 1: Towards a New Trade Synthesis, *Journal of Archaeological Research*, 16(4), 339–395.

Olalde, I., S. Brace, M.E. Allentoft, I. Armit, K. Kristiansen, N. Rohland, S. Mallick, et al. (2017), The Beaker Phenomenon and the Genomic Transformation of Northwest Europe. http://dx.doi.org/10.1101/135962

Olsen, B., M. Shanks, T. Wemoor and C. Witmore (2012), *Archaeology: The Discipline of Things*. Berkeley: University of California Press.

Papadatos, Y. (2007), The Beginning of Metallurgy on Crete: New Evidence from the FN – EM I Settlement at Kephala Petras, Siteia. In P.M. Day and R.C.P. Doonan (eds) *Metallurgy in the Early Bronze Age Aegean*, 154–167, Oxford: Oxbow.

Papadimitriou, I. (1955), Ἀνασκαφαὶ ἐν Μυκήναις. *Praktika tis en Athinais Archaiologikis Etaireias*, 110, 217–232.

Papadimitriou, I. (1957), Ἀνασκαφαὶ ἐν Μυκήναις. *Praktika tis en Athinais Archaiologikis Etaireias*, 112, 105–109.

Papamichelakis, G. and C. Renfrew (2010), Hearsay About the 'Keros Hoard'. *American Journal of Archaeology*, 114, 181–185.

Papazoglou-Manioudaki, L., A. Nafplioti, J.H. Musgrave and A.J.N.W. Prag (2010), Mycenae Revisited Part 3. The Human Remains from Grave Circle A at Mycenae. Behind the Masks: A Study of the Bones of Shaft Graves I–V. *Annual of the British School at Athens*, 105, 157–224.

Parker Pearson, M. (2012), *Stonehenge: Exploring the Greatest Stone Age Mystery*. London: Simon and Shuster.

Parker Pearson, M. and Ramilisonina (1998), Stonehenge for the Ancestors: The Stones Pass on the Message. *Antiquity*, 72, 308–326.

Parker Pearson, M., A. Chamberlain, M. Jay, P. Marshall. J. Pollard, C. Richards, J. Thomas, C. Tilley and K. Welham (2009), Who was Buried at Stonehenge? *Antiquity*, 83, 23–39.

Parker Pearson, M., J. Pollard, C. Richards, J. Thomas and K. Welham (2015a), *Stonehenge: Making Sense of a Prehistoric Mystery*. London: Council for British Archaeology.

Parker Pearson, M., R. Bevins, R. Ixer, J. Pollard, C. Richards, K. Welham, B. Chan, K. Edinborough, D. Hamilton, R. Macphail, D. Schlee, J.-L. Schwenninger, E. Simmons and M. Smith (2015b), Craig Rhos-y-felin: A Welsh Bluestone Megalithic Quarry for Stonehenge. *Antiquity*, 89, 1331–1352.

Parker Pearson, M., A. Chamberlain, M. Jay, M. Richards, A. Sheridan, N. Curtis, J. Evans, A. Gibson, M. Hutchison, P. Mahoney, P. Marshall, J. Montgomery, S. Needham, S. O'Mahoney, M. Pellegrini and N. Wilkin (2016), Beaker People in Britain: Migration, Mobility and Diet. *Antiquity*, 90, 620–637.

Parker Pearson, M., A. Chamberlain, M. Jay, M. Richards and J. Evans (forthcoming), eds, *The Beaker People: Isotopes, Mobility and Diet in Prehistoric Britain*. Oxford: Oxbow Books for the Prehistoric Society.

Peperaki, O. (2004), The House of the Tiles at Lerna: Dimensions of 'Social Complexity'. In J.C. Barrett and P. Halstead (eds) *The Emergence of Civilisation Revisited*, 214–231, Oxford: Oxbow.
Peperaki, O. (2007), Complexity, Power and 'Associations that Matter': Rethinking Social Organisation in the Early Bronze Age 2 Mainland Greece. University of Sheffield: PhD thesis.
Peperaki, O. (2016), The Value of Sharing: Seal Use, Food Politics, and the Negotiation of Labor in Early Bronze II Mainland Greece. *American Journal of Archaeology*, 120, 3–25
Pepys. S. (1668), *The Diary of Samuel Pepys*. https://www.pepysdiary.com/diary/1668/06/11/
Piggott, S. (1938), The Early Bronze Age in Wessex. *Proceedings of the Prehistoric Society*, 4, 52–106.
Piggott. S. (1939), Timber Circles: A Re-examination. *Archaeological Journal*, 96, 193–222.
Piggott, S. (1954), *Neolithic Cultures of the British Isles: A Study of the Stone-using Agricultural Communities in Britain in the Second Millennium B.C.* Cambridge: Cambridge University Press.
Piggott, S. (1959), The Radio-Carbon Date from Durrington Walls. *Antiquity*, 33, 289–290.
Piggott, S. (1965), *Ancient Europe from the Beginnings of Agriculture to classical Antiquity: A Survey*. Edinburgh: Edinburgh University Press.
Plog, F. (1977), Modelling Economic Exchange. In T.K. Earle and J.E. Ericson (eds) *Exchange Systems in Prehistory*, 127–140, London: Academic Press.
Pollard, J., P. Garwood, M. Parker Pearson, C. Richards, J. Thomas and K. Welham (2017), Remembered and Imagined Belongings: Stonehenge in the Age of First Metals. In P. Bickle, V. Cummings, D. Hofmann and J. Pollard (eds) *The Neolithic of Europe: Papers in Honour of Alasdair Whittle*, 279–297, Oxford: Oxbow Books.
Prag, A.J.N.W., L. Papazoglou-Manioudaki, R.A.H. Neave, D. Smith, J.H. Musgrave and A. Nafplioti (2009), Mycenae Revisited Part 1. The Human Remains from Grave Circle A: Stamatakis, Schliemann and two New Faces from Shaft Grave VI. *Annual of the British School at Athens*, 104, 233–277.
Pulak, C. (1998), The Uluburun Shipwreck: An Overview. *The Journal of Nautical Archaeology*, 27(3), 188–224.
Pulak, C. (2008), The Uluburun Shipwreck in Late Bronze Age Trade. In J. Aruz, K. Benzel and J.M. Evans (eds) *Beyond Babylon: Art, Trade, and Diplomacy in the Second Millennium B.C.*, 289–305, New York: Metropolitan Museum of Art.
Pullen, D.J. (2011), Before the Palaces: Redistribution and Chiefdoms in Mainland Greece. *American Journal of Archaeology*, 115, 185–195.
Pullen, D.J. (2013), 'Minding the Gap' Bridging the Gaps in Cultural Change Within the Early Bronze Age Aegean. *American Journal of Archaeology*, 117, 545–553.

Redman, C.L., M.J. Berman, E.V. Curtin, W.T. Langhorne Jr., N.M. Versaggi and J.C. Wanser (1978), eds, *Social Archaeology: Beyond Subsistence and Dating.* London: Academic Press.

Rehren, T. and E.B. Pusch (2012), Alloying and Resource Management in New Kingdom Egypt: The Bronze Industry at Qantir – Pi-Ramesse and Its Relationship to Egyptian Copper Sources. In V. Kassianidou and G. Papasavvas (eds) *Eastern Mediterranean Metallurgy and Metalwork in the Second Millennium BC: A Conference in Honour of James D. Muhly, Nicosia, 10th–11th October 2009,* 215–221, Oxford: Oxbow Books.

Reich, D. (2018), *Who We Are and How We Got Here: Ancient DNA and the New Science of Human Past.* Oxford: Oxford University Press.

Renfrew, C. (1968), Wessex without Mycenae. *Annual of the British School of Archaeology at Athens,* 63, 277–285.

Renfrew, C. (1969a), The Autonomy of the South-east European Copper Age. *Proceedings of the Prehistoric Society,* 35, 12–47.

Renfrew, C. (1969b), The Chronology and Classification of the Early Cycladic Figurines. *American Journal of Archaeology,* 73, 1–32.

Renfrew, C. (1972), *The Emergence of Civilisation, the Cyclades and the Aegean in the Third Millennium B.C.* London: Methuen.

Renfrew, C. (1973a), *Before Civilisation: The Radiocarbon Revolution and Prehistoric Europe.* London: Jonathan Cape.

Renfrew, C. (1973b), Monuments, Mobilization and Social Organization in Neolithic Wessex. In C. Renfrew (ed.) *The Explanation of Culture Change: Models in Prehistory,* 539–558, London: Methuen.

Renfrew, C. (1973c), *Social Archaeology: An Inaugural Lecture Delivered at the University 20th March 1973.* Southampton: University of Southampton.

Renfrew, C. (1975), Trade as Action at a Distance: Questions of Integration and Communication. In J.A. Sabloff and C.C. Lamberg-Karlovsky (eds) *Ancient Civilization and Trade,* 3–59, Albuquerque: University of New Mexico Press.

Renfrew, C. (1976), Megaliths, Territories and Populations. In S.J. De Laet (ed.) *Acculturation and Continuity in Atlantic Europe: Mainly During the Neolithic Period and the Bronze Age,* 198–220, Brugge: De Tempel.

Renfrew, C. (1977), Space, Time and Polity. In J. Friedman and M.J. Rowlands (eds) *The Evolution of Social Systems,* 89–112, London: Duckworth.

Renfrew, C. (1982), Explanation Revisited. In C. Renfrew, M.J. Rowlands and B.A. Segraves (eds) *Theory and Explanation in Archaeology: The Southampton Conference,* 1–23, London: Academic Press.

Renfrew, C. (1984), *Approaches to Social Archaeology.* Edinburgh: Edinburgh University Press.

Renfrew, C. (1986), Varna and the Emergence of Wealth in Prehistoric Europe. In A. Appadurai (ed.) *The Social Life of Things,* 141–168, Cambridge; Cambridge University Press.

Renfrew, C. (1991), Foreword. In C. Beck and S. Shennan (eds) *Amber in Prehistoric Britain,* 7–8, Oxford: Oxbow Books.

Renfrew, C. (1994), The Identity of Europe in Prehistoric Archaeology. *Journal of European Archaeology*, 2(2), 153–173.

Renfrew, C. (2001), Symbol before Concept: Material Engagement and the Early Development of Society. In I. Hodder (ed.) *Archaeological Theory Today*, 122–140, Cambridge: Polity Press (First Edition).

Renfrew, C. (2008), The Keros Hoard: Remaining Questions. *American Journal of Archaeology*, 11, 295–298.

Renfrew, C. (2013a), The Sanctuary at Keros: Questions of Materiality and Monumentality. *Journal of the British Academy*, 1, 187–212.

Renfrew, C. (2013b), The Role of the Settlement at Dhaskalio: An Overview. In C. Renfrew, O. Philaniotou, N. Brodie, G. Gavalas and M.J. Boyd (eds) *The Sanctuary on Keros and the Origins of Aegean Ritual Practice, Volume I: The Settlement at Dhaskalio*, 645–665, Cambridge: McDonald Institute for Archaeological Research.

Renfrew, C. (2013c), The Figurines from Dhaskalio. In C. Renfrew, O. Philaniotou, N. Brodie, G. Gavalas and M.J. Boyd (eds) *The Sanctuary on Keros and the Origins of Aegean Ritual Practice, Volume I: The Settlement at Dhaskalio*, 483–490, Cambridge: McDonald Institute for Archaeological Research.

Renfrew, C. (2015), Evidence for Ritual Breakage in the Cycladic Early Bronze Age: The Special Deposit South at Kavos on Keros. In K. Harrell and J. Driessen (eds) *THRAVSMA Contextualising the Intentional Destruction of Objects in the Bronze Age Aegean and Cyprus*, 81–98, Louvain: Presses Universitaires de Louvain.

Renfrew, C. (2018), The Sculptures from the Special Deposit South: The Finds. In C. Renfrew, O. Philaniotou, N. Brodie, G. Gavalas and M.J. Boyd (eds) *The Sanctuary on Keros and the Origins of Aegean Ritual Practice, Volume III: The Marble Finds from Kavos and the Archaeology of Ritual*, 19–42, Cambridge: McDonald Institute for Archaeological Research.

Renfrew, C. and J.F. Cherry (1986), eds, *Peer Polity Interaction and Socio-political Change*. Cambridge: Cambridge University Press.

Renfrew, C. and J. Lebegyev (2013), The Spools from Dhaskalio. In C. Renfrew, O. Philaniotou, N. Brodie, G. Gavalas and M.J. Boyd (eds) *The Sanctuary on Keros and the Origins of Aegean Ritual Practice, Volume I: The Settlement at Dhaskalio*, 491–504, Cambridge: McDonald Institute for Archaeological Research.

Renfrew, C. and M.J. Boyd (2018), The contrasting Material Worlds of Dhaskalio and Kavos. In C. Renfrew, O. Philaniotou, N. Brodie, G. Gavalas and M.J. Boyd (eds) *The Sanctuary on Keros and the Origins of Aegean Ritual Practice, Volume III: The Marble Finds from Kavos and the Archaeology of Ritual*, 533–46, Cambridge: McDonald Institute for Archaeological Research.

Renfrew, C., M.J. Boyd and C. Bronk Ramsey (2012), The Oldest Maritime Sanctuary? Dating the Sanctuary at Keros and the Cycladic Early Bronze Age. *Antiquity*, 86, 144–160.

Renfrew, C., G. Gavalas and P. Sotirakopoulou (2013), The Development of the Excavation: Stratigraphy and Phasing. In C. Renfrew, O. Philaniotou,

N. Brodie, G. Gavalas and M.J. Boyd (eds) *The Sanctuary on Keros and the Origins of Aegean Ritual Practice, Volume I: The Settlement at Dhaskalio*, 63–78, Cambridge: McDonald Institute for Archaeological Research.

Renfrew, C., O. Philaniotou, N. Brodie, G. Gavalas and M.J. Boyd (2013), eds, *The Sanctuary on Keros and the Origins of Aegean Ritual Practice, Volume I: The Settlement at Dhaskalio*. Cambridge: McDonald Institute for Archaeological Research.

Renfrew, C., O. Philaniotou, N. Brodie, G. Gavalas and M.J. Boyd (2015), eds, *The Sanctuary on Keros and the Origins of Aegean Ritual Practice, Volume II: Kavos and the Special Deposits*. Cambridge: McDonald Institute for Archaeological Research.

Renfrew, C., M. Marthari and M.J. Boyd (2016), The Curse of Looting: The Scourge of Cycladic Archaeology. In N.C. Stampolidis and I.G. Lourentzatou (eds) *Cycladic Society 5000 Years Ago*, 117–123, Athens: Museum of Cycladic Art & Ministry of Culture.

Renfrew, C., O. Philaniotou, N. Brodie, G. Gavalas and M.J. Boyd (2018), eds, *The Sanctuary on Keros and the Origins of Aegean Ritual Practice, Volume III: The Marble Finds from Kavos and the Archaeology of Ritual*. Cambridge: McDonald Institute for Archaeological Research.

Renfrew, C., M. Marthari, A. Dellaporta, M.J. Boyd, N. Brodie, G. Gavalas, J. Hilditch and J. Wright (forthcoming), eds, *The Sanctuary on Keros and the Origins of Aegean Ritual Practice, Volume VI: The Keros Island Survey*. Cambridge: McDonald Institute for Archaeological Research.

Renfrew, C., P. Sotirakopoulou and M.J. Boyd (forthcoming), *The Sanctuary on Keros and the Origins of Aegean Ritual Practice, Volume VII: Monumentality, Diversity and Fragmentation in Early Cycladic Sculpture: The Finds from the Special Deposit North at Kavos on Keros*. Cambridge: McDonald Institute for Archaeological Research.

Ribeiro, A. (2018), Death of the Passive Subject: Intentional Action and Narrative Explanation in Archaeological Studies. *History of the Human Sciences*, 31(3), 105–121.

Richards, C. (2005), ed., *Dwelling among the Monuments: The Neolithic Village of Barnhouse, Maeshowe Passage Grave and Surrounding Monuments at Stennes, Orkney*. Cambridge: McDonald Institute for Archaeological Research.

Richards, C. (2013), ed., *Building the Great Stone Circles of the North*. Oxford: Windgather Press.

Richards, C., R. Jones and S. Jeffrey (2016), eds, *The Development of Neolithic House Societies in Orkney: Investigations in the Bay of Firth, Mainland, Orkney (1994–2014)*. Oxford: Windgather Press.

Richards, C., J. Downes, C. Gee and S. Carter (2016), Materialising Neolithic House Societies in Orkney: Introducing Varme Dale and Muckquoy. In C. Richards, R. Jones and S. Jeffrey (eds) *The Development of Neolithic House Societies in Orkney: Investigations in the Bay of Firth, Mainland, Orkney (1994–2014)*, 224–253, Oxford: Windgather Press.

Ritchie, J.N.G. (1976), The Stones of Stenness, Orkney. *Proceedings of the Society of Antiquaries of Scotland*, 107, 1–60.

Robb, J. (2010), Beyond Agency. *World Archaeology*, 42(4), 493–520.

Roberts, B.W., C.P. Thornton and V.C. Pigott (2009), Development of Metallurgy in Eurasia. *Antiquity*, 83, 1012–1022.

Roberts, B.W. and M. Vander Linden (2011), *Investigating Archaeological Cultures: Material Culture, Variability, and Transmission*. London: Springer.

Rowan, Y., J. Dixon and R. Dubicz (2013), The Ground Stone Assemblage from Dhaskalio. In C. Renfrew, O. Philaniotou, N. Brodie, G. Gavalas and M.J. Boyd (eds) *The Sanctuary on Keros and the Origins of Aegean Ritual Practice, Volume I: The Settlement at Dhaskalio*, 557–595, Cambridge: McDonald Institute for Archaeological Research.

Rowlands, M. (1984), Conceptualizing the European Bronze and Early Iron Ages. In J. Bintliff (ed.) *European Social Evolution: Archaeological Perspectives*, 147–156, Bradford: University of Bradford.

Rowlands, M. (2010), Concluding Thoughts. In P. van Dommelem and A.B. Knapp (eds) *Material Connections in the Ancient Mediterranean: Mobility, Materiality and Mediterranean Identities*, 233–247, London: Routledge.

Rowlands, M. and J. Ling (2013), Boundaries, Flows and Connectivities: Mobility and Stasis in the Bronze Age. In S. Bergerbrant and S. Sabatini (eds) *Counterpoint: Essays in Archaeology and Heritage Studies in Honour of Professor Kristian Kristiansen*, 517–529, Oxford: Archaeopress.

Rowley-Conwy, P. (2007), *From Genesis to Prehistory: The Archaeological Three Age System and its Contested Reception in Denmark, Britain and Ireland*. Oxford: Oxford University Press.

Rutter, J.B. (2017), Partying in Prehistory: Social Drinking Behaviors in the Bronze Age Aegean, ca. 2600-1400 BCE. http://uu.diva-portal.org/smash/get/diva2:1071026/FULLTEXT01.pdf

Sahlins, M.D. (1968), *Tribesmen*. New Jersey: Prentice Hall.

Şahoğlu, V. (2011), Early Bronze Age Pottery in Coastal Western Anatolia. In V. Şahoğlu and P. Sotirakopoulou (eds) *ACROSS: The Cyclades and Western Anatolia during the 3rd Millennium BC*, 136–143, İstanbul: Sakıp Sabancı Museum.

Schliemann, H. (1878), *Mycenae: A narrative of Researches and Discoveries at Mycenae and Tiryns*. London: John Murray.

Schoep, I. (2012), Bridging the Divide between the 'Prepalatial' and the 'Protopalatial' Periods? In I. Schoep, P. Tomkins and J. Driessen (eds) *Back to the Beginning: Reassessing Social and Political Complexity on Crete during the Early and Middle Bronze Age*, 403–428, Oxford: Oxbow Books.

Service, E. (1962), *Primitive Social Organization: An Evolutionary Perspective*. New York: Random House.

Shanks, M. and C. Tilley, (1987), *Re-constructing Archaeology: Theory and Practice*. Cambridge: Cambridge University Press.

Shelton, K. (2003), The Chamber Tombs. In S.E. Iakovidis and E.B. French (eds) *Archaeological Atlas of Mycenae*, 35, Athens: Archaeological Society.

Shennan, S. (1986), Interaction and Change in Third Millennium BC Western and Central Europe. In C. Renfrew and J. Cherry (eds) *Peer Polity Interaction and Socio-political Change*, 149–158, Cambridge: Cambridge University Press.

Sherratt, A. (1981), Plough and Pastoralism: Aspects of the Secondary Products Revolution. In I. Hodder, G. Isaac and N. Hammond (eds) *Pattern of the Past: Studies in Honour of David Clarke*, 261–305, Cambridge: Cambridge University Press.

Sherratt, A. (1986), The Radley 'Earrings' Revised. *Oxford Journal of Archaeology*, 5(1), 61–66.

Sherratt, A. (1993), What would a Bronze Age World System Look Like? Relations between Temperate Europe and the Mediterranean in Later Prehistory. *Journal of European Archaeology*, 1(2), 1–58.

Sherratt, A. (1997), *Economy and Society in Prehistoric Europe: Changing Perspectives*. Princeton: Princeton University Press.

Sherratt, A. and S. Sherratt (1991), From Luxuries to Commodities: The Nature of Mediterranean Bronze Age Trading Systems. In N.H. Gale (ed.) *Bronze Age Trade in the Mediterranean: Papers Presented at the Conference held at Rewley House, Oxford, in December 1989*, 351–386, Jonsered: Paul Äströms Förlag.

Skinner, B.F. (1953), *Science and Human Behaviour*, London: Macmillan.

Smith, M.E. (2012), Archaeology, Early Complex Societies and Comparative Social Science History. In M.E. Smith (ed.) *The Comparative Archaeology of Complex Societies*, 321–329, Cambridge: Cambridge University Press.

Sotirakopoulou, P. (2004), Early Cycladic Pottery from the Investigations of the 1960s at Kavos-Daskaleio, Keros: A Preliminary Report. In E. Alram-Stern (ed.) *Die Ägäische Frühzeit. 2. Serie. Forschungsbericht 1975–2000. 2. Band, Die Frühbronzezeit in Griechenland mit Ausnahme von Kreta*, 1303–1358, Vienna: Verlag der Österreichischen Akademie der Wissenschaften.

Sotirakopoulou, P. (2005), *The 'Keros Hoard': Myth or Reality? Searching for the Lost Pieces of a Puzzle*. Athens: N.P. Goulandris Foundation.

Sotirakopoulou, P. (2008), The Keros Hoard: Some Further Discussion. *American Journal of Archaeology*, 112, 279–294.

Sotirakopoulou, P. (2016), *The Sanctuary on Keros and the Origins of Aegean Ritual Practice, Volume IV: The Pottery from Dhaskalio*. Cambridge: McDonald Institute for Archaeological Research.

Sotirakopoulou, P. (2018), The Pottery from Dhaskalio, the Special Deposit South and the Special Deposit North Compared. In C. Renfrew, O. Philaniotou, N. Brodie, G. Gavalas and M.J. Boyd (eds) *The Sanctuary on Keros and the Origins of Aegean Ritual Practice, Volume III: The Marble Finds from Kavos and the Archaeology of Ritual*, 435–443, Cambridge: McDonald Institute for Archaeological Research.

Sotirakopoulou, P. (forthcoming), *The Sanctuary on Keros and the Origins of Aegean Ritual Practice, Volume V: The Pottery from Kavos*. Cambridge: McDonald Institute for Archaeological Research.

Speak, S. and C. Burgess (1999), Meldon Bridge: A Centre of the Third Millennium in Peeblesshire. *Proceedings of the Society of Antiquaries of Scotland*, 129, 1–118.

Taylor, J.J. (1980), *Bronze Age Goldwork of the British Isles*. Cambridge: Cambridge University Press.

Thaler, U. (2015), Movement in between, into and inside Mycenaean Palatial Megara. In A.-L. Schallin and I. Tournavitou (eds) *Mycenaeans up to Date: The Archaeology of the Northeastern Peloponnese – Current Concepts and New Directions*, 339–360, Athens: Swedish School.

Thaler, U. (2016), Eventful Architecture: Activating Potentials for Movement and Segregation in Mycenaean Palaces. In S. Schmidt-Hofner, C. Ambos and P. Eich (eds) *Raum-Ordnung. Raum und soziopolitische Ordnungen im Altertum*, 111–139, Heidelberg: Winter Verlag.

Thomas, J. (1991), *Rethinking the Neolithic*. Cambridge: Cambridge University Press.

Thomas, J. (1999), *Understanding the Neolithic*. London: Routledge.

Thomas, J. (2010), The Return of the Rinyo-Clacton Folk? The Cultural Significance of the Grooved Ware Complex in Later Neolithic Britain. *Cambridge Archaeological Journal*, 20(1), 1–15.

Tomkins, P.D. (2008), Time, Space and the Reinvention of the Cretan Neolithic. In V. Isaakidou and P.D. Tomkins (eds) *Escaping the Labyrinth: The Cretan Neolithic in Context*, 21–48, Oxford: Oxbow Books.

Tomkins, P. (2012), Behind the Horizon: Reconsidering the Genesis and Function of the 'First Palace' at Knossos (Final Neolithic IV–Middle Minoan IB). In I. Schoep, P. Tomkins and J. Driessen (eds) *Back to the Beginning: Reassessing Social and Political Complexity on Crete during the Early and Middle Bronze Age*, 32–80, Oxford: Oxbow Books.

Triantaphyllou, S. (2010), Prospects for Reconstructing the Lives of Middle Helladic Populations in the Argolid: Past and Present of Human Bone Studies'. In A. Philippa-Touchais, G. Touchais, S. Voutsaki and J. Wright (eds) *Mesohelladika. La Grèce continentale au Bronze Moyen. Actes du colloque international Athènes 8–12 Mars 2006* (BCH Suppl., 40), 441–454, Athens: Ecole français d'Athènes.

Tsountas, C. (1899), Κυκλαδικὰ II. *Archaeologiki Ephemeris*, 17, 74–134.

Turner, V. (1967), *The Forest of Symbols: Aspects of Ndemba Ritual*. London: Cornell University Press.

Twohig, E.S. (1981), *The Megalithic Art of Western Europe*. Oxford: Oxford University Press.

Vandkilde, H. (1996), *From Stone to Bronze: The Metalwork of the Late Neolithic and Earliest Bronze Age in Denmark*. Moesgard: Jutland Archaeological Society.

Vandkilde, H. (2017), *The Metal Hoard from Pile in Scania, Sweden: Place, Things, Time, Metals, and Worlds around 2000 BCE*. Aarhus: Aarhus University Press.

Van Gennep, A. (1960), *The Rites of Passage*. London: Routledge & Kegan Paul.
Voutsaki, S., S. Triantaphyllou, A. Ingvarsson-Sundström, K. Sarri, M. Richards, A. Nijboer, S. Kouidou-Andreou, L. Kovatsi, D. Nikou and E. Milka (2006), Project on the Middle Helladic Argolid: A Report on the 2006 Season. *Pharos* XIV, 59–99.
Wace, A.J.B. (1923), Excavations at Mycenae. *Annual of the British School at Athens*, 25, 1–434.
Wace, A.J.B. (1932), Chamber Tombs at Mycenae. *Archaeologia*, 82, 1–242.
Waddell, J. (1976), Cultural Interaction in the Insular Early Bronze Age: Some Ceramic Evidence. In S.J. De Laet (ed.) *Acculturation and Continuity in Atlantic Europe: Mainly during the Neolithic Period and the Bronze Age*, 284–295, Brugge: De Tempel.
Wainwright, G.J. (1971), *Durrington Walls, Excavations 1966-1968*. London: The Society of Antiquaries.
Wainwright, G.J. and I.H. Longworth (1971), The Rinyo-Clacton Culture Reconsidered. In G.J. Wainwright, *Durrington Walls, Excavations 1966–1968*, 235–306, London: The Society of Antiquaries.
Wallerstein, I. (1974), *The Modern World System: Capitalist Agriculture and the Origins of the European World-economy in the Sixteenth Century*. London: Academic Press.
Weiberg, E. (2007), *Thinking the Bronze Age: Life and Death in Early Helladic Greece*. Uppsala: Acta Universitatis Uppsaliensis.
Wengrow, D. (2010), *What Makes Civilization? The Ancient Near East and the Future of the West*. Oxford: Oxford University Press.
Whitelaw, T. (2012), The Urbanisation of Prehistoric Crete. In I. Schoep, P. Tomkins and J. Driessen (eds) *Back to the Beginning: Reassessing Social and Political Complexity on Crete during the Early and Middle Bronze Age*, 114–176, Oxford: Oxbow Books.
Whittle, A. (1981), Later Neolithic Society in Britain: A Realignment. In C. Ruggles and A. Whittle (eds) *Astronomy and Society in the Period 4000–1500 BC*, 297–342, Oxford: British Archaeological Reports.
Wiencke, M.H. (2000), *Lerna: A Preclassical Site in the Argolid. Results of Excavations Conducted by the American School of Classical Studies at Athens. Volume 4: The Architecture, Stratification and Pottery of Lerna III*. Princeton: American School of Classical Studies at Athens.
Williams, A. (1948), Excavations in Barrow Hills Field, Radley, Berkshire, 1944. *Oxoniensia*, 13, 1–17.
Wilson, D.E. (1999), *Keos IX. Ayia Irini: Periods I–III. The Neolithic and Early Bronze Age Settlements. Part 1: The Pottery and Small Finds*. Mainz am Rhein: Philipp von Zabern.
Wilson, D.E. (2007), Early Prepalatial (EM I-EM II): EM I Well, West Court House, North-East Magazines and South Front Groups. In N. Momigliano (ed.) *Knossos Pottery Handbook: Neolithic and Bronze Age (Minoan)*, 49–77, London: British School at Athens.

Wilson, D.E. (2017), The Cycladic Marble Figurines from EBII Ayia Irini, Kea. In M. Marthari, C. Renfrew and M.J. Boyd (eds) *Early Cycladic Sculpture in Context*, 94–102, Oxford: Oxbow Books.
Wilson, D.E. and P.M. Day (1994), Ceramic Regionalism in Prepalatial Central Crete: The Mesara Imports at EMI to EMIIA Knossos. *Annual of the British School at Athens*, 89, 1–87.
Winch, P. (1964), Understanding a Primitive Society. *American Philosophical Quarterly*, 1(4), 301–324.
Woodward, A., (2002), Beads and Beakers: Heirlooms and Relics in the British Early Bronze Age. *Antiquity*, 76, 1040–1047.
Woodward, A. and J. Hunter (2011), *An Examination of Prehistoric Stone Bracers from Britain*. Oxford: Oxbow Books.
Woodward, A. and J. Hunter (2015), *Ritual in Early Bronze Age Grave Goods*. Oxford: Oxbow Press.
Wright, J.C. (1987), Death and Power at Mycenae: Changing Symbols in Mortuary Practice. In R. Laffineur (ed.) *Thanatos. Les coutumes funéraires en Égée à l'âge du Bronze*, 171–184, Liège: Université de Liège.
Wright, J.C. (2006a), The Formation of the Mycenaean Palace. In S. Deger-Jalkotzy and I.S. Lemos (ed.) *Ancient Greece: From the Mycenaean Palaces to the Age of Homer*, 7–52, Edinburgh: Edinburgh University Press.
Wright, J.C. (2006b), The Social Production of Space and the Architectural Reproduction of Society in the Bronze Age Aegean during the 2nd Millenium B.C.E. In J. Maran, C. Juwig, H. Schwengel and U. Thaler (eds) *Constructing Power - Architecture, Ideology and Social Practice*, 49–74, Hamburg: LIT.
Zapheiropoulou, P. (2017), The Complete Canonical Sculpture of Spedos Variety from Dhaskalio Kavos on Keros. In M. Marthari, C. Renfrew and M.J. Boyd (eds) *Early Cycladic Sculpture in Context*, 335–344, Oxford: Oxbow Books.

Index

Printed in Great Britain
by Amazon